Interfaces ▪ Studies in Visual Culture

Editors: Mark J. Williams and Adrian W. B. Randolph, Dartmouth College

This series, sponsored by Dartmouth College Press, develops and promotes the study of visual culture from a variety of critical and methodological perspectives. Its impetus derives from the increasing importance of visual signs in everyday life, and from the rapid expansion of what are termed "new media." The broad cultural and social dynamics attendant to these developments present new challenges and opportunities across and within the disciplines. These have resulted in a transdisciplinary fascination with all things visual, from "high" to "low," and from esoteric to popular. This series brings together approaches to visual culture—broadly conceived—that assess these dynamics critically and that break new ground in understanding their effects and implications.

For a complete list of books that are available in the series, visit www.upne.com.

Steve F. Anderson

Technologies of History

Visual Media and the Eccentricity of the Past

Dartmouth College Press
Hanover, New Hampshire

Dartmouth College Press

An imprint of University Press of New England

www.upne.com

CC 2011 by Trustees of Dartmouth College

Some rights reserved

All other permissions requests should be directed to:
Permissions Department
University Press of New England
1 Court Street, Suite 250
Lebanon NH 03766
fax: 603-448-7006
www.upne.com

Manufactured in the United States of America
Designed by Eric M. Brooks
Typeset in Melior and Francker
by Passumpsic Publishing

Library of Congress Cataloging-in-Publication Data
appear on the last printed page of this book.

5 4 3 2 1

Contents

Acknowledgments

This is a lungfish of a book. It was born in the great oceans of celluloid, Mylar, and broadcast media of the previous century but adapted itself to life ashore on the vast beaches of computational media, games, and networks; this evolution, with its richness as well as eccentricities, has infused this book at every level.

I would like to acknowledge the following people who have contributed directly or indirectly to the creation of this book. For the meticulous examples set in their own work and critical readings of early drafts and chapters, I would like to thank David James, Leo Braudy, and Marsha Kinder. My thinking about the materiality of cinema and its reciprocal relation to history has been indelibly shaped and inspired by Thom Andersen, James Benning, and Morgan Fisher. I am additionally grateful for key moments of intervention, support, and inspiration from Tara McPherson, Mark Williams, Anne Balsamo, and Greg Golley. For their extraordinary efficiency and personal attention, I am indebted to the editorial staff at the University Press of New England, especially Richard Pult, Amanda Dupuis, and Naomi Burns. My deepest gratitude is reserved for Robert Rosenstone and Marita Sturken, without whose foundational and genuinely transformative work in the fields of film, history, and cultural memory this book and the thinking it represents would not have been possible.

This book is dedicated to the memory of Chick Strand, Anne Friedberg, and Kenneth Forbes Anderson, the colleagues, mentors, and family members I have lost in the time it has taken to complete this book, and the one I have gained, Ginger Miranda Anderson-Willis.

It is beyond my ability to acknowledge the extraordinary insights, words, patience, and generosity that Holly Willis has brought to this project. If not for her, this book—and I along with it—would still be gasping for air in a primordial soup.

Technologies of History

Introduction

Each generation of media technology brings with it the potential to reimagine our relationship to the past. Conventional wisdom holds that visual histories are most effective at bringing the past "to life," inviting audiences to reexperience events and encounter historical figures as living people. But this rather limited view obscures far broader and more interesting questions about our most basic relationship to history and the diverse contributions of visual and computational media to conceptions of the past. History is now up for grabs in ways that were hitherto unimaginable; the past is routinely being remixed, reimagined, rescripted, and reappropriated in powerful and eccentric ways, often by individuals—fans, geeks, hackers, teens, and artists—who do not necessarily see themselves as engaged in the discourse of history at all. Tempting as it is to view this as a threat to both the order and discipline of history, we may equally see it as a sign of healthy, dynamically contested relations to the past. While historical uncertainty and disputation are sometimes viewed as the enemy of a respectful attitude toward the lived past, consensual histories run an even greater risk of becoming polite fables, the kind of cultural narratives that lead to rituals of remembrance rather than critical thinking and political agency. Media histories are all too easily misapprehended as tools for building passive consensus and foreclosing debate. This is due in no small part to the long shadow cast by Hollywood historical epics, documentary miniseries, and vast digital archives that offer grand visions and narrative closure rather than stubborn resistance, delinquency, and conflict.

But this is not the way it has to be. This book seeks out the cracks and fissures in historical consensus—those neglected, indigestible, contrarian imaginings that throw our whole historical sensibility into sharp relief. Emerging from an increasingly varied media sphere that includes film, television, games, and a whole spectrum of networked and computational media, these widely varied practices of history all see the past as a function of consequential, and above all *mutable*, materials: images, sounds, and architectures of information that are *both* expressive representation and tools for thinking and knowing. Simply put, we should not look to media for the truth about the past but instead examine them for clues about the way history is constructed and engaged through cultural products, memories, myths, and politics. The goal of this book is to move beyond the epistemological binaries that have dominated discourses of media and history during the past four decades to instead consider the myriad "technologies of history," the ways in which media practices broadly conceived help us think about the world, the past, and our potential to act as historical and political agents.

It is difficult to talk about what is at stake in the construction and dissemination of history through media without resorting to vague concepts such as "historical consciousness" or "historical awareness." We may assume that historical consciousness of a much re-created and increasingly distant event such as World War II, for example, is shaped significantly by the war stories repeated continuously in TV shows, movies, and games. But while the combination of anecdotal evidence and intuition supporting this assumption is convincing enough for certain kinds of observations, the actual relationship between these media and what people really know and care about the past should not be taken for granted. Although this book explores how viewers respond to film, video, and digital texts, its focus remains on the production and dissemination of cultural discourse rather than the more ethereal sphere of cultural consciousness. In order to avoid facile assumptions about reception, I will strive, whenever possible, to ground my analysis of media texts and systems in a clearly defined set of historiographical concerns or discursive systems.

I will also argue for a rigorously parsed understanding of an equally slippery term: memory. Terms such as "social memory" and "popular memory" are often used to describe what is at stake in a society's struggles over the construction of history, though efforts to define them precisely are rare. The working presumption for many writers is that the processes of remembering and forgetting that happen in people's heads on an individual scale are analogous to the way memory operates on whole populations.[2] In recent years, cultural theorists have argued for more complex and reciprocal models of interaction among the realms of memory, history, and media. Although it is easy to speak of film or television as creating or erasing something tangible called memory, I find it vastly more productive to accept the challenge posed by Marita Sturken, who describes relationships of "entanglement" that take account of the multiple narratives of history and memory as elements of a rich and complex morass of cultural practice.[3] Therefore, following Sturken, my preferred term to describe the functioning of memory across social groups and their behaviors will be "cultural memory."

It is also in the realm of practice—what Michel de Certeau calls "making history"—that we see the difference between "historiography" and its loosely deployed other, "history." The task of the historian, according to de Certeau, is a "repoliticization" of historical discourse, that is, a kind of writing that historicizes historiography itself. Historians, he argues, should apply their historicizing methods (i.e., a reading of socioeconomic and mental conditions) to their own work in order to show "how a symbolic system articulates itself in a political one."[4] On political grounds I will argue that all *history* is really *historiography*; that the separation of the object from its process of production obfuscates the ideological dimensions implicit in any treatment of the past. Thus, for the sake of clarity in the pages that follow, "historiography" and its derivates will be the preferred terms for any form of discursive construction concerned with events of the past. The term "history" will be used sparingly as a synonym for "the past," for example, when part of a vernacular phrase such as "history film" or "the construction of history." When the goal is to highlight the contested nature of "history" as a cultural formation, the term will appear—with no disrespect intended—in quotation marks.

Finally, in order to highlight the complicated effects of mediation on the relationship between images and the world—particularly the world of the past—I will attempt whenever possible to emphasize the constructive, rather than mimetic, aspects of film, video, and digital images. Roland Barthes argued that the indexicality of photographic images depends upon a visual referent, attesting to the fact that "something happened here." But even for Barthes, the content of a photograph was only complete when combined with memories expressed through spoken or written words.[5] In the digital era, this assertion must be further qualified, but the ontological status of photographic images has rarely spoken for itself, whether in the courts or among theorists of visual culture. Barthes's need to assert the indexical nature of photography demonstrates its contingent status long before the advent of digital manipulation. Henceforth, in order to underscore this contingency with regard to media-based histories, we will speak exclusively of the "construction," rather than the "representation," of history.

Mediated History

In our present age of technological proliferation, it often seems that what we call "history" flows more or less automatically from film, television, and computer screens, a by-product of the informational hemorrhaging of corporate-dominated media industries. Indeed, historiography depends on media for both raw materials and a means of conveying ideas from one moment or generation to the next. But the precise nature of the relationship between historiography and its medium is far from transparent. Within the American culture industry, "history" often functions primarily as a commodity to be packaged, sold, and consumed. Like all commodities, it may therefore be used and reused, mutated, revised, or recontextualized. While certain genres of all-inclusive, medium-effacing historiography attempt to conceal their origins through prodigious use of images from the past, others continually assert their status as ideologically invested artifacts that are invented, thought, made, and constructed. This book is concerned not with large-scale historical documentaries or costumed epics—"feather films" (as *New York Times*' Vincent Canby once described them), in which the main character writes with a large quill pen—but rather with instances of aberration, self-consciousness, and eccentricity. My focus will be on media that recognize that the construction of history is a complicated and sometimes ugly business.

Cinema, television, and digital media do not merely serve as vehicles for historical discourse; they also shape our basic relations to time, history, and memory.[6] It is arguably no more natural to conceive of "future" and "past" as entities successive and distinct from each other than to view cinema's succession of minutely varied images projected in rapid succession as representative of life. Film, indeed, includes the capacity to disrupt the evenly measured flow of time that we, at least since the modern era, believe ourselves to experience. Likewise, films that digress from established timelines and narratives open up possibilities for more diverse and controversial conceptions of the past. The potential for nonlinear or multiply linear temporal structures is, of course, exponentially greater in the realm of digital media, games, and computational systems. However, the extent to which the majority of these media have explored this potential remains disappointing with regard to the construction of history.

In order to adequately address the role of visual media in historiography, we will first address some theoretical contexts of motion pictures. Film theorists have argued that cinematic reception is partially defined through the perceptual apparatus of the brain and the unconscious. Cinematic devices such as flashback, flash-forward, slow motion, freeze frame, and so forth, suggest cognitive correlates produced through the imperfect activities of the brain's synaptic functions. I would add that the proliferation of historical images on film and television has led to the emergence of an equally intimate and reciprocal relationship between historical viewing and historical thinking. The language of cinema, like the languages of history, must be learned. Films instruct their audiences how they are to be watched, giving rise to reading protocols that vary from film to film and genre to genre. As such, films may also work against established communicative norms, subverting existing systems or offering alternatives of their own. Taking this one step further, the reading protocols from cinema allow us to "read history" in ways that may deviate from how the past is conventionally understood. Similarly, the widely varied reception contexts and interactive potential in television and video games exponentially complicate assumptions about how meaning is produced.

If we acknowledge that motion pictures have become an important part of the way "history" is disseminated and remembered, it follows that an understanding of the way viewers receive it should be factored into our understandings of cultural memory. Simply stated, historians should be more attentive to reception issues, especially when dealing with visual or popular cultural historiographies. A key aspect of this reception process is bound up with the processes and practices of memory as well as intertextual relations to other media. It is thus necessary to address questions of spectatorship, subject positioning, and the various ideologies embedded in the languages of film, television, and digital media such as games and online networks. These histories, then, are not limited to the media texts themselves, but they also bring with them all the problems of signification, subjectivity, and politics that have been articulated by media history and theory throughout much of the previous century.

Attention to these theoretical complications is sometimes elided within the subdiscipline of film and history, where realism, with its illusionist simulation of real-world experiences and emotions, remains the privileged mode of discourse. Films are praised for historical fidelity and accuracy of detail or denounced for anachronies and departures from the factual record. Long before historians began appearing on the History Channel to elucidate Hollywood's shortcomings, distinctions between mere historical "costumery"[7] and academic-style historiography were crucial to the formation of uppercase "History" as a proper academic discipline. Indeed, in Western universities, the discipline of "History" was not fully articulated until the early nineteenth century, concurrent with (and in opposition to) the rise of the historical novel. As numerous literary theorists have pointed out, the distinction is, to some degree, arbitrary. The basic relationship between "literary" (i.e., fictional) history and factual historiography is one of interdetermination rather than opposition.[8]

Western traditions of historiography have emerged from a combination of myth, fact, and imagination expressed through the revision and layering of textual systems. Contemporary struggles over the role of media in the construction of history restage many of the dilemmas that have been articulated and debated in the philosophy of history since the Enlightenment. Many of these arguments proceed from questions of whether historiography is best understood as a science or an art, or adequately described as a recapitulation of prevailing power relations reflected backward through time. Writings in the philosophy of history have situated historical discourse in terms of the philosophical and literary movements, political exigencies, and epistemological frameworks available to a given age. In other words, philosophical discourse attempts to historicize "history," to render it a congruous and integral part of our understanding of the world. At present, coherent understandings (those infamous "master narratives") of the world and of the past have rightly come under suspicion. Yet, the production and revision of historical discourse continues, in spite of the difficulty and apparent redundancy of the central questions of epistemology. Does their lack of resolution mean that these questions are "eternal" or simply no longer interesting to ask?

Visual History in Context

Why has interest in visual history increased in recent years? The answer is due in part to the emergence in the late 1980s of visual culture as a field,[9] and the ensuing interest in all things visual. The answer is also partly institutional. During the past two decades, it has become increasingly clear that film and its Mylar surrogates would continue to play a key role in historical writing and thinking well into the digital age. As a result, film has become widely integrated into the curricula of college and university history departments. In part, this responds to more general trends within academia toward interdisciplinarity and the need for differentiation among graduate students entering an increasingly competitive job market. The subdiscipline of "film and history" has also carved a small but persistent niche market within academic publishing. During the 1980s, film became a regular component of mainstream historical journals such as the *American Historical Review*, while seminal works by Pierre Sorlin (*The Film in History*, 1980) and Marc Ferro (*Cinema and History*, 1988) were first published in English. The specialty journal *Film and History* was founded in 1971, followed by the formation of the International Association of Media and History in 1981 and online manifestations such as the electronic journal *Screening the Past* (1997) and many others.

The past two decades have also brought a proliferation of book-length publications on the relationship between film and history.[10] However, much of this work emerges from deep within the disciplinary and method-ological boundaries of academic history, with relatively little engagement with the theoretical approaches developed by film, television, and visual studies since the 1970s. With some notable exceptions, historians have tended to deal with films as if they were in competition with traditional forms of academic writing. Certain works may be acclaimed for providing a sense of realistic experience or visual richness, but most often film is seen as a deeply flawed medium for historical reconstruction, with a low density of information and unfortunate tendencies to privilege narrative and character over fact. Even Robert Rosenstone, whose work redefined the discourse of film and history in the 1990s, stops short of dealing di-rectly with cultural memory and questions of reception.

The growing interest in the construction of history on media also re-sponds to a variety of less tangible social needs and circumstances. In his influential critiques of postmodernism, Fredric Jameson diagnosed the United States of the 1980s as a society that can no longer think critically about "the great metaphysical preoccupations, the fundamental questions of being and of the meaning of life."[11] He argued that the generalized state of amnesia afflicting American culture has eradicated not our desire for "history" but only our ability to understand and engage it in meaningful ways.[12] For Jameson, postmodernism's random cannibalization of images and styles from the past is symptomatic of the trivialized role of "history" in contemporary culture. The frustrated desire for "real history," which is sublimated into endless varieties of kitsch in architecture, design, and fashion, may also account for the continuing popularity of such nostalgic and fantastic histories as *Star Trek* (1966–69) and *Forrest Gump* (1994). If this diagnosis is correct (a question explored in some detail in the chap-ters that follow), historians and cultural critics must choose between ig-noring some of the primary ways that Americans engage the past and the

The Smoking Man, William B. Davis, contemplates his life as an assassin for the U.S. government in the *X-Files*' "Musings of a Cigarette Smoking Man." (Fox/News Corp., 1996)

unsavory task of addressing the contents and strategies of historiography as it is actually being practiced on film, TV, and digital media.

The increased interest in the construction of history since the 1970s in the United States also responds to a desire to regain control of historiography after Vietnam and the crises of governmental credibility that followed in the wake of the Warren Commission report and Watergate.[13] Subsequently, revelations of the disastrous legacy of Reagan's Cold War politics and supply-side economics, combined with the complicity of the news media in disinformation campaigns during the Panama invasion and the first Gulf War, provide a framework for the emergence of TV shows that center on conspiracy and paranoia, such as *The X-Files* (1993–2002), *Millennium* (1996–99), and *Dark Skies* (1996–97), as well as movies such as Oliver Stone's *JFK* (1991).[14] More recently, amid revelations about the violation of basic rights in conjunction with the "war on terror"—from Abu Ghraib and Guantanamo to eroding privacy rights within the U.S.—it increasingly seems that we are living through the inculcation of what

Giorgio Agamben calls the military and economic "state of emergency," in which fundamental rights are held in abeyance. These increasingly normalized "exceptional circumstances" are generally blamed on the terror attacks in Washington and New York by Osama bin Laden's al Qaeda network in 2001,[15] and have clearly set the stage for a spate of video games such as *Waco Resurrection* (2003), *Kuma\War* (2003), and *JFK Reloaded* (2004), in which players renegotiate their relationship to "history" via playable environments. As I will argue in subsequent chapters, a symptomatic reading of the relationship between such real-world events and their repetitions and metaphors in popular media offers a significant but ultimately insufficient strategy for historiographical interpretation.

The End of History and the Bounds of the Expressible

During the late 1980s and early '90s, it became fashionable for theorists from opposing ends of the ideological spectrum—as exemplified by French philosopher Jean Baudrillard and American political scientist Francis Fukuyama—to conclude that "history" itself was at an end. The extremes of postmodern culture, for both Fukuyama and Baudrillard, resulted in the loss, rather than the reconfiguration, of history. Baudrillard argued that this loss was due to the triumph of simulation over representation; the obviation of the category of the referent set any attempt at historical construction adrift in a sea of ungrounded signification. Baudrillard's assertion that "the [first] Gulf War did not take place," for example, arose from observations about its primary manifestation in the West as a media spectacle.[16] Baudrillard's admission that the events of the Gulf War (bombing raids, death, destruction, etc.) *did*, of course, take place reveals that, for him, it is not the denial of history at stake but rather a fundamental challenge to how it is constructed, disseminated, and assigned cultural value. For Fukuyama, it was the ultimate rationalization of historical "progress" that put an end to the struggles that previously defined teleological historiography. Although Fukuyama's "end of history" argument is rooted in specific economic and geopolitical changes of the late twentieth century—namely, the dissolution of the Soviet Union and the "worldwide triumph of democracy" and "free market" economics,[17] the thinking it represents is often uncritically applied to the role of film (and especially television) in the construction of history. Fukuyama's book *The End of History and the Last Man* touted the emergence of a "remarkable consensus" in favor of liberal principles of government and capitalist economics,[18] and declared California to be "the most post-historical part of the U.S."[19] Although Fukuyama does not address history films or TV directly, such assertions would be incomprehensible if not for the omnipresence of the film and television industries in Los Angeles. Hollywood, once synonymous with the production and destruction of dreams, now more commonly signifies the erasure or commercialization of history.[20]

Cultural theories that describe contemporary historical consciousness in terms of debasement and loss mendaciously imply that there was once a time when historical thinking was more firmly grounded in secure access to an authentic past, when past and present spoke to each other more directly.[21] But historical consciousness, like historiography itself, does not move forward through "homogenous, empty time," as Walter Benjamin put it.[22] Part of the difficulty—but also the intricacy and fascination—of dealing with texts from the past lies precisely in negotiating the gaps between the time of their origin and the present. We view the past through accumulated layers of historical sedimentation[23] and desires that underscore the fact of our own immersion in a concrete historical moment. The past, which David Lowenthal fittingly describes as a "foreign country," is no less complex or contradictory than the present. We should be suspicious of any theory of history that presupposes a past that was more naive than our own time. This is not to say that codes of historiography have remained consistent over time. Moments of rupture and realignment occur when historical construction and thinking are directly affected by the events of the past. As Hayden White argues, a "modernist event" such as the Holocaust is so dramatically disruptive of ordinary historical progression as to be "unrepresentable."[24] However, we must ask whether the challenge posed by the Holocaust and a handful of other historical events might be more productively addressed as a problem of epistemology rather than representation.[25]

In the case of Claude Lanzmann's nine-hour documentary miniseries *Shoah* (1985), for example, the goal is neither re-creation nor documentation of the Holocaust. Lanzmann's decision to eschew all archival imagery of the Holocaust represents a historiographical gesture of the rhetorical limits of photographic evidence. Instead, Lanzmann invites meditation on the circumstances and causes of this event and its implications for all humanity in the present as well as the past. *Shoah* exemplifies a model of historiography that is conceived as a process rather than a series of static, if reusable, documents. Lanzmann's historiographical approach arguably speaks to not the "unrepresentability" of its object but rather the potential of a film to approach what Noam Chomsky has termed the "bounds of the expressible," that is, those ideas constrained by an ideological or political order rather than the capacity of the medium itself. Rather than defying representation, the modernist event could be equally seen as challenging the fundamental means by which the past is constructed and imagined. Therefore, the net result is not a failure of representation but rather a call for renegotiation of the terms of the historiographical debate.

In this context, the challenge posed to historiography and epistemology by the "modernist event" may be taken as catalytic rather than catastrophic. The investigations of historical trauma and memory by Marcel Ophüls are exemplary of the potential for film to address even the most disruptive historical events without succumbing to historical exceptionalism. At this point, I want to make it clear that my emphasis on textuality in the construction of history does not mean relinquishing the ability to talk about certain functional and material conceptions of the past. The charge that poststructural theory diminishes history to mere relativism— "the product of competing narrative views with nothing to adjudicate between them"[26]—indicates a misunderstanding of the stakes of historical discourse. The competing textual systems through which we necessarily construct and gain access to ideas about the past need not be regarded as necessitating descent into indeterminacy. As Robert Young argues, "The reproach that poststructuralism has neglected history really consists of the complaint that it has questioned History."[27] Awareness of the operation of textual systems—together with their embeddedness in a matrix of institutional, cultural, and political power—is a perfectly good place to start thinking about the most vexing problems of media and history.

In practice, what I am suggesting aligns with Tony Bennett's assertion that meaningful historical debate can only take place between the horizons of determinacy and indeterminacy and therefore relies on "conditions of intelligibility" that are "grounded in a material conception of history."[28] The problem, of course, is that Bennett's material conception of history is not always so easily obtained—least of all without deploying some sort of textual system. Simply put, this book privileges textual conceptions of historiography with the knowledge that material consequences are at stake. I view this apparent contradiction as irreducible to a simple textual-material dichotomy and hope that the tension created by their intersection raises questions that are only resolvable through political action. The "conditions of intelligibility" to which Bennett alludes are a functional part of "meaningful historical debate" precisely, but only, to the extent they may be mobilized toward social and political praxis.

Historiography, Truth, and Narrative

If we consider the basic condition of historiography to be an ongoing process of discursive and cultural struggle, then we must look for meaning beyond the "footnotes, bibliography, and other scholarly apparatus"[29] of professional historians to the way historical evidence is culturally processed, disseminated, and remembered. To the extent that photographic reproduction bears an indexical relation to the world, photographs and film images may indeed capture a photochemical rendering of physical surfaces from the past. Fiction films that were shot in past decades, for example, reveal something about the time in which they were made, if only pertaining to set construction, costuming, acting, or lighting design. Location shots offer incidental evidence of the appearance of city streets or landscapes, the kinds of fashion that may have been prevalent, or the price of gasoline.[30] As Carlo Ginzberg argues, we understand the past by discovering and interpreting a series of often unintentional clues and cultural myths.[31] It is thus possible to extract evidence of social concerns and assumptions through analysis of recurring themes and narrative structures. Whether a film is of or from a previous era, it renders the past dialogically, through processes of negotiation and interpretation within which viewers can and should be construed as active participants. This layering of cinematic signification and interpretation bears an analogous relation to constructing and understanding "history."

To the extent that visual media operate mimetically to show us the world as it once was, these media also support the tendency to understand historiography as a way of reexperiencing or re-creating the past. This is as true of an entirely fictional story like *The Godfather* (1972) as a famed historical epic such as Abel Ganz's *Napoleon* (1927). In recent decades, historians and scholars have exhaustively debated the relative significance of these two historical modes.[32] Although some conflicts persist, it is now equally possible to discuss both fictional and fact-based histories in terms of their construction of the past. In both cases, films are evaluated in terms of not only their accuracy and faithfulness to the historical record but also their ability to capture and evoke something called the "spirit" of the past.[33] But, as decades of film scholarship have shown, motion pictures achieve emotional and psychological identification through codes and conventions, not by nature. Cinema and television contain within their representational apparatuses the simultaneous and inescapable marks of their own artifice, even in the most "realistic" historical epic. This allows for perhaps the most convincing reevaluation of the basic process of historical construction. Films that deploy historical conventions in order to subvert them reveal not only cinema's representational apparatus but also some of the assumptions that accompany historical thinking. The work of Jean-Marie Straub and Danièle Huillet—who are known for paying precise attention to historical detail while obstinately refusing to suture viewers into a naturalistic diegesis—is exemplary of this potential.

Among mainstream history films, the well-researched and documented case study remains the dominant paradigm. In recent years, the ancillary markets for history films have come to include books that detail the historical research upon which a film's story is based. In part, this reinforces the received wisdom that visual historiography is dependent upon written texts for its origin or justification or both.[34] Although not considered at any length in this book, there is much to be learned from the sociopolitical and ideological investments of "realistic" history films. In most cases, however, I have deliberately elided these films, which are treated extensively elsewhere, in order to focus on works that eschew or subvert conventions of historical accuracy and realism.[35]

Historiography Modes

If we map the practices of visual historiography along the axes of attention to factual accuracy and emphasis on narrative, we may visualize this book's areas of focus and exclusion in relation to prior academic work in visual history. Although such tools for visualization are problematic because they are necessarily reductive, the following diagram may help clarify this book's discussions of less well-known works of visual historiography. For the purposes of this visualization, I have selected certain exemplars and limit cases that illustrate the logic behind this mapping. These categories are not in themselves any way static or deterministic, nor is my placement of any given work within a single category without nuance or exception. Indeed, the most provocative examples are those that refuse neat categorization or that call for extending the limits of a category—hence the extraordinarily vibrant and contentious public discourse surrounding Stone's controversial historical revisionism, for example, or the fascination among historians with counterfactuals that fall far outside of their ordinary purview on the right half of the figure.

The area mapped in grey surrounds a zone of practice that privileges neither narrative nor factuality in its treatment of historical subject matter. I have labeled this general area "metahistory" for its reflection upon the act of writing history as much as the actual historical events, personages,

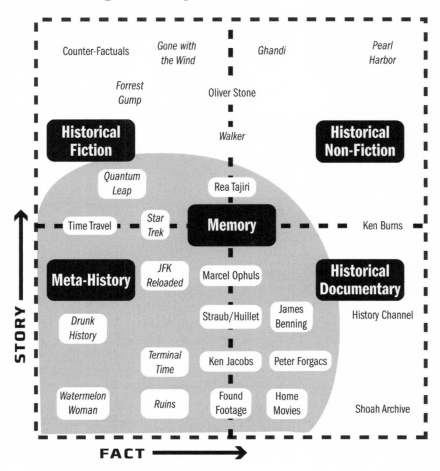

or interpretations represented. In contrast with White's use of the term "metahistory," however, I am satisfied to deploy the concept of reflective histories for categorizing alone. The works constellated in proximity to this term do not share any particular historiographical characteristics, and I will elucidate the widely varying ways in which these works contribute to my overarching argument. Finally, although it may result in consternation for some readers, I have taken the liberty of labeling the central zone of this figure "memory"—though I do not intend this to propose a consensual understanding of the term. For me, this multiply liminal space acknowledges the multivalent nature of memory and argues implicitly that we may best understand it through the conjunction and contradictions of fact, fiction, the desire for story, and resistance to unified narrative. My hope is that spatially locating some of the texts that are central to this discussion will clarify the focus of this book in comparison with its predecessors.

Discourses of Eccentricity

My goal is not to articulate a fixed relationship between historiography and various forms of media but rather to focus on certain, concentrated moments of interaction in which they—sometimes inadvertently—give each other away. The pages that follow do not attempt to construct a coherent narrative or to reconcile the multiple theoretical approaches developed in each chapter. Instead, the book as a whole addresses a set of historiographical problems raised with particular eloquence by group media texts that are connected by an uneasy relation to the construction of history. Each chapter intervenes in some aspect of ongoing debates over film, history, memory, or digital culture, most often to address the presuppositions and omissions of previous scholarship or to draw attention to the historiographical significance of neglected works. In all cases, my focus is on moments that cause us to reflect on the mechanics or the epistemological dilemmas of history writing itself—a metahistory of media histories if you will. Although much of the work considered here is admittedly obscure, exclusion from commercial distribution networks should not result in diminished critical attention. As David James has argued, the industrial and critical invisibility of alternative cinema "is the mark of its threat and also of its importance."[36]

To put it bluntly, I believe most visual histories have asked too little of their audiences, presumed too little knowledge and sophistication, and revealed too little about their processes of construction. Most Hollywood films construct their audiences primarily as consumers—both in the obvious economic sense and also ideologically—as vehicles for activating predetermined emotional responses. As consumers of commercial media, we are most often positioned as spectators rather than producers, critics, or agents of history.[37] Nonetheless, the histories produced by mainstream cinema and television are not without idiosyncrasy and moments of transgression. With existing boundaries of "legitimate" historical construction in a constant state of flux, the production and reception of historical discourse must be considered across as broad a range of cultural texts as possible. In some cases, this may involve making connections among widely divergent products of popular culture and the avant-garde. Although this strategy makes for alarming juxtapositions, the benefits of these discursive disjunctions far outweigh the detriments to scholarly convention. In any case, the traditional separation of high and low culture has always been of dubious merit. Virtually since the term's inception, the avant-garde has been demarcated against the realm of popular culture while harboring a not-so-secret fascination with it. By juxtaposing a disparate array of cultural texts I mean to erode the high/low and margin/center relations of commercial and experimental media, shifting emphasis toward works that challenge the discursive conventions of historiography or the cultural negotiation of the past.

The idea that meaningful generalizations about "history" and its telling may be made across such far-flung fields of media practice is both misleading and inconsistent with the type of historiography this book seeks to deploy. Inspired by Michel Foucault, the title of the book aims to focus attention on the mechanisms of history that are made visible through constant revision, contestation, and disruption. The *technologies of history* that interest us are those that are made to be broken, hacked, or reengineered. It is not a grand theory of history that we seek, nor even a stable relationship between the past and the media through which we engage it. If we are to speak meaningfully about the heterogeneity of the past, our method must be likewise heterogeneous. The goal here is not to reform narrative cinema's historical epics or to denounce the narrowness of concern in evidence on the History Channel and the reductive determinism of simulation games. Those who care about the construction and dissemination of "history" on film, television, and digital media should begin by articulating strategies of counterreading for the various histories that emerge across a range of commercial and noncommercial cultural practices. And perhaps most importantly, we must cultivate an awareness of too easily marginalized media practices, whether they are part of a self-consciously artistic avant-garde, informal networks of amateur creators, alternate history gamers, or pop-culture remixers.

1 Fantastic History

If you were a TV watcher in 1968, you might have seen an episode of the original *Star Trek* (NBC) series titled "Patterns of Force" in which Captain Kirk and his half-Vulcan first officer Mr. Spock visit the planet Ekos. There, they discover that a renegade Federation historian named John Gill has re-created a facsimile of Nazi Germany, with plans to deploy a "final solution" to annihilate the Zeons, a group of foreigners from a nearby planet inhabiting Ekos. The episode includes scenes of Kirk and Spock in Nazi uniforms and a struggle to derail the intended genocide while creatively interpreting the Federation's "prime directive," which prevents the Enterprise crew from any disruption of the planet's cultural development. The climactic scene provides an opportunity for Kirk to decry the evils of the Nazi regime and to express incredulity at his former history teacher having taken it as a model for a utopian society. This episode achieved near-legendary status in the decades to follow, and various incarnations of the *Star Trek* franchise itself have often revisited the narrative premise of an alternate outcome of World War II, along with countless other alternate history novels, films, and games.

The original *Star Trek* series was digitally remastered for the series' forty-year anniversary, and when "Patterns of Force" reaired in May 2007, the episode prompted a flurry of responses among *Star Trek* fans, who circulated shot-by-shot comparisons of the original episode online. A great deal of attention was paid to improved digital effects in the remastered version; however, fans also engaged in lengthy discussions regarding the timeliness of the episode, encouraging viewers to think about "history" and its repetition in relation to the ongoing war in Iraq. While few would consider *Star Trek*'s return to Nazi Germany culturally significant—and indeed, some might decry the trivialization of this particular historical period—I will argue the opposite. As a series and through its fan activity, *Star Trek* demonstrates a strong cultural desire to grapple with the deficiencies of mainstream historiography, as do many other works in the sci-fi and fantasy genres. This may be seen in the show's rampant, even obsessive, returns to key—if predictable—historical moments; in the frequent revisions of timelines to reimagine a different vision of our current world; and in a fascination with the "what-ifs" of history. Taken in aggregate, these returns and revisions constitute a culturally expressive

In *Star Trek*'s "Patterns of Force," Kirk and Spock go undercover as SS officers to overthrow a Nazi-esque regime instituted by a Federation historian on the planet Ekos. (Paramount, 1968)

practice of historiography and, as such, deserve critical attention rather than derision or neglect. In short, meaningful historiographical discourse takes place in many more places and cultural forms that we habitually acknowledge. This historiographical discourse generally and the particular histories enabled by digital, recombinant media in particular suggest provocative ways of reconceiving and interacting with the past.

In order to attain cultural and historiographical relevance, historical narratives need not aspire to factual accuracy or even plausibility. Instead, they may be "fantastic" (meaning that they may move well into the fictional realm, and even into fantasy), but in retaining a connection to history, they work to confuse the boundary between fact and fiction. In this sense, then, the term "fantastic" echoes the definition offered by Tsvetan Todorov in *The Fantastic: A Structural Approach to a Literary Genre* (1975), in which he argues that fantastic fiction provokes profound ambiguity between reality and fantasy within the narrative.[1] While Todorov deals explicitly with the supernatural, and his project is concerned primarily with codifying a genre, his emphasis on the blurring of boundaries and the ensuing state of indeterminacy experienced by the reader is productive for my purposes, insofar as fantastic historiography may similarly invite viewers to reconsider the ontological and epistemological categories—and supposed certainties—of traditional history.

More significantly perhaps, fantastic histories serve as a vehicle for expressing present-day obsessions, social anxieties, and cultural aspirations. Often, in their most outlandish configurations—for example, as science fiction—this type of historiography provides a forum for articulating ideal relationships with both past and future. By considering historical constructions that make no recognizable claim to authenticity, desire and fantasy in the imagination of the past is thrown into relief—a strategy of counterreading that is equally applicable to conventional historiography.

Fantastic historiographies help negotiate and reconcile cultural-historical contradictions and trauma. Painful events may be rewritten in terms of less-threatening relations of cause and effect: space aliens helped kill John F. Kennedy (*Dark Skies*); Adolf Hitler consorted with vampires (*Forever Knight*); Mussolini and Nixon gained power through the intervention of a mean-spirited genie (*The X-Files*); and so on. According to Anne Friedberg, "The proliferation of time-travel narratives in the 1980s seems symptomatic of anxiety about time and the loss of history,"[2] and Fredric Jameson diagnoses the prevalence of these narratives as the incapacity to imagine the future, arguing that they are "no doubt the symptom of social and historical impotence, of the blocking of possibilities that leaves little option but the imaginary."[3] The fabrication of unreal histories thus functions as both a substitute for the real past and an expression of the impulse to recover the power of history for the future. In either case, the past is invested with a redemptive or even healing capacity. In a reimagined or rerememered past, wrongs may be righted; tragedies that still resonate and haunt us in the present may be pacified.

The possibility of time travel postulated in science fiction narratives also renders the linearity of time and the inevitability of the present uncertain. If the present is changeable through actions in the past, then surely the same is true of the present—we are making our own "history-future" at every moment. The tendency within science fiction to focus on dramatic disruptions of the timeline reflects the ideologies of apocalypse and millennialism popularized in the 1980s and still echoing through paranoid cultures of the early twenty-first century. TV shows of the 1990s such as *The X-Files*, *Dark Skies*, and *Sliders* were all predicated on the possibility of radical historical change. However, since these fantasy constructions seldom addressed concrete aspects of everyday political struggle, radical or even progressive politics were not represented. Rather than inspiring audiences to action, these cultural texts articulated hopes, desires, and fears, which were perhaps inexpressible by other means. This revaluation of traditionally neglected artifacts of popular culture is a standard trope within postmodernist cultural theory, and indeed, the term "postmodern history" has gained a degree of recognition as a separate (and therefore contained and marginally interesting) category within the subdiscipline of film and history. So why is it not sufficient for us to simply follow Robert Rosenstone in labeling these sci-fi forays into the past as "postmodern" and be done with it?

On Postmodern History

As much as any other field of study, history is invested with hierarchies of meaning and authority. These hierarchies are rooted in cultural needs and consensus, and their attributes shift with political and social change. In his influential critiques of social and governmental institutions, Michel Foucault argues that authority is constructed through the combined exercise of physical and psychological power, reinforced through rituals and institutions, and largely consented to by the subjugated.[4] This authority holds no special relationship to what we call "truth," except as it is instrumental to the exercise of institutional power. The "truth" is thus equally deployed in the construction of counternarratives, although it does not need to be—nor does the striving for truth need to be the most important consideration in evaluating historical narratives.

Since the late 1970s, theorists of historiography have challenged the idea that the goal of history writing should be the progressive assembling of "larger historical truths" into grand libraries of fact and interpretation.[5] Hayden White argues that the work of the historian—as much as the chronicler or annalist—has never been merely the transliteration of a preexistent past into a documentary medium. Rather, "history" is constituted through the "emplotment" of historical information into recognizable narratives and literary tropes.[6] Although his work in the late 1970s was more readily assimilable within cultural studies than academic history, White's intervention ultimately served to redefine and legitimate the work of historians who were committed to narrative historiography in opposition to the scientific objectivism of the Annales School. Ultimately, the tropic convergence of historiography and literature described by White proved agreeable to the discipline of history in contrast with the greater threat posed by the immersive spectacle of the history film. Most literary and cinematic historiographies are indeed guilty of obscuring the "discontinuity, disruption and chaos"[7] of the past in favor of well-plotted narrative arcs and conflict-resolution structures. However, the answer lies not in a retreat into more detached or "objective" forms but rather in the complication and elaboration of existing narrative strategies. Furthermore, it should be remembered that the historical documents upon which documentary histories are based may not be considered naive or free of their own historical embeddedness. No record of historical events, whether a personal diary or a documentary newsreel, should be considered neutral—it is, as Dominick LaCapra argues, "always textually processed before any given historian comes to it."[8]

In spite of its reputation for conservatism and discursive sobriety, the discipline of history is far from monolithic. Ongoing challenges to historical research and writing protocols have resulted in a highly diverse and dynamically self-conscious array of competing methodologies. However, until the early 1990s, it was a rare historian who was willing to consider seriously the significance of film as a discrete and fully articulated form of historiographical practice. Hollywood's historical epics were—and still are—known for their factual inaccuracies, character composites, and elisions of historical complexity in favor of plot-friendly contrivances centered on personality, conflict resolution, and heterosexual romance. Although the value of historical filmmaking is often presumed to be its ability to bring the past "to life," a certain dishonesty attends historical narratives that undertake to present the past as an experience that may be recaptured, relived, or re-presented.[9] Put bluntly, the most interesting histories are those in which the past is fundamentally understood as a field of discursive struggle—a text that is open to revision and debate rather than delivering safe narrative closure. At times, "history" is rolled out like a carpet to cover gaps in knowledge or conceal atrocities committed in the interests of power. But historiography is not always reducible to discourses of domination. As feminist and postcolonial historiographies have demonstrated, revisionist histories also provide a source of empowerment and a means to erode centralized systems of authority.[10] Under certain circumstances, historiography also offers a means of escape into fantasy, an alternate form of mythology, or the expression of cultural needs and desires.

Perhaps the most influential and widely published figure in this movement is historian Robert Rosenstone who, as late as 1993, could justifiably declare himself to be the first to articulate the specific characteristics of historical films rather than simply treating them as a visual adjunct to written history. Rosenstone went on to break ranks with many in his field to focus attention on a number of films and videos that he regarded as examples of "postmodern history." Rosenstone's intervention marked a turning point in discussions of film and history, which had previously focused on questions of factual accuracy in large-scale historical epics. At the same time, theories of postmodernism that were once firmly predicated on assertions about the "loss of history" gave way to the troubling admission that, in order to be "lost," history would first have to be "found."

Within cultural studies, more sophisticated models for understanding cultural memory emerged in response to experiments with radical history[11] and the redefining of popular memory by Foucault and others.[12] The "culture of amnesia" associated with unreconstructed theories of television was gradually replaced with a notion of history and memory as fundamentally "entangled" with popular media rather than antithetical to it.[13] By the early 1990s, proclamations about "the end of history" following the collapse of the Soviet Union were revealed as cynical prevarications when Francis Fukuyama's "triumph of liberal democracy and capitalism"[14] led to an unprecedented and devastating economic crisis in Eastern Europe. Under the tutelage of Oliver Stone and Fox Mulder, American preoccupations with "history" came to be dominated by an amalgam of skepticism, conspiracy, and paranoia mixed with furtive, lingering hopes in the reliability of carefully executed, scientific research methods and technology.

In documentary film theory of the 1980s and '90s, already precarious connections between the real world and systems of representation were aggravated by the introduction and proliferation of digital imaging technologies. The popularity of Errol Morris's *Thin Blue Line* (1988) revived once-scorned strategies of re-creation and simulation in historical documentaries. Soon after the Rodney King verdict put the final nail in the coffin of visual positivism, the ontological status of images as historical evidence reached an all-time low, and a renewed critical attention to ideas such as "performativity" necessitated revision of Bill Nichols's venerable taxonomy of documentary modes.[15] With increasing access to personal computers and the Internet, databases and digital archives emerged as the primary means of storing, organizing, and disseminating historical information.

Some of the most diverse and challenging images of the past appear in movies and on television at the extremes of the high-low binary: in popular culture and the avant-garde. In a rare attempt to address the significance of some of this work to historiography, Rosenstone identifies a mode of what he calls "postmodern history" as that which "tests the boundaries of what we can say about the past and how we can say it, points to the limitations of conventional historical form, suggests new ways to envision the past, and alters our sense of what it is."[16]

However, Rosenstone limits his analysis to films that share the desire to "deal seriously with the relationship between past and present"[17] as it has been defined by more conventional modes of history writing. The representational strategies mobilized by postmodern history are, he claims, "full of small fictions used, at best, to create larger historical 'truths,' truths that can be judged only by examining the extent to which they engage the arguments and 'truths' of our existing historical knowledge on any given topic."[18]

Thus, Rosenstone essentially makes the argument that certain films and videos may be considered legitimate works of historiography because they try (with varying degrees of success) to do the same things that *real* historians do. Postmodern histories, though unorthodox, are recuperated by Rosenstone since they point to constructions of history that are verifiable through traditional means. Thus, ironically, Rosenstone reinscribes these film and video texts that he labels "postmodern" into a thoroughly modernist—rational and empirical—historical epistemology.

A more provocative strategy for drawing historiographical significance out of fantastic histories is to view them as moments of textual parapraxis. In other words, historiography that indulges in extremes of fantasy and speculation may reveal what is missing or repressed within conventional history writing or indeed the cultural unconscious. Present desires intrude upon the past and shape the various ways we choose to reconstruct it as well as the subjects we define as "historical." Seemingly involuntary choices, details, and slips may reveal more about what is desired from the past than the fully realized and deliberate discourses of documentary or realist historiography. Although such analysis may not teach us about the past as it was, we can catch a glimpse of its meaning and resonances for the present.

Where History Lies: Counterfactuals and Alternate Histories

In their most extreme form, historiographical constructions eschew facts altogether, creating willfully transgressive visions of the past. These include a rich and extensive body of popular literature known variously as alternative history, counterfactual history, allohistory, negative history, and uchronia. In 2000, Harvard professor of history Niall Ferguson edited a book called *Virtual History* that brought together essays by nine other historians, who speculate about what might have happened if certain key historical events had turned out differently.[19] The book suggests connections with chaos theory and ideas about multiple or nonlinear timelines but ultimately returns to a more sober form of historical discourse, arguing that we need to understand what might have happened if we are going to truly understand what did happen. As a result, submissions to the book are limited to speculations on alternative historiographies that are deemed plausible.

At the other end of the counterfactual spectrum are a huge number of alternative publications—zines, comic books, and Web sites—that explore many of the same issues in an unabashed and unfettered mode of science fiction fantasy. These include a group called the Interdimensional Transit Authority (ITA), a quasifictional organization that promotes travel between parallel universes and alternative timelines. The ITA publishes a series of "Alternate History Travel Guides" online and invites members to make use of a mechanism called the "Gridney Dimensional Conduit," which allows short-term visits to different worlds. Another organization called Point of Divergence operates as a forum and workshop for aspiring writers of alternative history.[20] In contrast with the anarchic spirit that underpins much counterfactual writing, Point of Divergence is clear about its desire to police the boundaries of its field and to refine alternative history as a literary genre. The Point of Divergence Web site asserts that they

> try to stay away from the same old stale topics that have been done to death (generally, what-ifs on the events of the American Civil War and World War II) and press on to fresh subject areas. One of the primary features of Point of Divergence is that it is designed for workshopping Alternate History stories—to offer criticism and suggestions on style, readability, and historical content as well as the realism/logic of the history created.[21]

Point of Divergence also advises would-be counterfactual authors to keep stories short, try to maintain a sense of logic, and not just sprinkle historical figures into improbable scenarios. Another typical strategy of this genre is to have readers encounter historical figures whose fortunes or circumstances have shifted. In one ITA story, Richard Nixon appears as a used car salesman in Whittier, California, while John F. Kennedy is a bloated, aging president, embattled over Vietnam. In another, Dennis Rodman is suspended from professional baseball for assaulting an umpire. In all these cases, part of the pleasure of the text lies in recognizing the deviations from "real history," creating a very large group of everyday

citizens who are "in" on the joke premised on a consensual understanding of both past and current events.

In the vast majority of this work, characteristics like imagination, thor-
oughness, and most importantly, the logical coherence of the alternate
world are valued. One organization, Uchronia, bestows annual "Sidewise
Awards for Alternate History," honoring the most convincing long- and
short-form works of fiction to appear on the organization's Web site. Interestingly, the standards to which writers of counterfactual history aspire
are nearly indistinguishable from those of academic historians; the only
difference is that they don't bother with adherence to so-called facts. Their
obsession with causality sometimes leads to the creation of elaborately
detailed timelines (beyond the initial point of divergence) that remove
any further historical disorder or disruption. Perhaps it is this respect for
linearity and causality that allows historians to take a somewhat more
indulgent attitude toward literary counterfactuals than cinematic ones.[22]

Ultimately, this type of fanciful revision serves to reinforce a fundamentally conservative view of historiography that maintains clear distinctions between truth and fantasy and a decided preference for linear and
coherent narratives. But at the same time, it allows for reexamination of
certain kinds of historical doxa that can and should be challenged, allowing, for example, the articulation of a narrative that portrays Kennedy as
the primary architect of the Vietnam War. Robert Young argues convincingly that historiography is an opportunity to escape from the either-or
binary of recapitulation or refutation of accepted narratives of the past:

> In Freud, the point is similarly not just the question—on which most
> attention gets focused—of whether the event "really" happened (a
> good copy) or was subsequently fantasized by the experiencing subject
> (a bad copy), but rather that it is repeated as a disruptive event that
> fissures ordinary forms of psychic continuity and therefore gains ana-
> lytic attention in the present. The same structure can be utilized by the
> historian so that the writing of history can itself become a disruptive
> event and consequently a form of political intervention.[23]

As a form of history writing, alternative and experimental historiographies thus function as the most promising vehicle for politicizing the
past, in part because these works access a wider range of expression and
creativity than fact-based historiography. Counterfactual histories' position in the margins of historical discourse makes them uniquely situated
to critique the conventions and power relations of traditional media and
historiography.[24]

Histories that deliberately lie pose a useful challenge to the most basic conventions of history writing and historical epistemology. In the most interesting cases, "history" becomes fused with metahistory in the creation of entirely new modes of popular historiography. At such moments, the lived past does not simply dissolve into a field of indeterminate signification; instead, it is reclaimed in the interests of clearly articulated historical and political imperatives. Histories that lie may be rightly situated within debates over postmodernism in film and history, but they should also be located in the context of a general cultural fascination with chaos theory and multiple-world scenarios that have appeared in films such as *Sliding Doors* and *Run Lola Run*, each of which explores an alternate sequence of events triggered by a single, seemingly trivial variable.

Television and Fantasy Narratives

A remarkable and misguided consensus exists among both historians and media critics regarding television's unsuitability for the construction of history. Notwithstanding the History Channel's original promise to provide access to "All of History—All in One Place," TV viewers are often characterized as victims in an epidemic of cultural amnesia for which television is both disease and carrier. Television, so the argument goes, can produce no lasting knowledge of the past; at worst, it actually impedes its viewers' ability to receive, process, or remember information of any kind. Raymond Williams's theorization of the "flow" of televisual discourse is frequently invoked to argue that the contents of television simply rush by like answers on the *Jeopardy!* board, without context or opportunity for retention. "Television," according to Mary Ann Doane, "thrives on its own forgetability."[25] And for George Lipsitz, television in the 1950s served to reinforce mass hegemony by creating "collective amnesia," "a loss of memory," and a "crisis of historical consciousness."[26] In one of the few books devoted explicitly to this subject, Colin McArthur describes with dismay the "tyranny of the moving image in tele-history,"[27] concluding that the ideological and institutional determinants of television production and history writing are virtually identical, thus ensuring their enslavement to the socioeconomic status quo.[28]

In spite of the old-fashioned, TV-hating prejudices that still underpin much of the writing about television and the widespread persistence of suspicion toward visual media for the construction of history, it is both possible and desirable to think more broadly about television's place in contemporary historiography. Simply put, television is no longer dismissible as a bad object detrimental to the development of "historical consciousness." In fact, American broadcast television has sustained an extremely active and nuanced engagement with the construction of history virtually since its inception. In particular, I believe TV has modeled highly stylized and creative modes of interaction with the past that, though subversive of many of the implicit goals of academic history, play a significant role in shaping compelling historiography.

Whether through reruns of shows and movies from previous eras or the innumerable series that are set in (or occasionally venture into) the past, TV has long been obsessed with looking back in time. The most obvious recent examples of this preoccupation may be found in the proliferation of overtly historiographical or nostalgia-oriented programming such as the History Channel, Ken Burns–style documentaries, and the '90s cable phenomenon TV Land (which originally touted its reproduction of programming schedules from the 1970s, complete with the original commercials). But it was public television, both in the United Kingdom and the United States, that most emphatically proclaimed itself to be the arbiter of historiography in popular culture. This was exemplified by shows such as *All Our Yesterdays*, a BBC series from the early 1960s that compiled and represented newsreels from twenty-five years earlier, and its American counterpart during the same decade *The Camera Explores Time*, which combined fictional reconstructions with archival footage.[29] Also on PBS in 1964 was David Wolper's *The Passing Years*, which provided "stimulating and nostalgic remembrance" of events, people, and times past. In its 1975 series *The Ascent of Man*, PBS took viewers on a "journey through intellectual history," and in 1984, Bill Moyers hosted a nineteen-part National Endowment for the Humanities (NEH)–funded documentary series, *A Walk through the 20th Century*.

In the 1960s, all three U.S. networks generated substantial quantities of conventional historiographical programming. These included the dramatized NBC series *Profiles in Courage* (1964–65), CBS's *Eyewitness to History* (hosted by Walter Cronkite from 1960 to 1963), and ABC's 1963–69 series *Saga of Western Man*, which presented dramatic re-creations of historical events such as the birth of Christ and Cortez's conquest of Mexico. By the late 1970s, however, the eight-part ABC miniseries *Roots* had revolutionized commercial TV's role in the construction of history, demonstrating that a historical drama connected with the right set of social issues could bring the past to life in ways that were profitable beyond the wildest dreams of public TV programmers.

The enormous popularity of *Roots* (which captured three of the top ten largest viewing audiences in television history at the time) and its numerous imitators[30] finally drew the attention of historians who were previously able to dismiss the role of television in the construction of history. The generally condescending attitude of historians toward TV and history was neatly and unapologetically summarized on the episode "History as an Act of Faith" (of the 1989 PBS series *The Open Mind*, hosted by Richard Heffner), in which Harvard professor of history Simon Schama described TV's penchant for narrative re-creation as ruining his discipline.

The pedagogical—one might even say didactic—function of much televisual historiography derives from TV's mandate, once an official part of networks' licensing by the Federal Communications Commission (FCC), to inform citizens. Indeed, historical pedagogy has occupied a privileged position within TV's program of national indoctrination, bleeding over into such obscure examples as the pilot for *The Monkees* (NBC, 1966–68), in which band members helped out with a high school history lesson between musical numbers, and an episode of *The Mod Squad* (ABC, 1969) that superimposed the lessons of ancient Greece and the Peloponnesian War onto the generational and political struggles of America in the 1960s, portentously resulting in the death of an elderly history teacher and the smashing of a plaster bust of Julius Caesar. Also symptomatic of TV's diverse engagements with historiography during this era were aberrant manifestations such as the "Improbable History" segments on *Rocky and His Friends* (ABC, 1959–61), an animated show in which a pedantic talking dog named Mr. Peabody calmly educates his naive human protégé, Sherman, in eclectic moments of world history ranging from the Trojan Wars to the development of the steam locomotive.[31]

But "history" also repeats itself on television in more subtle ways, often in the form of playful or fantastic narratives that may not give the appearance of being "about" historiography at all. This is particularly evident in the case of science fiction and time-travel narratives employed by shows such as the various *Star Trek* series of the '60s, '80s, and '90s,[32] as well as *Quantum Leap* (NBC, 1989–93), *Dark Skies* (NBC, 1996–97), and *Timecop* (ABC, 1997). The characteristics that unite these shows, rather than their historical accuracy or sincerity of purpose, are such factors as irreverence, creativity, and the willingness to utilize but also experiment with historical conventions. Underlying many fantastic histories are questions that are unanswerable through the channels of traditional historical work, such as the following:

- What if it were possible to not only reexperience the past but also change it?
- How might figures from the past understand and experience the present?
- What if history as we know it were a lie, created and maintained by a massive governmental or paragovernmental conspiracy?

While some of these questions come closer to the concerns of conventional historiography than others, each of them is expressive of a legitimate historiographical motivation. In the case of shows such as *You Are There* (CBS, 1953–57) and *Meeting of Minds* (PBS, 1977–81), fantastic narrative scenarios are incorporated into an explicitly pedagogical mode of address. Although the following examples are drawn from each of the past five decades, the threads of continuity connecting them are less dependent upon chronology or historical context than on the conceptual strategies and expression of shared desires.

Live from the Past: *You Are There*

In one of television's most remarkable products of the 1950s, the CBS television series *You Are There* offered a striking literalization of the link between television liveness and historiography. Adapted from a highly successful radio program that aired from 1947 to 1950, *You Are There* simulated full-scale network news reporting from the sidelines of notable historical events such as the Battle of Hastings, the execution of Joan of Arc, and Cortez's conquering of Mexico. Directed by Sidney Lumet and written largely by blacklisted writers, including Abraham Polonsky, Walter Bernstein, and Arnold Manoff, *You Are There* introduced the nation to CBS's future lead news anchors, Walter Cronkite and Mike Wallace. The show was structured to closely mimic a nightly news broadcast, complete with on-the-spot interviews and anchor desk commentary by Cronkite, who orchestrated the incoming reports and provided characteristically reserved commentary on the context and significance of the events reported. During the broadcast, field reporters ingeniously qualified conflicting historical opinions and disputed facts as being uncorroborated due to the immediacy of the live, breaking event. The show thus merged conventions of historical speculation and investigative journalism, while bringing present sensibilities to bear on the experience of the past.

You Are There created a dynamic and compelling form of "living history" that exploited the news format's ostensible commitment to fairness and objectivity. In an episode dealing with the assassination of Abraham Lincoln, for example, John Wilkes Booth agrees to do a live TV interview from the barn where he has barricaded himself after shooting the president, believing television will allow him to tell his story to an "impartial witness." Booth speaks rationally and eloquently of himself as a patriot of the Confederacy, whose actions were justified by a clearly articulated political goal. However, supplementary interviews with family members and associates emphasize personal motivations: jealousy of his brothers, desire for personal fame, and desperation or simple lunacy. The multiple perspectives offered by first-person interviews function as a surrogate form of historical analysis, offering precisely the kind of balanced presentation of the facts that links news reporting with more conventional modes of historiography.[33]

Although *You Are There* models an elaborate form of strategic anachrony, the show is structurally configured to reinforce the idea that historical events unfold according to familiar narratives, complete with well-timed elements of drama and suspense. Such factors undoubtedly contributed to the show's popularity; however, the opportunity to explore moments of historical discontinuity and chaos was thereby lost to a false sense of narrative closure. From Cronkite's opening intonation that "all things are just as they were . . . except *You Are There*" to the show's closing reassurance that "all events reported and seen are based on historic fact and quotation," *You Are There* strove for accuracy and fairness within the limits of accepted historical knowledge and pedagogy.

Past and Present Encounters

The desire to see the past through contemporary eyes, evidenced by shows such as *You Are There*, is paralleled by instances in which historical figures travel forward in time in order to observe and comment on the present.[34] Perhaps the most eloquent example of this was the public television talk show *Meeting of Minds* (PBS, 1977–81). Created and hosted by Steve Allen, *Meeting of Minds* brought together groups of actors portraying historical figures from various time periods and cultures to discuss contemporary topics and their relation to the past. The combination of personalities—including figures such as Socrates, St. Thomas Aquinas, Cleopatra, Florence Nightingale, Thomas Paine, Francis Bacon, Thomas Jefferson, Voltaire, Galileo, and Charles Darwin—were selected to ensure controversy and debate, with Allen acting as both moderator and provocateur. Describing the show, Allen proclaimed,

Host Steve Allen chats with Charles Darwin (Murray Matheson) and Galileo Galilei (Alexander Scourby) on *Meeting of Minds.* (PBS, 1977)

The idea is that every syllable will be part of an actual quotation. The degree of exact quotation varies from character to character. In the case of some people who played important roles in the drama of history, of course, there is no record of anything they ever said or wrote. Two examples that come to mind are Cleopatra and Attila the Hun. Nevertheless, they were both fascinating characters for our show. And there's nothing difficult in creating dialog for them. You bring factual information into conversational form—and commit no offense in doing so. The more scholars know about the people we're dealing with, the more impressed they are with how accurate our renderings are. It's remarkable how little negative criticism we've received.[35]

Interestingly, guests on the show spoke not only from their own imputed historical knowledge but also as well-informed students of U.S. history in the late 1970s, allowing them to make direct comparisons with the show's present. Thus, for example, the personages of Frederick Douglass and the Marquis de Sade discussed not only the relative merits of bondage and corporal punishment in their own times but also the debates over reform versus punishment in the American penal system of the '70s. Likewise, when introducing Karl Marx, Allen promised to hold him accountable for the atrocities committed in his name in the Soviet Union.

In a revealing juxtaposition, Marx was resoundingly booed by the studio audience that, moments earlier, cheered wildly for Marie Antoinette. Such moments betray the limitations of Allen's Cold War liberalism, as well as the show's framing as a vehicle for working out present contradictions through engagement with an imagined past. While such transparently contrived and quasihistorical constructs have generally been excluded from discussions of television and history, when taken in combination with the other fantastic scenarios considered here, they indicate a cultural need to imagine a type of historiography that is productive rather than merely reproductive and, perhaps most importantly, open to interaction with the present.

In its most literal manifestations, this interplay of past and present includes situations in which fictional characters inaugurate "real" historical events. In recent years, these causation narratives have driven two extraordinarily successful films directed by Robert Zemeckis, *Forrest Gump* and the *Back to the Future* franchise. In *Forrest Gump*, a slow-witted character played by Tom Hanks is digitally composited into archival film images as if he participated in historical moments such as the desegregation of the University of Alabama and teaching Elvis to dance. A nearly identical scene occurs in *Back to the Future*, when a time-traveling Michael J. Fox teaches Chuck Berry to play rock 'n' roll. And on the television series *Quantum Leap*, a temporally discombobulated Scott Bakula helps to free Martin Luther King's grandfather from slavery and teaches Chubby Checker to do the twist. Although clearly circumscribed by their fantasy constructs, the frequency with which these fictional scenarios involve white characters taking responsibility for (or facilitating) the historical achievements of African Americans underlines only one aspect of the problematic nature of this type of "playful" historical revisionism.[36]

While alternative histories may be granted a certain indulgence when they speculate on the historical impact of alien invasions and vampires, their intervention in politically charged discourses of race calls for a more rigorous critical standard. These violations of African American history do not merely disregard the factual record. No reasonable viewer could mistake the scenes described above for attempts at revisionist historiography rooted in even the most bizarre truth claim. However, these works' greater offense is the expropriation of a sphere of historiography that is under active, politicized contestation—the recognition of African American contributions to American history—to advocate the social agenda of "color blind" (white) liberalism. In both *Forrest Gump* and *Quantum Leap*, the white lead characters act as helpers in moments of black lib-

White time traveler Marty McFly (Michael J. Fox) teaches Chuck Berry
to play rock 'n' roll in *Back to the Future*. (Universal, 1985)

eration, symbolically solving complex race problems through a single
paternalistic gesture.[37]

Maintaining Order: *Star Trek*, *Quantum Leap, Timecop*, and *Sliders*

In the realm of fantastic or alternative histories, few genres open as many
possibilities as science fiction. Narrative devices such as the time machine
or accidental passage through ruptures in the "space-time continuum" (a

recurrent *Star Trek* phenomenon) offer endless opportunities for exploring the past. Other common motifs include the scientific experiment that went awry (the pretense of both *Sliders* and *Quantum Leap*) and the flashback structure (used to extreme effect in both the Euro-American *Highlander: The Series* and the Canadian police/vampire drama *Forever Knight*, in which immortal characters continually reexperience events from the distant past). On *Star Trek*, the historical periods revisited include such eclectic moments as the gunfight at the O.K. Corral; the outbreak of World War II; the crash landing of an alien spacecraft at Roswell, New Mexico, in 1947; the first U.S. manned space launch; and the computer revolution of the 1980s. Similarly, *Quantum Leap* re-creates events of the Civil War, the Watts riots, the Cuban missile crisis, the Francis Gary Powers U-2 spy incident, the assassination of Kennedy, the death of Marilyn Monroe, the discovery of Elvis Presley, and the Ali–Foreman "Rumble in the Jungle" boxing match in Zaire.

The extreme diversity and idiosyncrasy of these historical moments makes it difficult to define a single unifying characteristic or explanation behind them. However, it is possible to identify certain patterns and repetitions revolving around moments of trauma and those that lack historical certainty or closure. Whether due to the magnitude of the trauma or the sheer number of competing explanation theories, an event such as the JFK assassination provides fertile ground for the writing of counterhistories (in addition to Stone's *JFK*, both *The X-Files* and *Dark Skies* have recast the assassination in terms of government conspiracy and coverup). However, the significance of such revisionism is not its contribution to a final or even most accurate "truth" but rather the elaboration and perpetuation of cultural mythologies. The presumptive goal of this obsessive rewriting and fictionalizing is not historical closure but actually the opening of additional channels of discourse.

The persistent notion that the past is open to interpretation and modification is also expressed in a more literal sense on shows that explore the narrative trope of time travel. The *Star Trek* series, for example, have avidly pursued the logic of temporal causality and the possible existence of multiple timelines, with deeply conflicted implications for the construction of historical agency. On *Star Trek*, the idea that a single individual may cause dramatic social changes is axiomatic to numerous episodes, though it often proves inadvisable. In "Bread and Circuses," for example, a rogue Starfleet captain is responsible for transforming a planet into a culture of violence based on ancient Rome, complete with televised gladiator matches. Likewise, in the "Patterns of Force" episode noted at the opening of the chapter, a historian of "ancient" (twentieth-century) Earth becomes the ruler of a society that he models after Hitler's Germany, citing the efficiency and order of the Nazi regime. And in "City on the Edge of Forever," a lone female political activist is responsible for delaying the United States' entry into World War II, the unintended result of which is Nazi domination of the planet. Perhaps as a result, later episodes in the series extend the "prime directive" (which prohibits interference in developing cultures) to include the past, so that time-travel narratives invariably revolve around maintaining or reinstating the status quo.

Another overt example of this obsession with historical order may be seen in the ABC series *Timecop*, which premiered in the Fall of 1997 only to be canceled midseason after airing five episodes. On *Timecop*, "temporal criminals" were pursued through time by members of a top-secret government agency known as the "Time Enforcement Commission" (TEC). The show's opening warned that, "with history itself at risk," the TEC must fight to maintain law and order as well as the integrity of the "temporal stream" against time-traveling villains who revisit notorious historical criminals such as Jack the Ripper and Al Capone. In addition to its obvious connection to the 1994 movie of the same title, *Timecop* echoes the pursuit through time of Jack the Ripper in *Time after Time* (1979) as well as the PBS children's game show *Where in Time Is Carmen San Diego?* which pits junior historian-sleuths against a gang of thieves who rampage through time, stealing artifacts and altering the past. In all of these cases, the possibility of time travel is conceived simultaneously as a threat to the "natural progression of history" and an opportunity to go back and correct transgressions of the past according to a contemporary, enlightened sensibility.

The NBC television series *Quantum Leap* is unapologetic about its moralistic approach to the rewriting of history. In each episode, the show's main character, Sam (Scott Bakula), "leaps" uncontrollably from one moment in the past to the next, finding himself inside the bodies of various individuals (often of varying gender, age, race, etc.), "driven by an unknown force to change history for the better." Sam is accompanied on his adventures by a holographic companion (Dean Stockwell) who runs computer simulations in order to calculate which alterations to the historical timeline are necessary to "put right what once went wrong" and move on to the next leap/episode. Unlike typical *Star Trek* historical narratives, which operate on the level of geopolitical or eschatological conflict, *Quantum Leap* deals with more personal, emotionally laden struggles (e.g., an African American doctor must survive the Watts riots to help rebuild his community, and a boxer must win his last fight in order to finance a chapel for an impoverished group of nuns). On *Quantum Leap*, the past is malleable but only within the constraints of a prescriptive master plan, the execution of which is governed by statistical probabilities and the good intentions of white, male scientists.

The frequency of this narrative device—revisiting troubling moments in the past to correct wrongs—is a revealing expression of desires to work through the trauma of past events. The compulsive replaying of Nazi scenarios twenty years after World War II, for example, as well as the continual reworking of the Kennedy assassinations and a long list of other national traumatic events, suggests that one of the roles for these fantastic histories is therapeutic—the expression of a collective trauma and the suggestion that repetition may serve as part of the healing process.

While healing narratives motivate one large arena of fantastic historiography on TV, other strands favor a different variety of themes and objectives. For example, the short-lived NBC sci-fi series *Dark Skies*, perhaps the most overt and self-conscious example of fantastic historiography on American television, set out to reframe nearly every major news event of the post–World War II era in terms of a massive alien invasion. The series premiere of *Dark Skies* opens with a scene of a Cold War–era fighter pilot in pursuit of an unidentified flying object over Soviet air space. Shortly after making visual contact, the plane is shot down, forcing the pilot to eject while the UFO disappears without a trace. A TV news report uses archival footage to reveal that the downed pilot was Francis Gary Powers, the U-2 pilot shot down over the Soviet Union in 1960. Later in the same episode, the aliens (who are linked to a central "hive," bringing super strength and vacant stares to their human host bodies) are shown to be the cause of several other "real" historical events, including the Cuban missile crisis and the assassination of JFK.[38] Subsequent episodes deal with such events as the first U.S. manned space flight and the arrival of the Beatles in America, events that resonate powerfully in the cultural memory of the American baby boom generation.

Dark Skies' self-consciousness about its alternative historiography is made explicit in an opening credit sequence in which the series' main character intones ominously, "History as we know it is a lie." Promotional materials for the show similarly promise that *Dark Skies* reveals "the American history you never knew." And according to the show's creators, Bryce Zabel and James Parriott, "This is being presented as alternative history. Everyone has their favorite conspiracies, but we will challenge and expand on those by building a framework that adds consistency to the alien-awareness theories. . . . The series premise is simply this: Our future's happening in our past."[39] But clearly this show is not about historiography in any conventional sense—nor is *Dark Skies* adequately described as simply a show about memory or nostalgia, though it is both at times. The overriding tone of the show derives from 1990s paranoia and anti-government conspiracy cultures, bearing an uncanny resemblance to both *The X-Files* and Stone's *JFK*. However, *Dark Skies'* creators misjudged the extent to which alternative history is rooted in resistant cultural positioning and a kind of homegrown anarchy that is not easily accommodated to network marketing campaigns. The very consistency that the show's creators attempted to bring to "alien awareness theories" (still flourishing on the Internet and in subcultural communities) contributed to its downfall. In spite of a seemingly timely premise and NBC's strong commitment to the show, *Dark Skies* achieved consistently poor ratings and was canceled after only one season on the air.

Although it would be possible simply to dismiss *Dark Skies* as a show about neither "history" nor memory, it may also be understood as a text that effectively illustrates the inadequacy of these two terms as they are frequently constituted in historiography and cultural criticism. *Dark Skies* calls for a more mobile conceptual framework for dealing with the myriad ways in which historical information is culturally disseminated and processed. Although it never connected with the oppositional impulses of its prospective fan community, *Dark Skies* had strategies of "active forgetting."[40] Just as experimentation with language may display "the inherent oppressiveness of the symbolic order," histories that are "uncoupled from the instrumental need to signify" may reveal their own kind of creativity and anarchy.[41] TV shows such as *Dark Skies* and the historical impulses they manifest serve as indicators of the cultural processing and elaboration to which all types of historiography are subjected. As such, they create a new paradigm of "popular" historical thinking in which once heretical concepts (e.g., that present and past are mutually interdetermined, that time is nonlinear, and that "history" is open to multiple interpretations) are all but taken for granted.

Among the most sustained investigations of multiple-world phenomena is the TV series *Sliders*, which originally aired on Fox beginning in 1995; it was canceled by Fox after three seasons, only to be picked up by the Sci-Fi channel following a letter-writing campaign by fans. *Sliders* is a science fiction genre show based on the adventures of an unlikely foursome composed of a pompous professor, a hunky boy genius, an African American rhythm-and-blues musician, and a spunky tomboy, all of whom are trapped in a state of interdimensional flux, careening wildly from one parallel universe to the next, trying in vain to return home like the characters in a futuristic *Gilligan's Island*. Each world they visit is similar to our own, except for some more or less significant change in the historical timeline that renders it undesirable. These variables range from a world in which dinosaurs still roam the earth, to one that is perfect in every way except that humans are endowed with frog tongues, and to one in which J. Edgar Hoover executed a successful military coup following the Kennedy assassination, placing the United States under a perpetual state of martial law, enforced by machine gun–toting, cross-dressing government troops known as "skirt boys."

After several years in this state of dimensional flux, one episode suggests that the characters in *Sliders* are so out of touch with their original timeline that they wouldn't even recognize it if they saw it. With only a few minutes to decide whether the seemingly desirable world they have arrived on is truly their own timeline, one of the characters consults a newspaper and disappointedly reports that, on this world, Sonny Bono is a congressman and O. J. Simpson is on trial for murder. In this moment, the perceived "natural progression of history" is revealed to be a fundamentally arbitrary construction if not an outright fraud. In the end, the show's basic narrative trope of repeatedly attempting to return home from parallel universes, which are all revealed to be flawed in some way, supports a basically conservative and self-satisfied image of "our" reality; further, the show's underlying message asserts that, at any given moment, time and history as we know it are only a few molecular vibrations away from total chaos and anarchy. Although *Sliders*' engagement with more complex issues of historiography is admittedly limited, such episodes reveal the precariousness of "real history"—even slight shifts in the way events unfold can have enormous consequences—and the fears that we are culturally wont to project onto imagined ones.

Historical criticism that engages only with those types of historical construction, aspiring to conventions of academic historical writing, is singularly ill suited to theorizing many of the "historical" texts and practices that permeate American popular culture. Part of the power of these texts may lie precisely in their incomprehensibility and potential threat to more conventional historical forms, forcing—or allowing—viewers to choose their own path through the massively complex array of historical imagery and ideologies to which they are exposed. Rather than simply learning new ways to forget, TV viewers may be acquiring a much more specialized and useful ability—to navigate and remember their own past with creativity and meaning, even when it goes against the design of historians.[42]

This willingness to explore alternative, fantastic, or counterfactual forms of engagement with the past is also articulated with particular eloquence in the work of numerous independent and experimental film and videomakers. The remainder of this chapter is devoted to how alternative histories relate to the products and practices of the commercial film and television industries. Although some of these films are devoted to expressing a position that is diametrically opposed to dominant historiographical models, others opt for strategies of engagement and tactical appropriation.

Creating Your Own History: Cheryl Dunye's *Watermelon Woman* and Morgan Fisher's *Standard Gauge*

If television has suffered critical neglect based on the profoundly negative effect of the historical establishment's accuracy-based criticism, so too has the large and diverse body of experimental film and video work that directly engages and challenges the basic discursive strategies and tropes of Hollywood's history films. Many independent films also engage in an active critique and negotiation of industrial filmmaking practices while drawing upon them for both structure and content. In spite of the apparent connection between these works and mainstream cinema, the critical establishment—through marginalization in publishing and pedagogical practices—often simply reproduces the market-based segregation of "art" and "commercial" filmmaking. In reality, however, these two spheres of production are mutually determining, both formally and historiographically. As David James has argued, "The binary division between Hollywood and an avant-garde is itself misleading; non-industrial film is produced in a field that comprises multiple positions more or less close to studio production, with representational codes and production strategies continuously circulating among them."[43]

Films that construct experimental or irreverent images of the past are not *without* "history"; they are often simply expressing a familiar historiographical impulse through channels in which it is possible to understand the past as a field of competing discourses rather than an empirically established set of facts. In order to illustrate this point, I will now focus on two films in which Hollywood industrial practices become constitutive elements in the creation of historical counternarratives: Morgan Fisher's *Standard Gauge* (1984) and Cheryl Dunye's *Watermelon Woman* (1996).

Virtually all of Fisher's films to date are about the process of making and watching films. Many are composed in the style of structural film, with single, continuous takes and a total lack of editing and camera movement. In contrast, Dunye's *Watermelon Woman* deals with issues of race and sexuality, utilizing a kinetic and diverse range of styles (she shoots on video as well as film, combines documentary and fiction, uses handheld cameras and direct address, and occasionally cuts away to extra-diegetic performance sequences). In other words, these are two films that could not be more different in structure or appearance. But, while I think it's possible to regard them as occupying opposite ends of a stylistic spectrum, *Standard Gauge* and *Watermelon Woman* also share certain concerns regarding historiography and their relationship to commercial filmmaking.

In an interview with Scott MacDonald, Fisher says that, although his own films have fallen entirely within what is considered an avant-garde tradition,

> narrative filmmaking . . . has always been a part of my work, however obliquely. In fact if there were no narrative filmmaking and no industry I don't think I could do work. I don't mean this in the obvious sense: that without the Industry and industry in general, there would be no film or equipment and hence no independent filmmaking (in that respect, we are all at the mercy of industrial capitalism, whose sympathies and motives are directed elsewhere). I just mean that for me the Industry is a point of reference and a source, in both a positive and a negative sense, something to recognize and at the same time to react to.[44]

Standard Gauge is composed of a single, continuous, nearly thirty-minute-long take, (i.e., approximately one, complete 1,200 foot roll of 16 mm film). It was shot on an animation stand, in real time, while the director displayed various lengths of 35 mm film that he had collected over more than a decade working on the fringes of the Hollywood film industry. The film reveals that Fisher was a film editor for Roger Corman, did stock footage research for Haskell Wexler, and was an actor and second unit director for a cult film called *Messiah of Evil*. The soundtrack is dominated by a voice-over by Fisher, describing the significance of each piece of film that he momentarily positions in front of the camera. Sometimes, the stories are fairly long and complex—as in his description of the end of Technicolor processing—and other times he simply says, "Here are some pieces of film that I think are interesting to look at."

His treatment of these pieces of film is emphatically materialist but also nostalgic and fetishistic. In part, *Standard Gauge* documents a relationship to film images as physical, celluloid objects—a relationship that is threatened with erasure as the industry moves toward digital editing and projection. But most importantly, Fisher writes himself into his own version of film history and foregrounds parts of the filmmaking apparatus that are ordinarily suppressed. As in several of his earlier films, including *Cue Rolls*, *Projection Instructions*, and *Production Stills*, he is concerned with the technical processes of cinema and the invisible labor of those people who keep the system running (including color timers, lab technicians, and projectionists). Each piece of film testifies to some unseen aspect of the medium: optical soundtracks, printer notches, sprocket holes, head and tail leaders, color charts, camera flashes, and so forth. In these films, Fisher emphasizes all the things that are literally a part of every film but that are almost entirely excluded from the study of film and film history.

The story of Fisher's career in the film industry is refracted through his idiosyncratic collection of filmstrips, and this serves, in turn, as an excuse to ruminate on all of Hollywood history. However, Fisher's historiography is willfully subjective and fragmentary, as if he were attempting to prove Carlo Ginzberg's claim that the past reveals itself most eloquently in not grand narratives but rather tiny clues. Fisher admits that some of the filmstrips he displays were rescued at random from trash bins with no idea of their content. Yet, in these strips of film, he uncovers hidden discourses of institutional and gender politics—for example, in the suppression of the "China Girl" images used by labs to standardize flesh tones—as well as innumerable clues to the technological origins and uses of the films. In the end, Fisher does not attempt to construct a revision of any previously existing historiography but instead radically refocus his viewers' attention around his own personal and intellectual concerns. Alone among the filmmakers considered here, Fisher suggests that strips of film reveal multiple historiographical narratives regardless of their content and relation to overt historical construction.

An allegorical relationship exists between the suppression of the technical apparatus of filmmaking that Fisher articulates and the marginalization of women, lesbians, and African Americans in Hollywood that Dunye demonstrates in *Watermelon Woman*. Like Fisher, Dunye frames her attempt to recover a rapidly disappearing element of film history through the form of a personal narrative. Dunye herself appears in the film in a fictional persona who becomes fascinated with a young, African American actress from the 1930s known only as the "Watermelon Woman." Her research on the actress is impeded by the racism that inhabits both the industry and the archival/research institutions through which film history is defined and preserved.

Dunye's character is more successful with the alternative archives and individual recollections she finds in the queer and African American communities, eventually discovering enough pieces of the puzzle to identify the Watermelon Woman as an actress and nightclub singer known in various incarnations as Faye Richards or Faith Richardson. Almost incidentally, she also discovers that Richards sustained a long-term, lesbian relationship and creative collaboration with a white director named Martha Page (who is also fictional but transparently patterned after Dorothy Arzner). Their story is told through archival images, sequences from the films they were alleged to have made together, and, perhaps most interestingly, through a complex web of intertextual and historiographical allusions.

Dunye utilizes and, through her fictionalization, elaborates upon a historiographical process that Judith Mayne has described as "detection—an effort to rethink and reconstruct the various images, gaps and silences of the past."[45] The film simultaneously demonstrates the power of reclaiming identity through historiography while subverting the conventions of historiography's sober discourses. In conventional historiography, Nichols argues, the importance of archival footage is to offer a sense of the "body in history," allowing us to perceive the person as a real historical figure, and not merely a reconstruction. But he also warns that "when an actor reincarnates a historical personage, the actor's very presence testifies to a gap between the text and the life to which it refers . . . the extra body of the actor mediates our access to the historical event."[46]

Dunye avoids the problematic of the "body too many" by basing her story on a fictional character who is historically anchored by association with the lesbian and feminist recuperations of Arzner. Equally, the deficiency that *The Watermelon Woman* seeks to redress is that of the "body too few"—a lack that applies to both the nonexistent historical subject of *The Watermelon Woman* and the more general absent presence of African Americans in film history.

The pairing of the director, Martha Page (played by the film's producer, Alexandra Juhasz), and *The Watermelon Woman*, Richards, parallels the relationship of Arzner with her longtime collaborator Marion Morgan, creating a layering of historical narratives both inside and outside the film's diegesis. On one level, Dunye's enactment of the multiple roles of director and star of the film seems to represent a literalization of R. G. Collingwood's edict that the goal of all historiography is the reliving of the past by the historian. But the multiple identities of Richards speak most eloquently to the multiple layers of exclusion and marginalization experienced by the figure she represents, that is, someone multiply identified as female, African American, and queer.

In order to make this film, Dunye was forced to operate and seek financing and distribution outside the studio system, yet her film's content and the thrust of her historical revision remain focused on the world of commercial filmmaking and its cultural resonances. In creating the story of *The Watermelon Woman*, Dunye addresses many layers of deficiency in conventional historiography and in the persistent racism of the contemporary film industry. In the end, however, like Fisher, Dunye opts for a position of engagement rather than distance in relation to commercial filmmaking, while refusing to be confined by its conventions and expectations. Both *Standard Gauge* and *The Watermelon Woman* demonstrate the vast potential for film and video to problematize assumptions about the construction of history and to engage the past creatively—a process that seems to be most fully realized when these media are not constrained by conventions of narrative or factuality. For both Fisher and Dunye, the process of *film*making becomes analogous to and inseparable from the process of *history* making. For both filmmakers, "history" emerges from an intimate and reciprocal relation between life and cinema. As the on-screen text at the end of *Watermelon Woman* warns, "Sometimes you have to create your own history."

Camelot Revisited: *The Liberal War* versus *JFK*

The writing of history—the conception and reconstruction of the past—is a process that is subject at every level to the forces of politics and ideology. The mute distance of the past provides an easy target for appropriation and instrumentalization. But the past is neither entirely mute nor completely co-optable: it may linger in the memories of individuals with oppositional readings of events or send forth physical evidence that resists explanation by culturally accepted accounts. Furthermore, broadened access to media for marginalized members of society increases the potential for competing or counterhegemonic historiographies.

Although their filmmaking careers represent opposite ends of the commercial spectrum, Nick MacDonald and Oliver Stone have each sought to employ competing cinematic narratives of the 1960s and, in so doing, revise previously accepted historical accounts. Stone's *JFK* and MacDonald's *Liberal War* both examine the United States' involvement in the Vietnam War and its relation to the administration of President

The Zapruder film re-created in Oliver Stone's *JFK*. (Warner Brothers, 1991)

Kennedy. While Stone theorizes that the conspiracy to assassinate JFK was prompted in part by discovery of Kennedy's secret plan to withdraw troops from Vietnam, MacDonald asserts that JFK remained unwaveringly committed to victory in Vietnam and argues that postassassination efforts to distance him from the war he created constitute a disingenuous white-washing of the historical record. The "debate" suggested by the pairing of these two films is, of course, slightly misleading. Stone directed *JFK* a full twenty years after *The Liberal War*, and like most people, he has probably never seen it. *The Liberal War* never received distribution, has not been transferred to video, and is available only by contacting the filmmaker himself. The usefulness of juxtaposing these two films lies in comparing their rhetorical strategies—particularly their contrasting approaches to the construction of historical authority and their responses to the power of cultural consensus.

Stone's *JFK* followed the commercial success and critical acclaim of his Best Picture–winning Vietnam epic *Platoon* (1986). With this film, Stone had established his historiographical credentials and credibility as the voice of America in the 1960s. As a Vietnam veteran, he was authorized to speak about the war directly, without having to resort to the elaborately constructed metaphors seen in earlier films such as *Apocalypse Now* and *The Deer Hunter*. Above all, *Platoon* was praised for its immersive combat sequences. Veterans who saw themselves represented with relative dignity in the film reported that Stone had accurately captured the experience of participating in the war.[47]

In contrast, when MacDonald was filming *The Liberal War* with toy soldiers and paper cutouts in his living room in 1971, he elected to "set" the film in the future, in a utopian, postcapitalist society from whose perspective the twentieth-century's struggles over the division of global resources seems inconsequential and pathetic. Although the war was nearing its peak when he was making the film, MacDonald chose to imagine how Vietnam would be reconstructed as a history lesson. In fact, *The Liberal War* simulates an entirely conventional mode of historiographical discourse, unproblematically citing documentary evidence from the *New York Times* and statistics about Vietnam. However, I would contend that MacDonald's redeployment of these devices constitutes a problematizing rather than a simple endorsement of positivist, empirical historiography. The film's setting in a utopian fantasy future demonstrates the impact of a shift in interpretive context on the narrativizing of historical evidence. Seen through the eyes of the future, the dominant historiography of the Kennedy presidency in the late 1960s is thrown into relief as a series of neatly packaged stories about rich, beautiful young people. MacDonald emphasizes the textually processed nature of historical documentation and the power of historically situated desires. As a science fiction film, *The Liberal War* demonstrates the transformation of both evidence and historical narratives through the creative tension between science and fiction.

The juxtaposition of these two films highlights an important component of cinematic historiography related to representational conventions. One of the characteristics of history films is that they are recognizable in terms of style, language, and detail—even Stone's films, for all their stylistic excesses, at some level attempt to create the illusion that they are a "window on the past." The verisimilitude of *Platoon*, for example, brought enthusiastic endorsements from Vietnam veterans—its "realism" in many cases overshadowing its identification with an atypical (middle-class, white, volunteer) protagonist.[48] In contrast, *The Liberal War*'s reliance on toy soldiers, puppets, and crude animation makes it impossible to ignore the constructedness of the film. Awareness of MacDonald's representational and constructivist strategies is an integral part of the film's ideological investment in disrupting the automatic or preferred flows of history writing.

Stone's work has become emblematic of the capacity of motion pictures to provoke controversy over the construction of history. Although Stone describes his films as a combination of truth and fiction, he adamantly maintains that his work is nonetheless factually rooted. In conjunction with the release of both *JFK* and *Nixon*, Stone published thick books containing documents and research in support of the films' historical assertions and conjecture. Arguably, however, Stone's goal is not simply to overwrite accepted versions of events with his own set of revisions but also to open up historiography as a field of debate against the hermetics of official, governmental explanations.

Most unforgivable, however, is Stone's blinding commitment to the Camelot mythos, which leads him to overwrite a body of public evidence convincingly presented in *The Liberal War* that, at the time of his assassination, JFK was in fact planning to increase—not decrease—U.S. military presence in Southeast Asia.[49] In this case, Stone capitulates to precisely the kind of neatly packaged historiography he is otherwise committed to challenging: a beloved young president, tragically assassinated, simply *cannot* be responsible for the same era's most devastating political catastrophe. In the final analysis, the sophistication of the historiography practiced in *The Liberal War* does little to overcome its near total obscurity, while Stone's provocations and fomenting of useful historical debate does not forgive his mendacious canonizing.

Imagining Historical Spaces

The intersection of popular culture and historiography on television, as well as in other unlikely corners of popular culture, has generated innumerable, provocative experiments with "popular history." While certain examples have drawn critical attention—for example, Art Spiegelman's comic book/graphic novel about the Holocaust, *Maus*, and the Disney corporation's replication of ancient Jerusalem at its "Holy Land Experience" attraction in Orlando, Florida—more extreme cases, such as David Wilson's empyrean of anachrony, the Museum of Jurassic Technology (MJT), and Virtual World, a national chain of history-themed virtual reality entertainment salons, have been largely neglected. Like *Sliders* and the alternate histories cited earlier, these projects invite us to reconsider the parameters of "history" in compelling ways.

Founded in 1994 by experimental filmmaker and future MacArthur Genius grantee Wilson, the MJT appropriates and subverts the codes of museumization in ways that are at once utterly convincing and baffling to the imagination. With elaborately contrived and technologically sophisticated displays ranging from a human horn to X-ray bats, the MJT parodies the accoutrements and conventions of scholarly research and exhibition. Although less concerned with temporal paradox than the name suggests, the convincing implausibilities constructed by the museum demonstrate the codified nature of institutional discourses of natural history. Purportedly rare or ancient objects that logically must be fakes acquire an aura of historical gravity when presented in a carefully sculpted museum space, complete with dim lights and glass cases supported by meticulously composed texts. Most importantly, visitors are never allowed in on the joke—for all they (or I) know, fungus-inhaling stink ants may well exist in the rain forests of Cameroon. Wilson's virtuosity lies in his ability to mobilize conventions of scientific and historical authenticity in ways that invite us to question the foundations of the most readily accepted forms of knowledge.

The now defunct Virtual World franchise mobilizes a similarly bizarre, though considerably less elaborate, concatenation of historical signifiers as frames for an otherwise conventional arcade experience based on multiuser video games. Founded in 1995 by renowned designer Jordan Weisman and claiming to be the world's first virtual reality "theme park," Virtual World crafted each of its specific locations to resemble a nineteenth-century salon, complete with Victorian sofas, shelves of antiquarian books, and ersatz dinosaur bones on display. Visitors waiting for their turn to enter the virtual reality simulators were surrounded by documents and artifacts related to Virtual World's purported origination within the Virtual Geographic League (VGL). Purportedly founded in 1897 by Alexander Graham Bell and Nikola Tesla to explore the possibility of time and interdimensional travel, the VGL claims such illustrious members as Amelia Earhart and Sir Richard Burton (whose sword was displayed on the wall of the salon along with Earhart's flight goggles). Additional framed documents on the wall indicated that information about the VGL has been carefully suppressed by a government conspiracy that opposes unlocking the secrets to interdimensional travel. Virtual World's immersive BattleTech and Red Planet video simulators (typical multiplayer robot battle and spaceship race games) were positioned as technologies that allow ordinary people to safely simulate the adventures of VGL explorers without actually disappearing into another dimension.

Virtual World thus deployed a remarkable array of strategies to weave its patrons into a historical fantasy narrative connecting its multiuser video games with unsolved mysteries of the past and 1990s paranoid culture. Its panhistorical signifiers—from dinosaur bones to spaceship simulators—drew together prehistory with futurism, negotiating an imaginary relation to both past and future. But why turn to the past when constructing a narrative about futuristic technology? While some fantastic histories are about resolution of past uncertainties or trauma, Virtual World's pseudo-historical narrative about the VGL was less focused on "explaining" certain historical mysteries than implicating video-game players in a tantalizing narrative of government conspiracy and attempts to bridge spectral and dimensional barriers—all of which served primarily to compensate for the shortcomings of arcade game technology in the 1990s.

2 Cultural Memory

On Memorial Day weekend 2001, the world watched with anticipation as the first blockbuster of the summer film season, the Disney-owned Touchstone Pictures' *Pearl Harbor*, opened nationwide. Boasting the largest initial production budget in Hollywood history, *Pearl Harbor* promised to exemplify the kind of immersive, hyper-stimulating spectacle that has defined large-scale historical filmmaking in recent years. Even before the film was released, reviewers began discussing *Pearl Harbor*'s relative merits and adherence to the historical record—factors such as its omission of embarrassing details about inexperienced Navy antiaircraft gunners shooting down their own planes, its "compositing" of real-life characters, and allusions to previous images of Pearl Harbor, including iconic still photographs that reportedly served to guide the film's production design. Reviewers made comparisons to previous World War II spectacles such as *Saving Private Ryan* with its famed use of documentary-style camera work and graphic violence, a strategy that was explicitly replicated in *Pearl Harbor* for the forty-minute, action-filled centerpiece sequence depicting the attack.

The release of *Pearl Harbor* on Memorial Day weekend also coincided with a series of self-conscious attempts to weave the film and its reception into a larger fabric of national commemoration. Press materials indicated that *Pearl Harbor* marked the first time the U.S. Navy allowed filming in the actual waters around the USS *Arizona* Memorial where the bodies of hundreds of sailors killed during the attack remain entombed. The theatrical release of the film was also paired with a day of special programming on the Hearst Corporation's History Channel, promising to provide "The Real Story of Pearl Harbor" by screening films such as *Unsung Heroes of Pearl Harbor*, *One Hour over Tokyo*, and *Tora, Tora, Tora!* The National Geographic Channel, likewise, aired the films *Legacy of Attack* and *National Geographic behind the Movie: Pearl Harbor*, which offered a historically grounded supplement to the fictional narrative of the feature film.[1] And the day after the film's release, the American Movie Classics channel presented "A Day of WWII" featuring eight war movies, hosted by the cast of *Pearl Harbor* and a special "Cinema Secrets" segment devoted to the making of the film.

Within these juxtapositions one finds the continual slippage among spheres of authority, truth, and fiction that characterize the struggle for control of even the most mainstream historiographical discourse. In addition to inviting viewers to experience a lifelike and emotionally engaging rendering of the attack on Pearl Harbor, the film's broader cultural milieu continually reminds them of its constructed nature. This includes revelations about the film's intertextuality, behind-the-scenes documentaries, actors appearing out of character, and of course, the inevitable pronouncements by scholars and witnesses regarding the film's faithfulness to the historical record and its uncanny simulation of physical and emotional experiences. It is through this clash of historical signifiers and contradictions that the "history" of this event is constituted.

It is certainly no accident that so many historiographical films and TV shows revolve around moments of trauma, loss, uncertainty, or historical crisis. While this tendency highlights the powerful therapeutic potential of cinema and television, it may also reveal the limitations of the "cultural therapy" it purports to mobilize. The same traumatic events and crises continue to reemerge as the subject of Hollywood's most elaborately reconstructed history films. This repetition suggests either that historical trauma is not "curable" through the means available to film and television or, perhaps more likely, that the exorcism of cultural trauma is only part of the cultural significance of this type of work. Try as it might, Hollywood holds no more of the secret to reducing "history" to a single narrative than the most definitive of academic histories.

Creative Forgetting

As theorists of cultural memory have argued, the writing of history does not end with the creation of documents, narratives, or analyses. People consume and process written, filmed, televised, and played historiography within a web of cultural forces and interpretive contexts. The meanings that are encoded into a particular historical work may be decoded quite differently when they are received by an audience or reader. Further, historical meanings evolve over time, reflecting, among other things, the extent to which our relation to the past is conditioned by present circumstances. As reception studies of television have questioned assumptions about the passive spectatorship of TV viewers, memory studies provide a way of looking at historical reception, what people remember about the past, and how it is woven into the fabric of their lives.

The conception of memory as a primarily social rather than individual phenomenon allows for exploration of the ways in which memories are rescripted in relation to existing historical narratives. Like "history,"

cultural memories must be understood in the context of an array of political and ideological forces. Indeed, certain theorists have argued that
individual memories are determined by social context and not the other
way around. According to Maurice Halbwachs, individual memories are
always "interpenetrated" by "collective influences" that fill in gaps and
ascribe significance to lived experiences. By arguing that all memories
exist within a complex and fragmentary social milieu, Halbwachs's model
allows for a different conception of the relationship between remembering and forgetting. Elaborating on Halbwachs's sociologically neutral conception of "collective influences," Michael Bommes and Patrick Wright
politicize the discussion of cultural memory by insisting that

> memory has a texture which is both social and historic: it exists in
> the world rather than in people's heads, finding its basis in conversa-
> tions, cultural forms, personal relations, the structure and appearance
> of places and, most fundamentally, . . . in relation to ideologies which
> work to establish a consensus view of both the past and the forms of
> personal experience which are significant and memorable.[2]

The displacement and regeneration of memories, termed "creative
forgetting" by Friedrich Nietzsche[3] and "active forgetting" by Andreas
Huyssen,[4] is part of a continual process of revising the past in response
to changing social circumstances. While both Huyssen's and Nietzsche's
models are useful for undermining the oversimplified dichotomy of remembering and forgetting, I am more interested in critical efforts that
situate memories within not only a historical and individual context but
a political and ideological one as well.[5]

Through motion pictures and other media forms, memory and history
merge to form a circuit of construction and reception, and remembering
and forgetting. Cultural memory is thus constituted as a site of discursive
struggle that, like other types of historical construction, provides only mediated access to the past. Memories, on both a personal and cultural level,
acquire meaning in resonance with other historical constructs (images,
narratives, political, or personal beliefs, etc.).[6] Thus, the process of understanding how the past is transformed into memory through engagement
with popular culture may be best described as an archaeology in which
the goal is not simply to uncover something that has been buried but also
to discover how and why its meanings have changed and additional layers have been built up on top of it.

Memories that survive among individuals and communities may also
oppose historical discourse that is propagated from the top down via

cultural and governmental institutions. Recording and preserving these memories have proven to be extremely effective strategies for oral history projects that seek to incorporate marginalized voices—especially those of colonized or disenfranchised peoples—into the official record. Indeed, this somewhat essentialized vision of popular memory *in itself* is frequently politicized as a form of resistance to the suffocating constraints of "official history." This position is aptly summarized in a quote from Milan Kundera that opens *The Uprising of '34* (1995), a documentary about the formation of the garment workers union: "The struggle of humanity against power is the struggle of memory against forgetting." Even Michel Foucault argued that popular memory functions as a crucial site of resistance for oppressed groups. "Since memory is actually a very important factor in struggle, if one controls people's memory, one controls their dynamism. And one also controls their experience, their knowledge of previous struggles."[7] He also warned that institutional mechanisms work tirelessly to influence the content and transmission of popular memory. "Now, a whole number of apparatuses have been set up to obstruct the flow of this popular memory. . . . [Today there are] effective means like television and the cinema. I believe this is one way of re-programming popular memory which existed but had no way of expressing itself."[8]

Although widely quoted in support of the oppositional relationship between history and memory, these passages by Foucault demonstrate a surprisingly idealized view of preexisting social memories, untainted by the corrupting influence of mass media. Ironically, nostalgia for authentic, prelapsarian social memories outmatched in a struggle against official historical discourse implies the existence of precisely the sort of centralized institutions of social domination that Foucault elsewhere subordinates to localized applications of power and control.[9] This conception of popular memory also fails to account for memories that are formed through, rather than in spite of (or prior to), interaction with cultural apparatuses such as television.

The proliferation and repetition of certain media images at the expense of others undoubtedly influences what TV viewers consider to be "history" and what they remember of it. Under certain circumstances, then, television is acknowledged as a primary instrument in the production of memory. Americans are said to "remember" events such as the *Challenger* explosion because TV repeated it so many times. Likewise, memories of geographically or temporally distant historical events such as the Gulf War or the moon landing are likely to be based on television images. TV is also recognized for its facilitation of national remembrance and mourning, as during the funeral of John F. Kennedy and the proliferation of programming related to the fiftieth anniversary of World War II. In spite of these examples, critical work on television and memory often constructs elaborate arguments against the potential for television to engage productively with the development of cultural or individual memory. Fredric Jameson accuses cinema and television of being contributing causes to a "diminished capacity to retain the past," while for Anne Friedberg, there is a directly inverse relationship between the production of historiography on film and television and our ability to retain the past.[10] In some instances, television's " ideology of liveness"[11] and emphasis on the "now" is blamed for its disinterest in memory.[12]

However, television, as well as other media forms, does engage productively with cultural and individual memory. In recent years, cultural theorists have proposed models for understanding television and other constituents of popular culture as engaged in a relationship of mutual determination with the flow of cultural memory. For Marita Sturken, television is one among many "technologies of memory" that are "central to the interpretation of the past."[13] Likewise, John Caldwell claims that television can provide viewers with "a great deal of textual and *historiographic power*, traits not normally associated with the medium in academic accounts that aim to define television's essential qualities—presentness, amnesia, and lack of context."[14] And in a challenge to foundational television theory, Mimi White proposes a reconsideration of "liveness" as a structuring principle of TV, arguing that "history, banality and attractions" offer equally compelling paradigms for understanding television's basic structures.

> I want to insist that history, duration and memory are as central to any theoretical understanding of television's discursive operations as liveness and concomitant ideas of presence, immediacy and so forth. Indeed, liveness on television is routinely if variously imbricated with and implicated in history, momentous events, consumerism, and commodity circulation. Yet to make this claim flies in the face of certain influential theories of postmodernism which propose television as exemplifying, even propagating, the loss of history.[15]

Thus, for White, the privileging of liveness is not merely anachronous but also an active and semiarbitrary misconception that perpetuates TV's association with amnesia and ahistoricism. Caldwell and Sturken's acknowledgment of the existence of complex dynamics between popular culture and its consumers suggests not that all such practices are redeemable through mechanisms of popular memory but rather that, for better or worse, film, television, and other forms of cultural production constitute significant sites of engagement with the past.

The significance of popular memories does not necessarily lie in their opposition to official discourse, however, but in their functionality—the degree to which they are open to mobile and elastic deployment depending on historical circumstances and need.[16] Popular memory, thus conceived, highlights distinctions between the writing and the relevance of history, while simultaneously providing a crucial link between the two. How is historiography received and constructed through film and television, and what role do these media play in shaping popular memories? Further, how are these questions in turn asked by filmmakers in projects that interrogate memory and its construction? The four films analyzed below are explicitly concerned with the mutability and idiosyncrasy of individual recall. Together, they demonstrate that memory should be valued as a site of discursive, individual, and cultural struggle, rather than something that can be summarily erased, altered, or forgotten.

Excavating the Past: Rea Tajiri's *History and Memory*

Rea Tajiri is a third-generation Japanese American whose family was confined in American concentration camps during World War II. In her 1991 videotape *History and Memory*, Tajiri attempts to reconstruct her family's experience in the camps and to explore her own personal and cultural identity in relation to the internment.[17] Part conventional, part oral, and part experimental history, *History and Memory* presents the search for the past as a complex personal journey that cuts across the competing stories told by institutions and individuals. The tape is composed using multiple kinds of assets: voice-overs (oral history–type recollections by family members, Tajiri's own personal story, and a letter from her uncle); written texts (descriptions of images that cannot be re-created, a letter from the War Relocation Authority, and polemical statements or questions by the videomaker); stills (snapshots of family members in camp, her grandparents' alien registration photos, and images from the National Archives); archival footage (government documentaries, Hollywood features, and home movies taken in the camps); contemporary re-creations (Tajiri's restaging of her mother's trip to the camp in Poston, Arizona, and an image of her mother splashing water on her face); and artifacts (including logbooks, a piece of tar paper from one of the camp barracks, and a bird carved by her grandmother). The *story* of *History and Memory* is told through the interweaving of multiple threads of narrative—for example, government propaganda, stories told by family members, and Hollywood musicals—all in relation to Tajiri's own quest for her own family's past.

Near the beginning of the tape, Tajiri lays out the four types of historical events (and their possible forms of construction) of which the rest of the tape will be composed:

There are things which have happened in the world while cameras were watching: things we have images for [documentary records];

There are other things which have happened while there were no cameras watching, which we restage in front of cameras in order to have images [re-creations];

There are things which have happened for which the only images that exist are in the minds of the observers present at the time [memories];

There are things which have happened for which there have been no observers except for the spirits of the dead [imagination].

The conflict between the "representability" and "unrepresentability" of these four types of images structures the remainder of the tape: the screen is often black or shows only text; events that cannot be re-created (like the stealing of her family's house during internment) are described from the imagined perspective of her dead grandfather; and the numerous gaps in her mother's memory are filled with images from Hollywood films and Tajiri's own re-creations. Because internees were not permitted to have cameras, only a few unofficial photographs and another family's home movies of the camps appear. But rather than treat these lacunae of memory and limited resources as deficiencies, Tajiri transforms them into a structuring absence similar to the unseen (murdered) Japanese American Komoko in *Bad Day at Black Rock* (one of the films excerpted by Tajiri). By telling her family's story as much through images that *cannot* be shown (or remembered) as through ones that *can* be shown, Tajiri implicitly critiques the power imbalance between those who can and cannot represent themselves.

In the absence of many "popular" images of the camps, Tajiri includes a wide range of "official" images, from the reassuring documentaries of the War Relocation Authority to the only Hollywood feature on the subject of Japanese internment, *Come See the Paradise* (1990), in which romance substitutes for politics. The presentation of these overtly hegemonic materials is invariably inflected by Tajiri through vertical or horizontal montage. For example, government newsreels depicting Japanese making themselves at home in the camps are intercut with the patriotic musical

Yankee Doodle Dandy (1942) such that the newsreels are accompanied by the *Yankee Doodle Dandy* musical score and superimposed texts pose ironic questions about authority; voice-overs and image juxtapositions routinely recontextualize or directly contradict the "official" version of events; and images from *Come See the Paradise* (also intercut with newsreel footage) are accompanied by a full-length review trashing the film. In many cases, although she is critical of Hollywood constructions (especially those of and from the World War II era), these images seem to occupy a privileged space in *History and Memory*. Whether this is because of the significance of mass media to memory and identity formation or the fact that these constructions seek to engage the past as a coherent story (precisely what Tajiri is denied by her family), Hollywood feature films epitomize the textually processed nature of historical evidence. Tajiri's willingness to redeploy these films as a form of historical evidence reveals an important aspect of her historiographical method.

Throughout the tape, Tajiri vacillates between telling a story that is empirically grounded and one that expresses her own personal, mystical relationship to her family's past. For example, although she goes to the National Archives to research official, government records—films, photographs, and logbooks—from the camps, she also talks about having memories of events that happened twenty years before she was born and intuitively ("by some internal divining rod") locating the place where her mother's family lived during a visit to the camp in Poston. At one point in the narration, Tajiri says,

> I remember having this feeling growing up that I was haunted by something—that I was living within a family full of ghosts. There was this place that they knew about. I had never been there, yet I had a memory for it. I could remember a time of great sadness before I was born. We had been moved—uprooted. We had lived with a lot of pain. I had no idea where these memories came from, yet I knew the place.

Although Tajiri's mysticism and these "genetic memories" are somewhat problematic, they are clearly a part of the "zone of occult instability"[18] from which she speaks and, more importantly, consistent with her overall strategies of resisting what Homi Bhabha calls the "obligation to forget."[19] The politics of the tape revolve around not only knowing the past but also remembering it—of finding a way (in Foucault's terms) of "keeping it fresh and using it."[20] Historiography, for Tajiri, lies in not interpretation or narrativization but rather the struggle between modes of discourse both enabled and resisted by the idiosyncracies of human memory.

History and Memory benefits from a specific and contingent treatment of multiple layers of discursive construction. Her investigative mode is fundamentally archaeological, that is, a process in which both artifacts of official, historical discourse and personal, idiosyncratic ones are uncovered and relationships between them are articulated. It is in this liminal space, between what Bhabha termed the pedagogical and performative modes of discourse, that the tape's primary historiographical intervention takes place. If we extend Bhabha's metaphor of the construction of the nation to the construction of the past, *History and Memory* may be seen as an articulation of the split between the pedagogical and performative modes of discourse.

> The present of the people's history . . . is a practice that destroys the constant principles of the national culture that attempt to hark back to a "true" national past, which is often represented in the reified forms of realism and stereotype. Such pedagogical knowledges and continuist national narratives miss the "zone of occult instability" where the people dwell.[21]

Tajiri's insistence on negotiating her critique in the liminal spaces between the pedagogical and performative suggests (as does Bhabha about the nation) that the greatest potential for individual agency in the narrative.of history is in the struggle between them.

Issues of liminality and hybridity in *History and Memory* are apparent on many levels. A recurrent theme for the Japanese Americans in the tape is the conflict between their Japanese and American cultural identities. This includes Tajiri herself, for whom the entire tape may be understood in terms of cultural negotiation; her mixed-race nephew who questions his "moral authority" to speak as either a Japanese or a white person; and her uncle who became disillusioned and left America after the war but has thought about it "at least once a week for the past fifty years." The form of *History and Memory* is itself a hybrid, combining elements of personal autobiography, documentary, and fiction filmmaking.[22]

In expressing the difficulty of cultural transition and identity formation for Japanese Americans, Tajiri makes use of the autobiographical mode in order to describe an experience that is simultaneously generalizable and highly individual. Through this breakdown of traditional binaries—documentary/fiction, individual/group, and subjective/objective—*History and Memory* seeks to reconstruct a past that resists simple narrative coherence and allows for the coexistence of seemingly contradictory historiographical strategies.

Although media images represent only one type of intervention in the production of popular memory, they are consistently privileged for their impact on what individuals remember and the way groups perceive themselves. As Janice Tanaka argues,

> Memories are not always an understood compilation of linear ideas. They seem instead to be fragments of stored, synthesized, edited sensory stimuli; bits of personalized perceptions. Film and television often-times play a major role in the process of subliminal inculcation by creating criteria for self-evaluation. Consequently, our self-image, our role models, what we know and expect of our society and the world, are greatly influenced by the media. Somewhere, caught between the crevices of concept and production, lay the elements or perhaps the reflective shadows of who and what we are.[23]

For Tanaka, who is also Japanese American and a film/videomaker who has addressed the internment of Japanese Americans during World War II, both memory and media representations are crucial to the formation of personal and cultural identity. It is in these crevices and shadows, at the intersections of "history," memory, representation, and identity formation, that *History and Memory* makes its most significant contribution to experimental historiography.

Although Tajiri does not aspire to writing a definitive account of her family's internment, the concept of historical "truth" is not entirely absent. For all its emphasis on historiography as a field of discursive struggle, *History and Memory* does not simply advocate a simplistic historical relativism or indeterminacy. Indeed, Tajiri's historiography allows for something very close to historical certainty to emerge from her competing threads of discourse. One such moment crystallizes three separate strands of her family's past—personal memories, archival documents, and a physical artifact—around the figure of her grandmother's carved bird.[24]

In voice-over, Tajiri tells us that, as a child, she was fascinated by a small, colorful bird treasured by her mother. Her mother refused to let her play with the bird but offered no explanation. On the tape, the bird is photographed in two slow, dramatic zooms and carefully positioned on black velvet like a rare artifact. The fact that the bird was a relic from the camp, carved by her grandmother, is only discovered when Tajiri visits the National Archives and discovers a photograph of her grandmother sitting in a "bird-carving class." This momentary convergence of memory, document, and artifact—the "smoking gun" that brings together all the partial narratives told by individuals and institutions—demonstrates that, for Tajiri, a functional sense of historical truth *is* available to those who are willing not only to search for it but also to work to reconstruct it in its full context of contradiction, forgetfulness, and fragmentation.

Exteriorizing Memory: Daniel Eisenberg's *Persistence*

In his celebrated essay "In Defense of Amateur," experimental filmmaking icon Stan Brakhage wrote, "The entire act of motion picture making, thus, can be considered an exteriorization of the process of memory."[25] As Brakhage's characteristically hyperbolic statement suggests, representing the unrepresentable—especially internal states of consciousness, memory, and emotion—has been of particular concern to avant-garde filmmakers. Chris Marker's poetic ruminations on time and memory (e.g., *Sans Soleil* [1983], *La Jetee* [1962], *Grin without a Cat* [1977]) and Steina and Woody Vasulka's fluid electronic image processing in *The Art of Memory* (1987) exemplify a mode of visual discourse that conceives memory as an evanescent, dreamlike experience of the individual psyche. But how have experimental filmmakers dealt with memories that are linked to collective, highly politicized moments of historical or cultural trauma?

Daniel Eisenberg's 1997 film *Persistence* borrows many of the stylistic conceits of experimental film (including a fragmentary, nonnarrative structure and optically printed, sometimes abstract imagery) but addresses questions of memory and historiography in extraordinarily concrete terms. The film traces a series of parallels between two transformative moments in Berlin's past: post–World War II and postreunification. Visual alignments between the two eras merge into a seamlessly intercut tapestry of images, texts, and sounds composed of U.S. military newsreels from 1945–46, desolate landscapes stolen from Roberto Rossellini's *Germany Year Zero* (1948), and Eisenberg's own visual meditations on the landscapes, ruins, and reconstruction of 1990s Berlin.

Although it shares many thematic concerns with *History and Memory*, Eisenberg's film is remarkable for its near total suppression of any explicit reference to either history or memory. Although *Persistence* is a highly self-conscious essay film *about* postwar German history and cultural memory, the word "memory" is never used and no individual is ever asked to speak about the past. Except for a final sequence in which Eisenberg's voice-over refers to the importance of not forgetting, and a quote from Max Frisch about feeling shame at forgetting, the idea of memory remains entirely unspoken—invested in material things rather than psychic ones: landscapes, ruins, and the physical act of reconstructing the city. Unlike his counterparts in rereading German memories of the Nazi period (e.g., Marcel Ophüls, Claude Lanzmann, Debra Lefkowitz, and Steven Spielberg), Eisenberg refuses to locate the roots of memory in the people who lived through this era. Instead, he documents the reconstruction of the city as an attempt at historical erasure that is eternally doomed to failure.

In a literalization of the film's metaphorical relation to historical construction, cranes, scaffolding, and workmen appear throughout the film, accompanied by the ubiquitous sounds of jackhammers and construction. However, the construction Eisenberg highlights is not the resurrection of buildings or monuments but rather the erection of massive scaffolds around the perimeter of a downtown skyscraper—the structures by means of which the real reconstruction will eventually take place. This work, like the film itself, is preparatory and contingent. At one point, Eisenberg's voice-over describes the firebombing by neo-Nazis of a human experimentation facility in Sachsenhausen (near Berlin) and the morally and historiographically ambiguous question of whether such a structure should be rebuilt. Eisenberg's goal is not to answer these questions but instead to lay out the stakes of reconstruction, the absences and presences that form the central contradictions of the city, the inevitability of loss, and the noble futility of preservation.

Although Eisenberg's wanderings through the city are less random than those of the little boy in Rossellini's film, the image of the city that emerges remains fragmentary and idiosyncratic. He visits sites where political changes have left concrete traces: a tank proving ground and an abandoned Soviet air force base littered with rusting carcasses of helicopters and jet engines—skeletons of the Soviet era that haunt the place as palpably as the Nazi ones. The film notes that when Hitler was overseeing the plans for Nuremberg, his architect, Albert Speer, also created models of the ruins that would remain a thousand years after the Reich had fallen, perhaps to be revived in its own neoclassical era. Political shifts and the passing of time bring material consequences; they leave scars on the landscape no less revealing than the scars of war on minds and bodies.

Aerial shots of the ruined city from 1946 are simultaneously beautiful and appalling for the total devastation they reveal. Virtually no buildings appear to have survived the bombardment. Accompanied by the discordant strains of violins that merge with air-raid sirens, the images are both haunting and portentous of the possibility of future catastrophe. In Eisenberg's footage, finely groomed parks and topiary bushes are juxtaposed with abandoned ruins, posing a domesticating threat to the overgrown, uncrafted landscapes that signify the past. In another sequence, Eisenberg photographs a winged monument from a fast-moving vehicle—a figure that evokes Walter Benjamin's "Angel of History." The viewer is positioned hurtling forward through both time and space, while the winged figure appears to be blown violently backward, helplessly observing the train wreck of human history, crystallized with fearful intensity in the city of Berlin.

Memory Pictures: The Long, Sad Films of Marcel Ophüls

Since the 1970s, Marcel Ophüls's production company, Memory Pictures, has created a vast and underrated body of work devoted to interrogating the role of memory in the writing of history. Averaging over four hours in length, each of Ophüls's documentaries focuses on moments of historical trauma. At least three of his films deal directly with the Holocaust, including *The Sorrow and the Pity* (1969), *Hôtel Terminus* (1988), and *The Memory of Justice* (1976), while others have addressed wars in the Balkans (*The Troubles We've Seen*, 1994) and Vietnam (*Harvest of My Lai*, 1970). But more than merely chronicling the Holocaust, Ophüls's films grapple with the way these moments have been processed—written, remembered, obscured, revised, or forgotten—by historians, media practitioners, and the public. Although Ophüls's work frequently highlights the imprecision and the instrumentalization of individuals' memories, the goal of his work is not to debunk oral history per se or to render the past unknowable. Meaningful engagement with the past, he suggests, requires an investment of time (at least four hours), intelligent skepticism, and a willingness to engage with the contents of both history writing and film on a processual level. The responsibility for preventing the erasure, forgetting, or denial of history, Ophüls argues, lies not in the creation of a total archive but rather with the cultivation of a formidable audience-public capable of thinking, remembering, and constantly questioning what and how we know.

In Bill Nichols's terms, Ophüls's primary documentary "mode" falls squarely within the realm of the "interactive" (though he also employs "observational" and "reflexive" strategies throughout). The filmmakers' biases, beliefs, and motivations are foregrounded from the very beginning, and these serve to provoke nearly all the action in the film. Ophüls is rude, sarcastic, manipulative, and confrontational with his interviewees. For example, when interviewing an acknowledged friend and former bodyguard of Klaus Barbie, Ophüls kept the man waiting for nearly an hour while his crew surreptitiously filmed him fidgeting and checking his watch. Ophüls then conducted the interview wearing a bathrobe, explaining that he had been taking a nap in the next room. Ophüls once compared his on-camera persona to that of Peter Falk's Columbo, a frequently disheveled, always irrepressible detective, forever asking just one more question.

Some of Ophüls's greatest strengths as a historiographer have, interestingly, also brought him some of the harshest criticism. By conceiving "history" as something that lives among us, existing only in a dialectical relationship with the present, Ophüls is able to make connections across time, demonstrating ways in which the past manifests itself in the actions, beliefs, and memories of individuals living in the present. For example, following the release of his 1978 film *Memory of Justice* (about the Nuremberg Trials), Ophüls was attacked for creating linkages between Nazi genocide and the more recent imperial wars in Vietnam and Algeria. Ten years after the Russell Tribunal and public recognition of the massacre at My Lai, it is difficult to imagine that such connections would seem far-fetched or misplaced. The offense Ophüls had committed was treating "history" as something that cannot and should not be isolated in time.

Hôtel Terminus: *The Life and Times of Klaus Barbie*

Nichols writes, "Excess in documentary is that which stands beyond the reach of both narrative and exposition. . . . Does this excess have a name? I would argue that it has a simple and familiar one: history. As the referent of documentary, history is what always stands outside the text."[26] The notion of excess is extremely useful in thinking about Ophüls's films, though perhaps not in the sense described by Nichols. In fact, I would argue exactly the opposite, namely, that the only meaningful "history" for Ophüls is an act of engagement, constructed in and through the text of the film rather than something that stands outside it. The referent that *Hôtel Terminus* works to signify is not an abstract conception or even a material "truth of history" but rather the combination of truth and lies through which we negotiate our present existence against the past.

Early in *Hôtel Terminus*, Ophüls explores in detail the question of how Jean Moulin, leader of the French Resistance, came to be captured by the Gestapo unit led by Barbie in Lyon. Here we have a concrete series of historical events: Moulin was betrayed by someone in the movement, captured, and tortured to death by Barbie. There is no doubt that this is "what happened," but I am reluctant to call this the "referent" of this section of the documentary.

As the film is being made, René Hardy, who is widely thought to have betrayed Moulin, is a dying man who answers questions cryptically. He appears evasive when confronted with the same questions he has obviously been answering for forty years. Is his exhaustion the result of so many years of guilt or merely the burden of the accusations? At one point, it would seem that he has confessed, but he also contradicts himself, denying us the closure and certainty that he alone could (perhaps) provide. A number of witnesses and surviving members of the resistance speak passionately about what they believe happened, what they saw, what might have happened, and their own experiences under torture by Barbie. If Hardy turned in Moulin, it was most likely a result of Barbie's expert application of physical and psychological torture. Survivors recount torture sessions after which they could not remember what they had said or even how they survived. Finally, Ophüls challenges one of Hardy's accusers, "Isn't it incredibly arrogant to try to form an opinion—to presume to judge the behavior of those who were tortured or faced with the threat of torture? It's an indecent question!"

The film reaches no conclusion about Hardy's guilt or innocence—really it provides no new information at all, just a synthesis of the same memories, stories, and suspicions that have hovered around the case for decades. Why, then, does Ophüls spend so much time on it? The answer may be simply that Moulin was Barbie's most famous victim. Without him, Barbie would have been just another run-of-the-mill Nazi thug—an "ordinary torturer" as one survivor puts it. But this sequence serves a more significant purpose in the film by establishing the stakes of Ophüls's historical investigation. After thirty minutes of the Hardy-Moulin case, we are made to understand that this film is not about uncovering the truth about Barbie or providing more direct or certain access to the "history" that exceeds the film text.

As a historical figure, Barbie is "textualized" from the outset of the film. A montage of disembodied voices describes him as "brutal," "jovial," "ruthless," "frightening," "a sadist," and "a decent boy." Although we learn early on that Barbie has recently been arrested and is awaiting trial for war crimes in France, he is seen only in a few black-and-white stills for the first three hours of the film. The "real" Barbie thus becomes displaced by a composite of memory fragments, accusations, and disjunctive, smiling images. Barbie's absent body throughout the early part of the film reinforces the impression that, at some level, his story is a vehicle for investigating the things Ophüls is really interested in: the inability in both France and Germany to live with the memory of the Holocaust and the continual rewriting of history to cover up or rationalize wartime atrocities (from French collaboration during the Nazi occupation investigated in depth in Ophüls's *The Sorrow and the Pity* to the recruitment of ex-Nazis by American intelligence after the war). At the same time, however, Barbie's fate is not exclusively instrumentalized. He is present through much of the film by his conspicuous absence, by the determination with which people refuse to talk about him, and by the mythic status he attains through the proliferation of contradictory accounts regarding his life and character.

As the subject of the film, Barbie is significantly mobilized along all three of the "axes" (history, myth, and narrative) identified by Nichols for the treatment of "bodies in history."[27] As a person whose notoriety is defined by the pain and death he inflicted on others, it is impossible not to understand Barbie as a physical, historical being. Nearly all of the stories about him involve physical brutality as evidenced by scars on the bodies of survivors and stories of ice baths, beatings, and killing. Within the context of the film, he also serves as the focal point of a fairly straightforward historical narrative: a seminary student joins the Nazi party, discovers an aptitude for torture and murder, oversees the death of Moulin and the deportation of Jewish schoolchildren from the town of Izieu, is recruited after the war by American intelligence, relocates to Latin America, and many years later is extradited to France, found guilty of war crimes, and imprisoned. All of this may be ascertained from the film—the "what happened" of Barbie's life—but these details are revealed almost incidentally. And finally, as a mythic figure, constructed through numerous and contradictory personal accounts, Barbie attains a kind of mythological status as an icon of Nazi barbarism and cruelty. In keeping with Ophüls's strategy of creating meaning through the conflict and convergence of various discursive tactics, Barbie's "historical body" may be understood only through the convergence of these multiple frames of reference.

The Troubles We've Seen

Both *Hôtel Terminus* and *The Troubles We've Seen* are structured as a series of encounters (as opposed to conventional interviews that are framed and edited to minimize the presence of the film crew) between Ophüls and various individuals related to the story. One result of this is to shift "textual authority" toward the film's "social actors," who are perceived only in terms of their interaction with the filmmaker.[28] Another is to emphasize the dynamic and highly mediated relationship between past and present. Since Ophüls is primarily concerned with working back through the memories (and revised personal histories) of his subjects, we do not often, for example, cut away to archival footage while they are talking. This practice, which is a convention of documentary filmmaking, serves to verify and authorize the account of the person who is talking. In Ophüls's work, our only measures of the veracity of someone's testimony are their own performance and the (often quite expressive) reactions of the director himself.

As Nichols notes, use of the interactive mode may lead to situations in which "the logic of the text leads less to an argument about the world than to a statement about the interactions themselves and what they disclose about filmmaker and social actors alike."[29] Ophüls, it must be remembered, does not set out to tell us the whole story. Indeed, a viewer who entered *The Troubles We've Seen* without prior knowledge of Balkan history could easily remain mystified about who was fighting whom (and why) for the duration of the film. But throughout the film, we get a clear sense of the people toward whom Ophüls feels sympathy or respect and those he holds in contempt or disregard. Indeed, the film is so heavily invested in personal feelings and idiosyncracies as to border on the essay-istic. In a memorable but narratively superfluous scene at the conclusion of the first (two-hour) segment, Ophüls returns to Italy from a three-day trip to Sarajevo. We see him shaving and chatting about the trip while a nude woman lounges on the hotel bed, smiling coyly at the camera. Here, Ophüls is deliberately outrageous, flaunting his hedonism and detach-ment when away from the deprivation of a besieged Sarajevo. Yet, the relation of this scene to the "argument" made by the film should not be casually dismissed. The war continues, but life in the rest of the world goes on. In a film that refuses to employ narration or expert witnesses, how better to make the point about the isolation of the Balkan people and the opacity and irrelevance of their struggle to much of the world?

Ophüls's work continually reminds viewers that they are watching an elaborate historical construct. The strong sense of continuity between Ophüls's "history films" and (the primarily present-tense) *Troubles We've Seen* demonstrates the mutual imbrication of past and present implicit in all of his work. Just as his historical films are about the interactions between present and past, the "history" of wartime journalism haunts his investigation of news reporting in Bosnia at every turn. "History," this film argues, does not just appear, nor is it written first or exclusively by historians. Historical events are first textualized through a media ap-paratus that, although heavily influenced by corporate, economic, and national interests, is also created by individual news reporters. The film tells us that, while it is important to know about the world around us, in order to understand the meaning of "the news," one must first understand the conditions of its production—including the daily struggles over the exercise of power that take place between individuals and institutions.

The members of the foreign press who are the film's "main characters" bring with them a diverse array of personal histories and agendas. In many cases, they are professional war correspondents—veterans of the press corps in Vietnam and other international conflicts—who have clearly mastered the discursive conventions of war coverage. Like the Bosnians they are here to cover, they get shot at, they suffer from shortages and discomfort, and some of them get killed. Ophüls's respect for their commitment, personal sacrifices, and the work they do is obvious. I believe he also recognizes in them a group of people who experience on a daily basis the same problematic relationship to representation and historiography that Ophüls himself has devoted his career to. These reporters know what they can and cannot say about the war—what will and will not be published or broadcast in their home countries—and understand at a very practical level that these decisions have little to do with the "truth" of what is happening. The message is clear: "history" is a construct, even when it takes place in the present; even our best, most immediate channels of representation must be regarded with an informed and skeptical eye.

In one of many digressions from the immediate subject, Ophüls recounts the story of Robert Capa's famous "Moment of Death"[30] photograph from the Spanish Civil War. The photograph shows a young soldier at the precise moment of receiving a fatal wound—his body is contorted, head back, arms outstretched, a rifle falling from one hand. The image quickly achieved iconic status and greatly enhanced Capa's already respectable reputation as a photojournalist. Ophüls presents evidence that this icon of photojournalism may have been a fake, including another image of a soldier striking a "dead" pose in the same location moments later. A number of impassioned and credible witnesses attest to the fact that Capa would never have perpetrated such a fraud or allowed such a misunderstanding to occur. But cherished "truths" that could go unchallenged in 1936—Capa was an honest reporter, and camera images do not lie—no longer suffice in a new millennium, in the face of new but familiar genocides.

To the extent that history writing is related to remembrance, Ophüls's films pose perhaps their greatest challenge to traditions of oral history. For oral historians, film and video play a special role in the enunciation and preservation of "history"—especially when it involves traumatic events that are most prone to denial or repression.[31] However, the goal of Ophüls's work is not to displace other types of historiography or to render the past unknowable. They ask only that audiences complicate their understanding of and relation to it. Memories lie. People lie. Both may attempt to tell us what we want to hear.

Taken together, the projects discussed in these first two chapters stake out a position between two contradictory perceptions regarding historiography and cultural memory: one that claims that popular media—especially television—contribute to the creation of a "culture of amnesia," and another which invests unproblematic authority in the testimony of witnesses and participants in historical events. Both Ophüls's audacious, interrogatory documentary filmmaking and Tajiri's interwoven strategies of appropriation, re-creation, and personal narrativizing lead to a deeply politicized understanding of how the past is processed and made relevant in people's lives. Cultural memory, according to the model put forth in these works, is a product of political and social construction, processes that take place in dialogue with, rather than in opposition to, official historical discourses and individual recollections.

3 Found Footage

Opening title cards identify the setting as the Yucatán Peninsula in 1931, where Sylvanus G. Morley, a legendary archeologist who began studying Mayan artifacts in 1904, is teaching a Mayan woman to speak English. The young woman stands in front of a pyramid dressed in traditional Mayan garb and phonetically pronounces these words: "We are dressed as our ancestors were, who lived here in peace and contentment 700 years ago." The scene ends with a somewhat awkward bow toward the camera, followed by another title card stating simply "Fake Documentary." The next shot is a pan from the ancient Mayan pyramids of El Rey to the pyramid-shaped hotels of contemporary Cancun, emphasizing that yes, indeed, this is not a real documentary film but instead a film determined to upset the codes and categories that delimit documentary discourse.

The film is Jesse Lerner's *Ruins*, a feature-length documentary from 1999 that in its "fakeness" illustrates some of the central tenets of "history" as an open text. The opening sequence functions as a metaphor for the historiographical strategies of the entire film in which past and present are dialogically imbricated in relations of space, time, language, and ideology. In order to truly understand the past, *Ruins* shows us, one must first grapple with both the desires of the present and the awkward mechanisms—some more insistently awkward than others—through which historical discourse is rendered.

In an age of digital reproduction and recombinant media, film, like "history," occupies an intermediary condition in an inevitable process of revision, recontextualization, and reuse. This is perhaps no more true than in films that use found footage, meaning footage shot for one use but then "found" and repurposed, and thus redirected toward new uses. Found footage films are a staple of the American avant-garde and include experiments with "revised" films made by Joseph Cornell from the 1930s, to the work of Bruce Conner as exemplified by *A Movie* from 1958, and to art-oriented practices of the 1990s and a new millennium in which artists such as Douglas Gordon revisit existing films to explore dimensions of temporality, spatiality, and narrative, subjecting films to scrutiny and meta-analysis.

Why has found footage been so important to the American avant-garde? The answer is at least partially economic. Found footage films do not require cameras or the purchase and developing of film stock. For the most part, among marginal film- and videomakers, the copyright of appropriated works is disregarded or—as in works such as Conner's 1976 *Crossroads* (which makes use of footage declassified by the federal government) or Hollis Frampton's *Public Domain* (1972)—irrelevant. In extreme cases such as Ken Jacobs's *Perfect Film* (1986) or William Jones's *Tearoom* (1962/2007), the filmmaker did little more than retrieve a complete roll of film from obscurity, make a minor adjustment, and sign his name to it. Although the legacy of Marcel Duchamp's "ready-mades" is clearly in evidence in these examples, found footage is more frequently subjected to transformative processes such as optical printing, reediting, tinting, and so forth. As the title of Jay Leyda's book *Films Beget Films: A Study of the Compilation Film* suggests, the easy (one is tempted to say *natural*) reproducibility of film images makes them ideal sources for duplication and rejuvenation. He argues that the process of found footage filmmaking resembles the process of biological reproduction, indicating an almost genetic proclivity for images to be copied, mutated, or recontextualized in the course of perpetuating the film "species."

Leyda's organic model, however, provides little insight into the political and historiographical implications of found footage works that develop an antagonistic relationship with the texts they appropriate. Although this is clearly not the case with all instances of recycled imagery, a tendency toward oppositionality has contributed to its privileging in the American avant-garde, where alterity has been a defining and sustaining impulse. In James Peterson's *Dreams of Chaos, Visions of Order: Understanding the American Avant-Garde Cinema*, for example, oppositionality is clearly at the heart of his focus on found footage as one of the three primary discursive strands in the American avant-garde.[1] However, there is good reason to avoid this type of binary thinking about the relationship between commercial and experimental cinema, particularly in light of the discursive complexity and interdetermination of much found footage practice.

Film (need I say again, "like history"?) is both material and functional in nature, and found footage films underscore this materiality and functional use directly, inviting us to ask not only what films about the past *are* but also what they *do*. Viewing a found footage film invites us to engage in a doubled reading that juggles the disparate temporal registers suggested by the footage, as well as the varied authorial functions. The numerous cultural uses for recycled footage provide evidence of the multiple meanings and potentially infinite rewritings that are immanent in any image. This polyvalent and mutable existence results in not a flattening of filmed historiography but rather a layering and textualizing that reverberates through the process of historical writing. Just as it is impossible to frame a shot or select a film stock without being implicated in a system of ideological values and industrial production, one cannot select an image to be reused without creating a historiographical argument. What is an image's relationship to its referent? How do we ascertain that relationship? And what happens when that relationship is forcibly revised—and makes evident that revision, inviting now a cascading sequence of assessments?

The technological and ideological underpinnings of cinema and photography—which have equally significant implications for the historiography produced through these media—are usefully argued in works such as John Tagg's *The Burden of Representation: Essays on Photographies and Histories*, which questions how and why photographs were adopted as documents and evidence, and Brian Winston's *Technologies of Seeing: Photography, Cinematography and Television*.[2] Winston argues that the development of film stocks and lighting practices that are oriented to the reproduction of Caucasian skin tones bears the burden of racism, an argument that might be echoed in examining the privileged mode of storytelling on film, namely, linear, causal, realist narratives. How does this mode prefigure and parallel a mode of historical thinking that similarly narrows the range of expressible histories? And, to follow this set of comparisons, how might a mode of historiography that operates outside of—or in constant danger of transgressing—the bounds of conventional narrative similarly complicate our understanding of history? The appropriation and reuse of "found footage" inaugurates multiple possibilities for reinscription and critique of previously articulated codes of representation, and invites us to question the manner and extent to which "history" may be constituted through images at the most basic level.

In compilation films, motion pictures operate through a discursive paradox. The desire for coherent and orderly historiography is related to antiquated notions of what "history" is and how we experience it. Visual media, which are now understood to be the primary bearers of "historical consciousness," must negotiate a sometimes conflicted alliance between the specificity of documentary or historical imagery and the fluid contingence these images acquire when they are reinscribed and viewed in a cultural context. A fixed relation between history writing and the historical world is the central dilemma of empirical historiography, unprovable by the discourse it enables, but essential to the functioning of the entire system. The appropriation and use of found footage may be understood as a tactical maneuver within which the simultaneous deployment and subversion of ontological certainty is a crucial factor. The discursive import of found footage thus relies upon its claim to a prior, indexical connection to the world, at the same time that it is inscribed in a fully articulated and conventionalized system of filmic signification.

Traditional historiography operates according to the same basic codes that prevail within the legal system, emphasizing presentation of physical evidence, expert testimony, and verifiable modes of documentation. According to this model, historians function as detectives engaged in solving a puzzle or uncovering and narrativizing a series of preexisting facts. This type of archival thinking is characterized by Michel de Certeau as a form of historiography comparable to epistemological conquest, a campaign of mastery aligned with the strategies and goals of European colonialism.[3] It is in resistance to this totalizing impulse that much found footage work originates, frequently resulting in fragmented and chaotic reworkings that open up spaces for alternative voices or readings from *within* received historical texts.

Found Footage as Historical Evidence

In spite of its ubiquity both on TV broadcasts and in avant-garde compilation practices, the recycling and recontextualizing of film and video images remains critically neglected. William Wees's *Recycled Images: The Art and Politics of Found Footage Films* remains the only widely available book-length treatment of this subject published in the past thirty years.[4] Wees bases his work on the articulation of three categories of found footage use, which he correlates to three political positions. The uncritical reproduction of images from the past as evidence (e.g., the use of stock footage in documentary film) is dubbed "reproduction." Films that perform an interrogation of previously photographed images he calls "critical appropriation." And the reuse of images that seems to be more or less random he labels "postmodern appropriation."[5] Wees's straightforward taxonomy of these categories of appropriation describes a great deal of found footage practice, particularly by North American male filmmakers during the 1960s and '70s. Although he brings together a range of interesting work—some of it admittedly obscure and in need of attention—Wees's writing remains largely observational and inattentive to the politics of appropriation that his book's subtitle suggests, ultimately providing little insight into the challenge posed by reused imagery to the fundamental relationship between images and the world.

Theorists who invoke the vocabulary developed by postmodern theory to deal with the consequences of appropriation (principally the disappearance of stable categories of authorship, originality, and authenticity) have diverted discussions of found footage and historiography away from thinking about appropriation as a rhetorical strategy. In cinematic historiography, the use of found footage is more productively viewed as a speech act in its own right, a rhetorical gesture that draws on a vocabulary of preexisting images and visual syntax. The tension created between the found image as a historical artifact (therefore "true") and the potential for multiple meanings implied by its appropriation and reuse (therefore of indeterminate referentiality) lies at the heart of some of the most interesting—and historiographically disruptive—work with found footage.

At the extreme end of this spectrum, the rhetorical power of found footage is sometimes invoked as parody, via the simulation or recontextualization of archival imagery. Particularly inspired examples that mimic the documentary mode include Peter Jackson's *Forgotten Silver* (1995), Andy Bobrow's *Old Negro Space Program* (2005), and Cheryl Dunye's *Watermelon Woman* (1996). Each of these projects deploy humor and irony to "rewrite history" by claiming to have discovered previously forgotten film images. In *Forgotten Silver*, Jackson claims to have unearthed a body of film work by a fictional New Zealand filmmaker that proves New Zealanders were actually responsible for nearly all major innovations in cinema technology, from the invention of color and sound to the narrative structure of feature films. In *Watermelon Woman*, Dunye claims to have rediscovered the life work of an African American actress whose career defies the traditional invisibility of women and people of color in cinema history. And, billing itself as "A Film Not by Ken Burns," Bobrow's short, *The Old Negro Space Program*,[6] precisely mimics the form of a Ken Burns documentary, telling the forgotten history of an African American space program formed in protest to the exclusion of negroes from NASA (National Aeronautics and Space Administration) in the late 1950s. In Bobrow's alternative history, footage from the Prelinger Archive and NASA's own image archive are manipulated and renarrativized to tell the story of the NASSA, the Negro American Space Society of Astronauts. In addition to ambiguous found footage that purports to record a failed space launch by NASSA, a series of doctored still images depict real NASA astronauts in a capsule labeled "Whites Only," while a room full of NASA workers are depicted wearing KKK (Ku Klux Klan) hoods. In voice-over, two separate narrators explain that "it was a different time" in the late 1950s, when blacks were excluded from the space program. This repetition ironically draws attention to the fact that African Americans remain underrepresented in the space program. Like *The Watermelon Woman*, *The Old Negro Space Program* invents an imaginary history in order to shed light on the "history" we accept as real, highlighting the exclusion of racism from mainstream, teleological historical narratives.

The many uses to which found footage is put, especially in documentary and avant-garde films, provide useful challenges to assumptions about the relationship between film images and the world. In historical documentaries, for example, the distinction is often marked according to whether or not the original sound is used in conjunction with the picture.[7] If the original sound (e.g., a newsreel voice-over or "March of Time"–style music) is used, the effect is to draw attention to the datedness of the visual material. The absence of these sounds, in contrast, allows the images to be read as direct signifiers of something in the world. This preferred reading may be reinforced by the addition of postsynchronized audio effects, music, or narration which resutures and naturalizes the image into the present film. When original sound is used, the images are more likely to present themselves as a construction in which a new "argument" or diegesis appears to be layered over an underlying one. The relationship between these two layers, then, highlights the artificiality of the relationship between the "original" filmed material and the world that it purports to signify.

However, such moments of historiographical self-consciousness are not unheard of in commercial productions. A remarkable scene occurs in an episode of *The X-Files* in which a government employee reveals to Agent Fox Mulder (David Duchovny) the existence of a massive conspiracy to control and rewrite "history." With each mention of a historical event, the image cuts to a corresponding stock footage image, for example, reference to the first exploding atomic bomb is accompanied by an image of a mushroom cloud. Likewise, references to Nikita Khrushchev, the moon landing, and the Cuban missile crisis all trigger cuts to iconic stock footage images. The narrative generated is entirely fictional (according to the dominant discursive regime), illustrating the ease with which such iconic representations are redeployed and recoded within a narrative that is overtly concerned with the writing and rewriting of history.[8]

In popular culture, postmodernism's predilection for perpetual "present-ness" resulted in well-known sublimations of the persistent desire for history into endless varieties of kitsch, pastiche, and nostalgia. However, new modes of cinematic historiography emerged most actively from the other end of the high-low culture divide. Indeed, the revision and politicization of history and memory have been frequent obsessions among experimental filmmakers of the past three decades. The most interesting of these undertake an interrogation of not only the strategies of authentication deployed by documentary filmmaking but also the material and epistemological premises of "history" itself. This chapter is devoted to more esoteric instances of appropriation. Few of the reused images discussed here possess a significant degree of iconic status. Most are obscure, forgotten, or ignored, and rescued from trash dumpsters, pornographic video stores, government archives, or personal collections. The histories they construct—with some exceptions—are correspondingly specific in nature, speaking to larger issues of historiography allegorically, via the mobilization and challenging of discourses of historical authenticity.

The Real in the Fake: Jesse Lerner's *Ruins*

It is a truism of postmodern culture that the difference between truth and fiction is not what it used to be. But in Lerner's *Ruins*, this is more than an empty slogan; it's a point of departure. *Ruins* is a self-proclaimed "fake documentary" that exposes the persistence of colonialist ideology in pre-Hispanic histories of Mexico and calls into question the processes by which the disciplines of archaeology and art history are constituted. In *Ruins*, Lerner is as much concerned with historiography—the processes of writing history—as with "history" itself. The film mobilizes a multiplicity of historiographical and documentary strategies, ranging from archival footage compilation and hidden camera interviews to cutout animation and fictional re-creation. *Ruins* puts forward a scathing revelation of the racist and colonialist underpinnings of ancient Mesoamerican historiography and offers in its place an enlightened critique and alternate vision of the region's past. The film succeeds brilliantly in snatching Mexican history from the jaws of colonialist discourse, while simultaneously interrogating the conventions of authenticity and authority in the historical documentary.

Ruins is constructed in three movements. The first poses the basic questions of Mesoamerican historiography, debunking both the colonialist naïveté of nineteenth-century accounts and the arrogance of the "definitive" archaeological histories written in the 1940s and '50s. The second part of the film illustrates what is at stake in the history of this region and the ongoing instrumentalization of Mexican history in the interests of growing U.S. internationalism during World War II, followed by tourism and other corporate incarnations of Manifest Destiny. The final movement consists of a sustained meditation on questions of originality, authenticity, and competing discourses of art and culture as refracted through the practice of forgery. The film's visual syntax is a blend of American avant-garde and essayistic documentary, combining strategies of found footage collage with a handheld, home movie vernacular. The structure of *Ruins* is fundamentally intertextual, referencing other historical texts as well as fiction films, advertisements, music, newsreels, and Hollywood feature films. Audiences must work to make meaning out of the diverse juxtapositions and layers of historical revision embedded in the film, a process consistent with its implicit critique of dramatic narrative historiography.

The opening sequence of *Ruins*, described at the start of the chapter, presages the film's pedagogical intent, uniting space, time, language, and ideology in a move that insists we acknowledge the desires of the present. Following the preamble, a feature film–style credit sequence introduces each of the film's major "characters," thereby announcing one of Lerner's guiding ambiguities—the fluidity of fact and fiction in terms of performance, evidence, and documentation. *Ruins*' "elaborate web of artifice" begins with a sequence of crude, cutout animations, accompanied by voice-over narration from several nineteenth-century histories of Mexico and Central America. The animations depict events for which no documentary record exists—the expropriation of ancient Mexican objects and their installation in American and European art museums.[9] The animations are accompanied by inconclusive speculations on the origins of the Mayan people (with theories ranging from the lost tribe of Israel to Vikings and Pygmies). These histories attempt to reconcile the reputed savagery of Mayan rituals with the magnificence of their architectural and artistic accomplishments. A final voice-over admits that, in the absence of definitive proof, all historians can rely on is "probabilities and conjectures," while on screen the pages of a history book are systematically shredded, another metaphoric rendering of the historical revision that will be enacted in the film.

Ruins borrows its overall rhetorical strategy from postcolonial theory to highlight the power relations implicit in the gaze of the ethnographer and the cultural narratives that are their stock in trade. The film implicitly argues that the act of viewing and theorizing "primitive" cultures cannot take place outside the paradigms of colonialist ideology. Appropriating the past in order to render it in a coherent, linear narrative, the film argues, is equivalent to the cultural appropriation of the colonizer. By labeling the film a "fake," Lerner distances himself from the problematic histories of visual anthropology and ethnographic filmmaking. *Ruins* proceeds to mobilize discourses of documentary accuracy and historical authenticity along divergent trajectories, a destabilizing gesture that leads to reflexive questioning of the filmmaker's own process. Interestingly, Lerner's disruption of the fact-fiction binary is only a temporary rhetorical strategy that allows him to distinguish his project from the outmoded pedantry of his racist predecessors, while eventually articulating his own revision of the historical record. In spite of repeated proclamations that the film is a "fake," by the end of *Ruins*, a senile, old history has essentially been replaced with a smarter, newer one. *Ruins* functions as an open rather than a closed text—one that suggest fissures and contradictions in its own argument and ultimately stretches beyond the critique of historiography to pose an indictment of tourism, colonialism, ethnography, and documentary itself.

The story told in *Ruins* is dispersed into a multiplicity of voices, some of which are linked to on-screen characters and texts while others are presented as disembodied fragments, quotations, re-creations, and fakes. Lerner's role as filmmaker thus comes to resemble that of a ventriloquist rather than a unifying consciousness.[10] Indeed, Lerner speaks from a position of omniscience only in rare moments throughout the film. The most notable examples are when a female narrator's voice ruminates on the similarities between documentary and forgery, and when recurring intertitles remind viewers they are watching a "Fake Documentary" made in 1998. In the latter half of the film, *Ruins* becomes increasingly idiosyncratic in the range of voices it presents, eventually quoting figures as disparate as Orson Welles, Margaret Meade, Rod Serling, and Allen Ginsberg. This panoply of voices metaphorically references the associative montage of historical consciousness and creates a web of textual connections and collisions. Lerner thus establishes a contract with the viewer based on not trust that he is presenting reliable information but rather a tacit agreement to collectively investigate and draw meaning from a range of historical perspectives, images, artifacts, and documents.

The first and last sections of the film are anchored by contemporary interviews with two individuals representing opposite ends of the spectrum of historical authenticity. The first interview is with a woman named Maria Elena Pat, who is identified as an eyewitness to the mid-twentieth-century excavation of Mayan cities by archaeologists Sylvanus Morley and Eric Thompson. Speaking to the camera, Pat refutes and ridicules the accepted histories of Mayan culture, arguing that Morley and Thompson fundamentally misunderstood Mayan language, culture, and politics. Pat speaks as a cultural insider but also as a well-informed critic of Morley and Thompson's outmoded research methods. Her monologue is intercut with archival footage of Morley and Thompson presenting their theories as well-established archaeological facts. In juxtaposition with Pat's critique, however, Morley and Thompson's once authoritative accounts are made to appear preposterously speculative and transparently rooted in projections of their own cultural anxieties.

Interestingly, however, Pat's analysis is not simply presented as an unproblematic correction of the historical record. In order to undermine the authority of her (somewhat unlikely) testimony, Lerner positions Pat against a rear projection screen on which appears a series of images by Laura Gilpin depicting scenes of Mayan civilization.[11] This strategy lends a highly constructed, performative feel to the interview, suggesting that Pat's testimony may be as much of an artificial construct—a potential fake—as everything else in the film. This layering of discourses of authenticity and artifice underscores *Ruins'* operating premise that the past is accessible only through accumulated layers of historical sedimentation[12] and competing interpretation. Historical consciousness, as Walter Benjamin argued, does not move forward through "homogenous, empty time."[13] The chaotic structure and contradictory discursive strategies of *Ruins* function as a metaphor for historical sedimentation and the need to sift through layers of evidence and interpretation in order to understand both the past and the construction of history.

In the latter part of the film, Lerner's interest in the relation between reality and artifice is most clearly embodied in the heroic, but ultimately tragic, figure of the forger. *Ruins* tells the story of an art forger named Brigido Lara who, in the 1960s and '70s reputedly created thousands of sculptures that came to define the art of the Totonac culture, a pre-Aztec society in Mexico's Gulf Coast region. Lara's forgeries were so convincing that many of them were sold to museums as ancient artifacts, and Lara was arrested and temporarily jailed as a looter (rather than a forger) of antiquities. Many of Lara's pieces are now in New York's Metropolitan Museum of Art and other high-profile collections—an unintentional joke at the expense of connoisseurs of "primitive" art. In one remarkable sequence, Lara looks at images of his own work in a coffee table book called *Masterpieces of Primitive Art* and proudly presents some of his sculptures to the camera, caressing them lovingly while the narrator ruminates on the nature of forgeries. Are they "worthless embarrassments or treasured pieces of art"?

Unlike the clearly staged interview with Pat, Lara is shot verité style on location in his studio and in the field as he meticulously seeks out exactly the right kind of clay, tools, and conditions for creating his sculptures.

Lara tells the story of his life as a forger in an earnest voice-over, noting that, although his intention was not to deceive, his work has significantly shaped the museum's definitions of authenticity. Lara is ultimately unapologetic about his role in the falsification of Totonac history, remarking simply, "It's their problem if they were fooled. It's supposed to be a healthy experience." Like Lerner's film, Lara's forgeries transcend the presumed limitations of their inauthentic origins. It is not simply questions of truth versus fiction under investigation but also the institutions of authority and authenticity exemplified by the art museum and its self-perpetuating—sometimes self-serving—curatorial practices. Expanding beyond questions of historical value and authenticity, *Ruins* thus articulates a withering indictment of the art world's systems of authority and claims to cultural relevance.

The latter part of *Ruins* also presents etymological exegeses of words such as "reproduction" and "replica," distinguishing them from forgeries by their relation to deception and embeddedness in the power dynamics of cultural appropriation. The trade in replicas and reproductions—presented as an important part of the tourism industry in contemporary Mexico—operates through a tacit agreement between buyer and seller that the objects offer primarily symbolic or sentimental value. By contrast, the collecting of original artifacts by wealthy foreigners (including Nelson Rockefeller, whose private plane was reputedly so heavily laden with Mayan sculptures it was unable to take off) constituted a clear gesture of economic and cultural exploitation. The irony that an unknown percentage of the artifacts collected under these circumstances were forgeries is not lost on Lerner who positions this fact among other discourses of resistance and tactical response to U.S. cultural hegemony. In what appears to be a hidden camera interview, a replica seller insightfully theorizes that Americans are interested in the indigenous cultures of Mexico because they are a nation of immigrants with no real history of their own. This fleetingly incisive moment of nonexpert analysis throws into relief the convolutions and pretenses of academicized history and its endless revisions.

In *Ruins*, the overt parallels between the art forger and the documentary filmmaker suggest that fiction and artifice may come closer to "staging the real" than the faithful reproduction of documentary facts. The film argues implicitly that histories not subject to revision and debate are thereby drained of their dynamism and cultural relevance. More importantly, static histories are removed from the arena of politics, where meaning is formed in relation to the needs of the present and desires to transform the future. The conception of historiography deployed in *Ruins* does not simply recover or preserve a factual history but also actively engages in the conflicts and uncertainty of the past. Historians should not understand themselves to be constrained by the impossibility of total historical preservation. Rather, *Ruins* demonstrates that they may be equally freed by it to construct a relationship with the past that is imperfect and improvisational and to understand "history" as constituted through multiple voices and cascading layers of meaning.

Little Stabs at History: Ken Jacobs's Projection Performances

A central figure in American experimental film of the 1950s and '60s, Jacobs has, since the late 1990s, devoted himself to working with a unique, projection apparatus called the "Nervous System." Utilizing dual projection and an auxiliary shutter mechanism, Jacobs's live performances produce 3-D and other perceptual effects that challenge the most fundamental assumptions about cinematic reception. Beyond its relevance to cognitive and phenomenological film studies, Jacobs's work with historical footage enacts a complex reading of key historical moments since the birth of cinema. From the Spanish-American War (*Making Light of History: The Philippines Adventure*, 1983) to the assassination of Malcolm X (*Perfect Film*, 1986), Jacobs unravels the naturalized bonds of cinematic convention and historical construction. In his projection performances, Jacobs asks us to view both the film image and "history" itself in a new light.

In Jacobs's work, we witness the birth of not only cinema via direct allusions to Eadweard Muybridge and Auguste and Louis Lumière (*From Muybridge to Brooklyn Bridge*; *Opening the 19th Century*) but also cinematic movement and a redefinition of perceptions of time, depth, and space. From his late 1950s collaborations with Jack Smith (*Little Stabs at Happiness*; *Star Spangled to Death*, etc.), to his elaborations on structural filmmaking in the 1970s and '80s (*Tom, Tom the Piper's Son*, *Disorient Express*, *Georgetown Loop*, etc.), and to the Nervous System, Jacobs has created a wildly disparate body of work unified nonetheless by a powerful sensitivity to the medium of film, the practice of historiography, and the possibilities for experimentation with each.

The centerpiece of Jacobs's recent work, the "Nervous System," utilizes two projectors loaded with identical strips of film and an auxiliary, propeller-like shutter mechanism that creates a flicker effect reminiscent of early cinema. One projector remains unchanged, while the second is subjected to every possible form of manipulation: lateral shifts, tilts up and down and side to side, focus, zoom, and occasional obstruction or addition of lenses. The "propeller" is also subject to a range of adjustments, affecting the speed and rhythm of the flicker. Jacobs controls the frame-by-frame advancement of each filmstrip in varying relation to the other. In addition, the projectors' internal shutter mechanisms have been removed so that the flicker and persistence of vision effect is entirely manually imposed. On rare occasions during a performance, Jacobs adjusts the propeller to mimic an ordinary projector shutter, causing the flicker effect to all but disappear, producing a disconcerting effect on eyes that have grown accustomed to the pulsing. The "trick" that is played on the viewer's perceptions and expectations defies conventional intellectual or emotional response, while the incessant flickering between blackness and image offers the promise of continually renewed ways of seeing. The effects of the Nervous System range from a powerful sense of three-dimensionality to a hypnotic state of semiconsciousness that allows viewers to create their own meanings and narratives.

For my purposes, two of Jacobs's projects stand out, essentially using the Nervous System to make history nervous. *Loco Motion* and *Opening the 19th Century* both transform straightforward historical documents into perception objects, so we relearn how we look at even the most familiar objects. Jacobs's project changes the way we see—not merely in how we reconsider the evidentiary foundation of the documents subjected to his system but also in how we "see" them cognitively and retinally.

The original footage of the Sarnia Tunnel from which Ken Jacobs's performance of *Loco Motion* derives, was shot by Biograph cinematographers in 1903 and is unexceptional among early films of its kind. Indeed, at the time, it was probably barely a novelty—simply one among many films photographed from the front or back of a moving train. Motion was the point of these films and its ability to dazzle audiences with a sensation reminiscent of the experience of riding trains.[14] At the time this footage was shot, cinema was also coming into its own, making the transition from mere novelty rides[15] to a more complicated mode of presentation. Dozens of these films are preserved in the Library of Congress's Paper Print collection, depicting ordinary train routes, traversed at normal speed with real passengers. For contemporary audiences, these shorts offer little excitement or novelty. However, in Jacobs's hands, they become a thrill ride to rival the experience of the earliest film showings.

Loco Motion begins with a camera apparently mounted on the back of a train, pulling slowly away from a tunnel.[16] Before long, another train appears and heads toward us, passing on the right. By this time, the Nervous System's rendering of space has become so disorienting that what appeared to be motion *away* from the tunnel, photographed from the back of the train, now appears as motion *toward* the tunnel, photographed from the front of the train. As the performance progresses, it becomes apparent that Jacobs is deliberately manipulating these sensations, moving his audience backward and forward through both time and space. The only consistent point of reference, the tunnel, appears to be simultaneously advancing toward and receding from the camera.

Then, in a sudden burst of speed that causes the audience to jerk back in their seats, we enter the tunnel. Light changes to dark, and a pulsating synthesizer score rises all around. The sound is loud and enveloping, emanating from all corners of the room. The rhythm of the pulses seem perfectly matched to the Nervous System's flicker. The "light" at the end of the tunnel takes the shape of a huge, dark mushroom cloud. The supports of the tunnel seem to mark the train's progress through space but, again, the sensation of motion does not correlate with the distance traveled. Together with the surrounding sounds, the tunnel appears to be a totally articulated physical space as we are swept into the darkness. The synthesizer fades down gradually just as we reach the end of the tunnel, but the show isn't over yet. The train continues its impossible journey past another train and a platform peopled with travelers. A man standing atop a passing train strikes a heroic pose that, impossibly, never changes as we pass him. Time and motion again fluctuate back and forth. The straight track appears at times to bend, causing the audience to lean in anticipation of a centrifugal force that never comes. The experience has become physical as well as mental.

Next, we approach a train station, and the synthesizer begins again with an electronic approximation of a train whistle, pulsing and droning ominously. The sound seems to be a warning to the human figures that dart out of the way of the oncoming train and float dreamlike back into danger. We momentarily appear to be on a collision course with another train, and I have to remind myself, as the Lumières' audience must have over a hundred years ago, that the oncoming train poses no real danger. It's only a movie. Jacobs rides the suspense of this moment for all it's worth before jerking us onto another track and allowing the train to pass harmlessly by. We change tracks a couple more times, or perhaps it is just more spatial manipulation. Our speed fluctuates between whiplash-inducing acceleration and what seems to be full reverse. We pass another train with people frozen like mannequins, waving to us without moving a muscle, yet we move past them in what can only be a series of advancing frames. The droning pulse of the synthesizer becomes a full orchestra winding down, and the train coasts gently to a halt.

In *Loco Motion*, Jacobs comes close to creating an utterly immersive, installation space. The sensation of moving forward (or backward) through the tunnel provides a powerful, somatic experience similar to an amusement park ride or virtual reality simulator for its immersive intensity. In addition to the perceptual trickery and obsessive pleasure in simply re-viewing these images, Jacobs's work challenges their historical content and the very process by which film is used to construct the past. While most contemporary debates over film and history focus on issues of accuracy and responsibility, Jacobs's work insists that cinematic historiography raises more fundamental questions of epistemology and representation. "History," for Jacobs, cannot be separated from the present or understood except through the innumerable layers of perceptual and historical sedimentation that build up over time. The "Nervous System" offers an important intervention in reconceiving the fundamental relationship between archival images and the construction of history.

In addition, Jacobs's Nervous System constantly draws attention to the mediation of the cinematic apparatus and his own role as an "interpretive paleographer"[17] of images. He invites us to think about not only the events and people shown in historical images but also how historical meaning is created cinematically. The extreme manipulation of the imagery and analysis of motion enables a critique of even the tiniest gesture or most fleeting moment. Unique among cinematic performances, the Nervous System allows for simultaneous engagement with the material properties of the filmstrip and the content of the images.

In *Opening the 19th Century*, Jacobs reworks images believed to be the first tracking shots in film history, photographed by the Lumière brothers in the 1890s. The camera moves through streets, rivers, and canals in Cairo, Venice, and other unidentified cities. Images are taken from boats, streetcars, trains, and so on. The performance utilizes the "Pulfrich effect," an obscure neurological effect that creates the illusion of three-dimensional space from two-dimensional images. The effect is achieved through the use of a neutral density filter that is positioned over one eye, effectively slowing the responses of the brain to the information captured by one retina and thereby throwing off synchronization with the other.

Jacobs claims that this performance is designed to allow audiences to see the nineteenth century in a more lifelike way.[18] But he also makes it strange by turning alternate sequences upside down so that we see the same exact footage twice, once right side up and forward, once inverted and backward. The motion is thus rendered continuous from either left to right or right to left for each half of the film. The two halves are separated by a red flash and a train whistle that cue the audience to move the filter from one eye to the other. Jacobs's performance of *Opening the 19th Century* is silent except for the train whistle and the noise of Jacobs's Nervous System apparatus deliberately situated in the room with the audience, creating yet another allusion to early cinema exhibition. While the images in *Opening the 19th Century* lose the geographical specificity that they originally had as travelogues, the 3-D effect that Jacobs creates (via Pulfrich) ironically fulfills the goal of three-dimensionality ordinarily denied to cinema tourism.

In Jacobs's performance work, the negotiation and rescripting of film history runs in parallel with that of "real history." Jacobs's project makes film history and material history inseparable, achieving seemingly impossible effects with the aid of simple pieces of grey plastic. His performances echo a time when filmmaking required one to be part inventor, part scientist, and part showman, reminding audiences of cinema's origins in vaudeville and traveling sideshows. The Nervous System, as Phil Solomon has noted, is a contraption reminiscent of traveling magic lantern shows of the nineteenth century. And like those early operator-entrepreneurs, Jacobs delivers not just images but also an experience, something fantastic that summons up the thrill of the first motion picture projection and the frenetic impossibility of moving images.

The histories rendered by the Nervous System are constituted through an encounter, a momentary set of perceptions and uncertainties. Each performance is tied to its own particular time and place as well as the physical presence of Jacobs himself. This is part of what makes these performances difficult to describe and situate critically. Though bounded by certain parameters, each performance is different and perceived differently by individual viewers. Each spectator brings his or her predispositions and perceptual context to any given screening. The Nervous System, however, accentuates these distinctions by both defamiliarizing the images being viewed and disrupting the basic experience of cinema viewing. In all cases, Jacobs requires his audiences to work for their experience, to not take "history," film, or perception itself for granted.

Craig Baldwin's *O No Coronado*

Although stylistically distinct from the other found footage films considered here, Craig Baldwin's *O No Coronado* digs into an equally rich source of images drawn from popular culture and film archives to construct a counterhistory that is deeply politicized. In *O No Coronado*, Baldwin recounts the horrors of the Spanish conquest of the Southwest driven by Coronado's futile search for the "seven cities of gold." The film employs re-creations with a modern-day Coronado and absurdly costumed conquistadors, as well as Baldwin's signature found footage from widely disparate sources. In addition to footage from historical films about Spanish expeditions and the Inquisition, Baldwin utilizes images from the *Lone Ranger*, B-grade science fiction movies, corporate videos about mining and nuclear waste disposal, and occasional contemporary interviews with tourists to the pueblos decimated by Coronado, indicating the extent to which this region's past has been commodified and trivialized. "Coronado," the tape points out, is now the name of a shopping mall in Arizona patronized by tourists who visit the pueblos while remaining oblivious to the genocidal conquest that happened there some five hundred years earlier.

Baldwin's historiography is assembled through fragments of images, re-creations, and narratives, accompanied by spoken accounts of Spanish atrocities. The voice-over offers both a questioning of the means by which "history" and ideology are constructed and a sincere effort at revision—a reminder of the cruelty, obsessiveness, and greed of colonial conquest. Baldwin's style also poses a critique of the Ken Burns style of history telling in which a spoken narrative simply elaborates upon the historiography materialized on screen. Although a few of Baldwin's sequences deploy a similar strategy, others clearly undermine it. Shots from the *Lone Ranger* TV series, for example, illustrate the persistence of colonialist ideology through the image of the docile native sidekick, Tonto. Likewise, a fifteenth-century account of terrible beasts in the southwest wilderness is accompanied by clips from a science fiction movie in which two alligators fitted with prehistoric-looking dorsal fins attack each other. And in a strategy that recalls Jean-Marie Straub and Danièle Huillet's hilltop dialogue in *Othon*, re-creations of the Coronado expedition take place on top of a hill overlooking a modern urban cityscape.

In virtually all of Baldwin's work, appropriation plays a key role in larger strategies of cultural, legal, and historiographical transgression. Baldwin's disregard for copyright laws (dealt with explicitly in his documentary *Sonic Outlaws*) allows him to attack the hegemony of corporate-controlled media over images of the past. He says, "In any event, I don't care what's happening legally. Some people might, but I'm interested in leaving that question behind and doing my own work despite the laws. As far as I'm concerned, the situation calls for more ingenuity and more crime."[19]

Along with earlier films such as *RocketkitCongokit* (1986) and *Tribulation: 99 Alien Anomalies under America* (1992), Baldwin's *O No Coronado* models a historiographical mode that insists that—in a free society—the ownership of images should not dictate who is allowed to write history.

William Jones's *The Fall of Communism . . . as Seen in Gay Pornography*

Also deeply invested in questions of appropriation, experimental filmmaker Jones has created a remarkable and iconoclastic body of film and video work that deals explicitly with the writing of history. In his rigorously structured and densely erudite work, Jones has developed a unique mode of historico-etymological exposition that highlights the entangled operations of historiography, politics, economics, and sexuality. His work is both highly personal—by turns confessional, autobiographical, and analytical—and politically charged.

The appropriation of images—from both domestic and industrial sources—plays an important role in much of Jones's work, ranging from the reuse and replication of his father's frantic home movies in *Massillon* (1991) to the operatic power plays enacted in an Eastern European porn video that he excerpts in *The Fall of Communism . . . as Seen in Gay Pornography* (1998). Likewise, in *Finished* (1996), Jones pairs images of gay porn star Alan Lambert with scenes from Frank Capra's *Meet John Doe* (1941), in order to investigate the relationship between Hollywood and the porn industry and the complex interplay of images and desire. Jones's mode of historiography is metonymic, highlighting the ways human history is written on and through individual bodies. His work insists that even the most marginal images, people, and places—an obscure town in Ohio, a French-Canadian porn star, and a collection of low-budget porn tapes—may be used to construct a meaningful historical critique.

The writing of history, for Jones, is also about appropriation on textual and cultural levels. In *The Fall of Communism*, images of "appropriated" bodies are charged with eroticism derived from the knowledge and mastery of others. The tape is entirely composed of images from gay porn videos imported from the three cities that have become the centers of porn production in Eastern Europe since the collapse of the Soviet Union: Prague, Budapest, and Moscow. In these tapes, Jones offers a remarkable articulation of the power dynamics that develop between viewer and viewed. The power disparity between consumer and consumed in commercial pornography—those who sell their bodies and those who buy them—becomes a metaphor for the economic "shock therapy" of the post-Gorbachev era and the devouring of the regions' economic resources by hastily formed capitalist institutions.

In voice-over, Jones notes that "symbols of the old and new coexist in the fantasy world of gay porn. Anachronisms may go unnoticed by consumers who fast-forward through the boring parts. But patience has its rewards." The first part of Jones's video is composed exclusively of "the boring parts" excerpted from these videos: street scenes, landscapes, and iconic locators such as Moscow's St. Basil's cathedral—elements that are clearly secondary to the tapes' primary purpose. This is followed by a protracted montage of looks at the camera that Jones reads as indicative of the contempt the tapes' subjects have for the videomakers. Jones notes that Eastern European sex workers, who receive one-tenth the wages of their counterparts in the West, "have been absorbed into the international labor market" in ways that go unmentioned in official discourses about post-Soviet economic reform. The tape concludes with a protracted series of excerpts from porn "screen tests" in which young boys respond to questions about their sexual preferences and allow themselves to be posed and fondled by an English-speaking director. The painful dehumanization of these boys by a Western movie director (who appears on screen only as a pair of disembodied hands) parallels the exploitation of Eastern European markets by Western business interests in the wake of the region's economic collapse. Extracted from their original context, these images seem to reveal all the contradictions that inhere in capitalism—the hopes, fears, and disappointments of a new economic order.

As the opening line of narration in *The Fall of Communism* states, "Even in an unlikely place, it is possible to find traces of recent history." Jones's tape thus argues that larger historiographies may be inscribed in even the most liminal and specific documents. The selection of gay porn videos privileges a mode of historical reading that emphasizes discourses of power and desire, but Jones's method is also highly portable. Complex readings may be drawn from virtually any collection of images or historical texts. More explicitly even than most radical, subcultural histories, Jones's work argues that, when we talk about sex, desire, or "history," we are really talking about politics.

Found footage, in its tendency to deploy and undermine its own claims to historiographical authenticity, is key to the construction of visual historiography. Although digital technology has heightened cultural skepticism regarding the ontological origins of photographic reproduction, these forms of appropriation and reuse operate most powerfully through the tension between their status as originary artifacts from the past and infinitely reusable signifiers in the present. Irreducible to discourses of postmodern pastiche or quotation, found footage films and other appropriative practices constitute strategies of counterreading that illustrate the potential for multiple voices and interpretations within preexisting images.

4 Home Movies

Some of the most provocative forms of history writing take place in the least expected places. This is nowhere more true than in the realm of amateur film and videomaking—the massive body of work that we call "home movies" or "home videos." This chapter focuses not on home movies themselves but rather on a range of instances when home movies are reappropriated and recontextualized in the interests of self-conscious historiography.[1] With the proliferation of high-quality consumer cameras, amateur video footage now routinely appears on television news reports and reality programming as well as in a new generation of reflexive documentaries in which video cameras are distributed to documentary subjects as a counterpoint to the "outside" perspective of the show's producers.[2] With the explosion of online video sharing and distribution sites including YouTube, the accessibility of video by nonprofessionals has increased exponentially and with it the range of perspectives from which any given event may be captured for posterity. As raw historical documents, this type of amateur footage provides an enormously rich archive of images that are imbued with a presumption of authenticity nearly unique among contemporary motion picture practices.[3]

Clearly, the "truth claim" these images make may be called into question on many levels. But within the family, home movies have occupied a privileged position, both in terms of their capacity for archival preservation and their active function in family identity formation. In defining the role of home movies in family life, anthropologist Richard Chalfen identifies a system of representation that he terms "home mode communication." The "home mode" is a "pattern of interpersonal and small group communication centered around the home" that emphasizes its function in a "process of social communication."[4] For Chalfen, this centering on the home includes the exclusive circulation of images among individuals who have intimate, personal ties to the family. Chalfen's home mode is thus a recognizable—one is tempted by the normative logic he deploys to say "universal"—form of social representation that only makes sense within the context of the family.[5]

Patricia Zimmermann, one of the earliest film theorists to write extensively about home movies, argues that home movies function within families very much like ethnographic records, serving a ritualistic role in the way families construct themselves and their sense of a shared past. Zimmermann also notes the near total suppression of "unpleasant" events such as funerals, divorce, hospital rehabilitation, and so on, within the home movie repertoire.[6] Chalfen similarly argues that, by emphasizing the sunny side of life, home movies have an agenda-setting function for the family. Repeated viewing of idealized images creates an often mythological sense of family unity and reinforces behavior that is meant to be socially productive or desirable.[7] This view is echoed by Maureen Turim, who notes her own family's obsession with photographing her as the bride of a heterosexual coupling with boy children, "wedded to a fifties' prediction of a future marriage."[8] Images of the family constructed through home movies are thus both reflective of and overdetermined by idealized desires that fetishistically compensate for the absence of an ideally unified family in the real world.

While Zimmermann and Turim address the contents and social history of home movies, anthropology-minded theorists such as Chalfen have tended to limit their analysis to the function of home movies within family rituals: the "deep-structure" patterns that emerge, the social circumstances of their exhibition, and the layers of reading motivated by intergenerational screenings and live, voice-over narration. While all of these factors to some extent underlie my reading of appropriated home movies, I am ultimately more interested in the process by which this appropriation articulates a dialectical relation between the images' old and new contexts. How can we understand the seemingly unique power of home movies that so many filmmakers have chosen to redeploy?

In *The Imaginary Signifier*, Christian Metz uses Jacques Lacan's theory of the mirror stage as a paradigm for understanding spectator identification in cinema. According to Metz, the film viewer has been prepared to identify with the gaze of the camera (and cinematic images in general) by the pleasurable experience during early childhood of recognizing his or her image in the mirror as an ideal unity. Cinema, then, re-creates a feeling of transcendent wholeness for the spectator by presenting coherent, recognizable images from the perspective of a ubiquitous Other. However, Metz's focus on commercial cinema leads him to assume that the typical film spectator is not viewing his or her *own* image on the screen.[9] This absence of the image of the self from the screen constitutes for Metz a position of power and transcendence. The spectator, he argues, is "all perceiving" and "all-powerful"; it is the spectator who "make[s] the film."[10]

In the case of home movies, the converse is true. The spectator often *does* appear on screen and is therefore (by Metz's logic) placed in a position of relative nonpower and vulnerability.[11] It is this disempowerment that is mobilized and reversed when home movie images are appropriated.[12] Another way of thinking about the transformation of home movie images is in terms of a shift from imaginary to symbolic identification. The idealized images preserved in home movies activate both types of identification: imaginary identification, in which we identify with the image of ourselves that appears desirable or lovable, and also symbolic identification in which we identify with the position from which we are viewed so as to *appear* desirable, lovable, and so forth. In the first instance, we imagine our lives to be congruent with the happy, unified image we see on the screen; in the second, we place ourselves in the position of the photographer, carefully constructing that ideal image.[13] So, as Slavoj Zizek notes, "Apropos of every imitation of a model-image, apropos of every 'playing a role,' the question to ask is: *for whom* is the subject enacting this role? Which *gaze* is considered when the subject identifies himself with a certain image."[14]

The examples of appropriated home movies I will consider offer a range of responses to this question. In addition, these films perform a complex interrogation of the power relations embedded in the home mode along with their historiographical "truth claim." Within experimental film practice, home movies are frequently mobilized for two distinct, but dialectically related, projects pertaining to questions of historical writing:[15]

Films that attempt to negotiate individual or social group identity
    through collective or personal memory
Films that seek to come to terms with some aspect of personal or
    collective history

Removed from the closed circuit of intrafamilial production and reception, appropriated home movie images become "declassified," that is, opened to a different kind of public scrutiny and historical revision, and it is to these appropriations we now turn.

Peter Forgacs's *Private Hungary*

For nearly two decades, Hungarian film and videomaker Peter Forgacs has been compiling and reediting home movies shot in Europe (mostly by Jewish families) between 1920 and 1960. The first major result was an eight-part series funded by Hungarian television and the Bela Balazs Studio collected under the title *Private Hungary* (1988–94). The series provides glimpses of otherwise undocumented historical moments, as well as highly personal and often emotional family dramas. Each segment follows a similar trajectory: a family is introduced; relationships are established; and footage of holidays, weddings, vacations, and leisure activities gradually give way to military parades, work camps, and deportations, followed by accounts of deaths and disappearances.

To gather footage for the project, Forgacs ran ads in Hungarian newspapers seeking families whose home movies span several decades—usually from the 1920s or '30s to the '40s or '50s. He bought the rights to use the movies, reedited them, added music and sound effects along with sparse narration or text, then packaged them as a unique kind of historiography in which personal stories are entwined inextricably with national histories. The series thus domesticates Hungarian national history at the same time that it publicizes and historicizes individual stories into a national context. In addition to the Hungarian series, Forgacs has completed several structurally similar films, including *Meanwhile Somewhere* (1996) and *The Maelstrom* (1997), which tell similar stories using footage from families in other European countries.

Throughout the series, Forgacs draws attention to the class status (mostly upper) of the families he selects. Many are entrepreneurs or professionals whose wealth and privilege are evidenced by frequent trips abroad and vacation homes (in addition to the obvious fact of being able to afford to produce the movies themselves) and the dramatic changes in material circumstances that accompany the beginning of the Nazi era. Death is a part of every film. The enormity of the Holocaust looms over each individual deportation, home forfeiture, and ruined business. By the midpoint of each segment, every smiling image of a family member is darkened by the possibility that it will be the last time they are seen alive.

Forgacs's attempt to express the enormity of the Holocaust through the stories of a handful of families leads him to favor images and moments that refer metaphorically to this historical period. In the opening shot of *The Maelstrom*, for example, huge waves crash violently against a concrete pier while spectators lean perilously over the edge. Forgacs slows these portentous images down and repeats them throughout the film as a metaphor for the violence poised to descend upon Europe and the naïveté of Jews who are later shown carefully following packing instructions for their deportation to death camps. Such moments also highlight the uncertain division between a simple home movie and the splendor of "professional" cinematography. In addition, throughout the series, Forgacs eliminates all remnants of the unedited visual idiom of home movies (jump cuts, flash frames, etc.), even going so far as to create sequences based on shot-reverse-shot patterns. Thus, Forgacs's project simultaneously offers a celebration of individual, amateur vision and a reification of cinematic conventions. In Forgacs's hands, these images speak directly to private moments from the past, but they also assert the beauty and elegance of home movies as a rival to commercial spectacles.

Forgacs's composer, Tibor Szemzo, achieves a similar effect through the omnipresent musical score that accompanies each part of the series. Although ranging in tone from droning minimalism to orchestral richness and jazzy riffs, the music adds emotional resonance and grandeur to the fragmented and disparate family histories on display. Likewise, the sound effects added by Forgacs to the otherwise silent images are stylized and exaggerated, rather than serving to naturalize the images they accompany. The overall effect is an audio environment that transforms the quotidian nature of the home movie into something decidedly larger and more resonant.

Forgacs describes *Meanwhile Somewhere* in terms of poetic collage, resulting in a "mosaic" of "the intimate, the brutal, the happy, the rare."[16] The mosaic strategy Forgacs deploys leads to some remarkable juxtapositions. A typical sequence from the first segment of *Private Hungary* called *Dusi and Jeno* illustrates the imbrication of the daily activities of the segment's main characters, a middle-aged couple named Dusi and Jeno, with larger historical events:

Dusi washing the dog
the movie theater across the street
a Nazi military convoy rolling past on its way to invade Yugoslavia
Dusi watering the garden
Dusi beating the rugs
Jeno in his reserve officer's uniform
Nazi soldiers on the streets of Budapest
Jewish families from the neighborhood packing for deportation
Dusi and Jeno walking the dog
aerial bombardment of Budapest by allied planes
Budapest in ruins
statues of Stalin appearing around the city

It is impossible to tell whether these disturbing juxtapositions (repeated in many similar sequences) were manufactured by Forgacs through editing or whether they are simply reflective of the chronological order in which the images were captured by the camera. This uncertainty opens questions that undermine the truth claim and the presumptive innocence of the home movie images. Interestingly, as the series progresses, Forgacs becomes increasingly willing to reveal his editorial control over the footage, abandoning the apparent chronological structure of *Dusi and Jeno* in favor of the repetitive and metaphorically resonant sequences of *The Maelstrom.*

In addition to careful editing, Forgacs subjects his appropriated home movie images to multiple levels of processing, ranging from slow motion, freeze frames, and color tinting to the addition of text and superimposed images. Sometimes the transformation is clear, as when extreme slow motion turns a celebratory political parade into a death march, or when freeze frames and a haunting musical score create a disturbing counterpoint to the repeated, forceful kisses to which a vacationing businessman subjects his wife in *Either/Or.*

Questions of authorship and identification are also played out with particular complexity in the *Either/Or* segment of *Private Hungary.* Many of the images in this segment are related to performance—the clowning of adults on vacation, a seemingly endless series of parades, and especially the photographer's daughter "Baby" who, after years in front of the home movie camera, becomes a performer in a chorus line. In all cases, Zizek's question "For whom is the subject enacting this role?" is open to multiple and contradictory interpretations depending upon the level of authorship that is privileged (i.e., that of the original photographer or that of the editor-director, Forgacs). For the contemporary viewer, it is possible to slide in and out of identification with various spectator positions, viewing the films at times for historical "content" and other times as a loving family record. This breakdown of spectatorial and authorial stability is aligned with the politics of Forgacs's project, which questions the authority of official historiography and the presumed homogeneity of its recipients.

The use of other people's home movies in constructing his critique of historical spectatorship and authorship poses a fundamental problem for Forgacs. On one hand, the images are accessible and recognizable to viewers precisely because of their generic appearance and familiar content dominated by the preoccupations of the bourgeoisie: home, possessions, children, pets, family vacations, and so on. Indeed, viewers in the context of Western capitalism may see the images as cross-cultural and transnational, united by class and economic privilege across time. On the other hand, Forgacs is careful not to simply reinforce norms of bourgeois representation, and he continually highlights the class discourse embedded in the images and his own controlling intervention as editor and (re)producer.[17]

While the inevitable layering of authorship mobilizes competing discursive priorities throughout Forgacs's work, many of the home movies he selects claim a much more direct ontological relation to the historical events they capture. In a particularly chilling sequence from *The Maelstrom*, for example, a handheld camera records Nazi troops overseeing the deportation of Jews from a Dutch neighborhood. Photographed from a distance and partially obscured by tree branches, the images at times seem to quiver with terror—perhaps that which was felt by the photographer at the risk of being discovered. In such moments, the raw power of Forgacs's project becomes apparent, if only for its ability to rescue such images from their obscure status as family keepsakes.

The genius of Forgacs's project is his reclamation of documents within a narrative that includes both the act of their creation and the subjectivity of their creator. The significance of images captured and reproduced under these circumstances lies not so much in their contribution to the historical "record" but rather in their preservation of gestures of defiance. Perhaps most importantly, Forgacs's work with home movies demonstrates that "history"—even the grandest, most traumatic, and incomprehensible events—loses power when it remains an abstraction. Historiography that is useful and alive takes place on a microlevel, as experienced by individuals and families in a daily struggle with existence.

The Rhythm of Memory: Yervant Gianikian and Angela Ricci Luchi's *From the Pole to the Equator*

Also working with footage from the early 1900s, Italian avant-garde filmmakers Yervant Gianikian and Angela Ricci Luchi offer a meditative look at a troubling collection of images in their feature-length essay film *From the Pole to the Equator*. Composed entirely of footage that was either shot or collected by turn-of-the-century Italian cinephile and cinematographer Luca Comerio, *From the Pole to the Equator* both mobilizes and subverts the pleasure of revisiting the past through motion pictures. Drawing from Comerio's massive personal archive, which included fiction films as well as documentaries, Gianikian and Ricci Luchi selected images that emphasized the imperialist and colonialist underpinnings of Comerio's collection. These include images such as a hand-tinted cock fight, big game hunting, missionary work in Africa, an expedition to the South Pole, the coronation of George V, Mussolini entering Tripoli in 1927, and British military parades in India. A droning, minimalist score creates a melancholic counterpoint to the exuberance of the original images and points to the filmmakers' intended critique without overinscribing it. Interestingly, Gianikian and Ricci Luchi offer no explicit commentary in the form of voice-over or on-screen text; the editing is languorous and restrained to preserve the grand, sweeping nature of the original images. In a rare gesture of faith in the intelligence and perspicacity of their audiences, the filmmakers simply provide the opportunity to contemplate a distant collection of images and invite viewers to draw their own conclusions about the meanings embedded in them.

The filmmakers describe their work as a process of transformation—not only of the physical appearance and context of the film but also of its meaning and relation to the past. "We use ready-mades," Ricci Luchi states. "We transform the old into the new." Gianikian adds, "By changing the speed, the colors, the meaning, we make the film new. By 'old' and 'new,' we don't just mean the physical material of the film. It's a question of meaning also: the old *means* in a new way. . . . The relationship between Then and Now is always central to our films."[18]

Through optical printing, Gianikian and Ricci Luchi continually alter the speed of the action, sometimes creating pulsing rhythms and patterns within a single shot, what they call the "rhythm of memory."[19] This processing nearly doubles the length of Comerio's original footage from 57 to 107 minutes. The film's lack of explicit commentary requires audiences to perform their own critique of the images and their immanent colonialist ideology. According to Richi Lucci,

> We reread, rewrote, re-edited the original Comerio film, overturning the original meaning and ideology. Our film was centered on the metaphor of amnesia: the amnesia of Comerio's last years, the general amnesia about primitive cinema, and the desire of early audiences for exotic spectacles, which reflected their dreams of conquest and cultural pillage (their "amnesia") about early cultures.[20]

The "metaphor of amnesia" in *From the Pole to the Equator* is specific to Comerio's footage and the colonialist ideology it evidences, but it applies equally to the more general distance of contemporary audiences from primitive cinema. *From the Pole to the Equator* is at once a film about spectacle and a critique of the distracted mode of viewership it invites. Unlike Jacobs's experiments with 3-D and somatic responses, the film plane in *From the Pole to the Equator* remains flat and distant, an object for contemplation and dissection rather than immersion.

Su Friedrich's *Sink or Swim*

Home movies constitute only two of the twenty-six segments (plus the coda) in American avant-garde filmmaker Su Friedrich's account of her troubled relationship with her father, *Sink or Swim* (1990). Interestingly, the film is structured around not a narrative or a chronology but rather a sequence of words in reverse alphabetical order, from Zygote to Athena. Friedrich's father, a linguist, was a domineering and sometimes violent presence in the filmmaker's life, and *Sink or Swim* represents an attempt to come to terms with the emotional scars of her upbringing and serve as an object lesson in parental behavior. Although it is less overtly "political" than several of her other films, *Sink or Swim* marks a rare convergence of a narrative devoted to highly traumatic personal experiences and the rigorous order of a structural film.

The two home movie sequences, which are associated with the words "witness" and "memory," are privileged by being the only times we actually see Friedrich's father in the entire film. The first time, he is tossing his infant daughter into the air—the motion is slowed, emphasizing the total helplessness of the child. Because of distance, it is impossible to know whether the game is a source of pleasure or terror for the girl, though the latter is strongly suggested by the fact that the image freezes before we see whether or not her father succeeds in catching her on her way down. In the second instance, a similar kind of emotional dissonance occurs when playful home movie images of Friedrich's father as a child are accompanied by the tragic story of his sister's death. Immediately after this, we see the only close-up of Friedrich's father as an adult, carrying his very young daughter on his shoulders. Once again, the shot ends in a freeze, perhaps suggesting that their relationship was arrested in this state of total paternal control.

But it is the final, multiply superimposed image of the young Friedrich, performing for her father, that marks the most complex instance of reinscription of a home movie image. In this climactic scene, the pirouetting image of the filmmaker, combined with the incantation "tell me what you think of me,"[21] effectuates a reversal of the camera's gaze that conjures for us the stern countenance of Friedrich's father, peering judgmentally through the camera viewfinder. In this moment, Friedrich catches her father looking, but at the same time, she reveals her own childish complicity in the dynamics of parental approval. Thus, both father and daughter are implicated in a quest for identity through images and, at a certain level, embroiled in a struggle for authorship of this final image.

Such appropriations of home movies may be read as moments of hyper-awareness of the power and directionality of the gaze. The filmmaker who implicates herself in the process of identification does not do so simply to retake control of the representational apparatus and thus make the shift from imaginary to symbolic identification. For example, Friedrich does not identify the position of her father as the preferred site of self-recognition. Rather, both positions are rendered suspect and their mutual dependence and interaction is foregrounded. Although the act of inserting oneself into the realm of the symbolic (i.e., language—in this case, film language) constitutes for Lacan the crucial moment in the realization of subjectivity, the film/videomaker who appropriates family images for this purpose has taken only the first step toward identity negotiation through film or video.

Implicit in this "confessional" mode of home movie appropriation is the possibility that the film/videomaker will be forced to occupy a position of vulnerability in relation to his or her audience. Unlike the traditional ethnographic subject, this individual is in control of the images included in the final work. However, a standard trope of the confessional essay (which is reinforced by the frequency with which film/videomakers literally expose themselves to the camera[22]) seems to require the maker to allow for a degree of authorial vulnerability through self-exposure. In *Sink or Swim*, Friedrich disavows the detached safety of omniscience and exposes herself to the camera in order to redeploy the power of a confessional mode of discourse. The result is a work that underscores the power dynamics that inhere not only in the home mode and her own father-daughter bond but also within any relationship between viewer and viewed.

William Jones's *Other Families* and *Massillon*

Like Friedrich, William Jones, who in addition to his found footage films uses home movies in his work, makes explicit links between etymology and historiography in telling a story about his own past. In order to speak with precision, Jones's work argues, we must first grasp the available systems of signification in their entirety. The construction and conveyance of "history" through linguistic systems—words, images, and movies—is itself historical and therefore subject to shifts in connotation and ideology. In two remarkable works, an autobiographical feature film named *Massillon* after the town where he grew up and a short video called *Other Families* (1992), Jones practices an explicitly Marxist historiography, rooted in a critique of the social dynamics, constraints, and power structures of American family and economic relations.

Jones's *Other Families* is composed entirely of home movies that have been transferred to video, edited, and systematically analyzed in terms of sexual politics and class. Jones's narration throughout *Other Families* is delivered in a restrained monotone, continuing his meditations on words and images developed in *Massillon*. In *Other Families*, Jones takes on ideologically loaded terms like "traditional" and "capitalism," and uses them to construct counterreadings of some of American culture's most cherished formations. Jones's commentary on images of children opening presents on Christmas morning, for example, proclaims, "Often, when we believe we are speaking about love, we are really speaking about economics." Images of a little girl excitedly displaying a new outfit are also shown repeatedly in order to denaturalize them and suggest a subtle critique about the conventionalized association of happiness with material objects.

Interestingly, Jones waits until the final credits to acknowledge that the home movies presented in *Other Families* are actually of his own family (and the family of his collaborator, David Jensen). In addition, the voice-over commentary deliberately avoids constructing any kind of family or personal narrative that would reduce the project to an "explanation" of the videomakers' adult, gay sexual identities. Instead, the implied queer reading of the images remains extremely ironic and subtle, even subtextual: in one repeated sequence, Jensen is kissed on the cheek by his older brother; in another, we see the nonprocreative couple formed by Jones and his sister standing outside the fence at a rabbit farm. Jones's goal is to inscribe the development of sexual orientation into social, political, and linguistic discourse rather than the ideology of biological determinism. By dealing with images of childhood *without* claiming that they reveal some innate gay*ness*, Jones creates an argument on behalf of not merely one or two individuals but also a range of people who may recognize themselves in the (Midwestern, white, middle-class) images of the Joneses and Jensens.

Jones's work with home movies also engages questions about the relation between images and memory. In *Massillon*, Jones paraphrases Chris Marker's claim in *Sans Soleil* (1982) that intangible memories of the past are easily overwhelmed by the concrete traces captured by motion pictures: "My father shot home movies which made such a strong impression on me that my memories of these [family vacations] are actually memories of the home movies." Neither Jones nor Marker laments the "loss" of originary memories to those constructed in dialogue with film or video images. Rather, this loss is understood to be an integral part of remembering, embedded in a continual process of revision and interpretation.

Home movies are invoked twice in *Massillon*. At the beginning of the film, we see typically touristic images of Washington, D.C., photographed in the 1960s by Jones's father. And at the end of the film, we see a sequence in which Jones photographs the same sites with his own camera, attempting to mimic his father's frenetic camerawork. Jones's replication of his father's images reflects his desire expressed throughout the film (as a gay man subjected to legal constraints and moral condemnation symbolized by a tracking shot that circles the Supreme Court in Washington, D.C., and accompanied by an extended recording of a Christian radio evangelist praising court decisions that limit or deny gay rights) to control his own representation through the layering of textual systems. But it also locks him into the same kind of authorial struggle with his father articulated by Friedrich in *Sink or Swim*. For both filmmakers, however, the appropriation and rereading of "home mode" images provide them with a decisive sense of control.

In a certain sense, the compilation film that appropriates home movie images may be said to constitute a kind of evil twin of "home mode" representation. Although Jones's work is frequently concerned with the destruction and defamation of societal myths, his process of appropriating and rethinking the idealism that pervades home movies offers a much-needed counterpoint and subversion of their representational power. Filmmakers who appropriate and recontextualize images of themselves take advantage of a situation that is unavailable to the traditional subject of ethnography, namely, the ability to say, "These images are mine—they are *of* me, therefore they *belong* to me." This critical reversal illustrates how appropriated images can expose the relations of power and privilege that condition our most basic understandings of the past.

As the projects in this chapter illustrate, there is a depth and complexity in amateur film practice as a whole that bears reconsideration because, in the realm of cinematic and televisual historiography, control over the writing of history is at stake in the appropriation and reuse of film and video images.[23] In an age when increasing numbers of people carry video-enabled mobile devices, the potential significance of everyday acts of documenting is poised to expand dramatically. However, as we have seen in the examples in this chapter, the presumptive spontaneity and lack of intentionality in such documents does not exempt them from the same type of analysis to which we subject other forms of historical media.

Although it is beyond the scope of this book to consider the full range of historiographical implications of the emerging practices of present-tense self-documentation and sousveillance, the appearance of these technologies is worthy of note, particularly amid a culture of continuing fascination with present-tense historiography—the sense that we are, each of us, at any moment, potential agents in making our own history.

5 Materialist History

Not all history films strive to recapture a sense of lived experience from the past or emplot historical data into narratives to be readily consumed by passive viewers. For some filmmakers, past and present are always already mutually implicated through the material and textual nature of historiography. While some films slice through the incongruities and complications of the past from a position of asserted knowledge, others embrace their own indeterminacy and speak of process and contradiction; politics and preconceptions; or systems of signification, knowledge, and power. From this perspective, the "literal past," at stake in historiography, is an unrecoverable fiction, a prevailing myth to which it would—in the event it were desirable to do so—be impossible to return.

Cinematic historiography is most provocative when it recognizes the limitations of its own asymptotic relation to the possibility of historical truth. Films that refuse to create a psychologically or emotionally immersive simulation of the past draw attention to the necessary contrivances of cinematic historiography. Proceeding from the assumption that "history" is best understood in terms of discursive struggle, they construct a relationship with the past that operates in and through the tension between discursive relativity and a certain kind of "truth claim." Viewers are thus invited not to reexperience the past but rather to interrogate its meaning and the conditions of understanding constructed by the film. In particular, this chapter seeks to recognize and examine a type of historiographical filmmaking that engages the past along three interrelated critical axes: textuality, politics, and materialism.[1]

The now commonplace assertion of poststructuralist theory that there is no "outside" to texts offers a starting point for understanding the work considered in this chapter. However, overt concern with textuality does not necessarily imply disengagement from material consequences and motivations. History writing, according to this model, is not scientifically dictated or entirely materially determined. Historiography is a process of articulation resulting in a "discursive surface"[2] upon which one may read inscriptions of ideological and material origins. Accordingly, most Hollywood history films provide images of the past that reflect and reinforce the comfortable desires of Western, capitalist liberalism—for example, causal, linear narratives that are reassuringly familiar, especially when spoken in a language of cinematic realism. Other films, however, choose to confront the "strangeness" of the past as it appears in otherwise famil-iar objects, people, or events.

In order to come to terms with the past, Robert Young argues, "The initial gesture must be to confront its strangeness, rather than to seek for similarities and continuities so that it can be equated with the present and thus, in effect, dehistoricized."[3] In a medium—indeed an industry—defined and sustained by the endless renewal of historical imagery and readily evoked nostalgia, the defamiliarization of the past and its modes of construction on film requires a radical break from the conventions of both historiography and cinema. Although such work is obscure relative to the overwhelming majority of history films in commercial distribution, a substantial body of work exists for which the articulation of a political position with regard to historiography is as important as the "contents" of the "history" it constructs. In order to understand this work, one must grasp the multiple systems of signification and layers of discourse that—although a part of every film—these films bring explicitly into play. His-torical films risk not only an epistemological argument but also a politics of historiography unique to historical filmmaking.

But what does it mean for a film—or indeed any form of historical construction—to "be political"? For Dana Polan, the answer lies in the extent to which a work provides both images of the past and the means for acting upon it. "Against history as mechanistic repetition, another form of history is imaginable: history as a living of a moment in/through an ac-tive transformative relation to the past, a relation of practice in which the materiality of historical existence is not merely cognized but changed."[4] Polan argues that the ability of "history" to define and transform our rela-tion to the past is most profound when brought to bear on the material circumstances of life. Cinematic historiography is thus most effectively politicized through attention to its material origins and consequences, when it demands a parallel rethinking of concrete historical events along with their systems of construction. All cultural forms, even (maybe espe-cially) those that deny they are engaged in politics, have political implica-tions and thus the potential for material consequences in the world.

In considering the politics of American film in the 1960s, David James argues that at no other point in film history have the mechanics and ma-teriality of filmmaking taken on such relevance to the process of produc-tion. Citing parallels with art movements of the same era, James identifies a polarization of the two most active legacies of experimental filmmaking. The structural film movement of the late 1960s may be understood as a retreat from the tumultuous 1960s political arena into the minutiae of the cinematic apparatus, with filmmakers investigating ever more arcane constituents of film and laboratory processes. At the other end of the political spectrum, activist film collectives such as the Newsreel organizations largely abandoned formal and aesthetic concerns in order to advocate direct political action related to the Vietnam War and Civil Rights movements.[5] Although radically divergent politically, both movements suffered a similar fate during the following decade. While structural filmmaking had largely exhausted itself by the early 1970s, most activist coalitions found themselves splintered into innumerable, sometimes factionalized, micropolitical identity groups by decade's end.

Although the form of each of the movements that James identifies was indeed polarized and largely isolated from the other during the 1960s, subsequent decades saw the emergence of a provocative mode of hybrid practice that introduced explicitly political content into work that retained an interest in structural and materialist principles. In the United States, this may be seen most clearly in the work of filmmakers such as Jon Jost, Su Friedrich, and James Benning, and in Europe in the work of Jean-Luc Godard and Jean-Marie Straub and Danièle Huillet. In part, I believe this hybridization was enabled by the integration of experimental films and their makers into academic institutions—a move that, for some, marked the death of a particular, romanticized mode of avant-garde filmmaking[6] while providing historical context and economic support for continuing experimental practices. Both of the connotations that I have attached to the term "materialism" bring useful concepts to bear on the works examined in this chapter. Marxism and structuralism are both predicated on the perception and theorizing of systems that underlie an existing set of socioeconomic relations. In commercial filmmaking, as in capitalist economics, institutions and codes of signification invite—and to some degree rely upon—suspension of critical analysis. Films that illuminate their material origins work in harmony with a Marxist ethos that views historiography as a process entwined with other systemic factors. The challenge of historiography thus becomes not merely adherence to standards of factuality but also the unveiling of historical processes and the obfuscations of existing systems of representation.

Films that take the past as their subject may or may not draw attention to their own conventions and artifice. "Materialist" history films draw upon strategies developed by writers of experimental history in which the process of telling is integrated into or positioned at odds with the story being told. This is a tension that has long been present within historiography, finding its most eloquent noncinematic articulations in works such as

Norman Mailer's *Armies of the Night*, a novel in two parts: "The Novel as History" and "History as a Novel," each telling the same story in a discursive mode that subverts the conventions and claims to authenticity of the other. Such examples are rare in Hollywood, however, where Alex Cox's inventively anachronistic but financially ruinous *Walker* (1987) stands as a warning to studio executives against disregarding historical conventions. More recently, commercial aberrations such as Quentin Tarantino's *Inglourious Basterds* (2009), in which Adolph Hitler and Joseph Goebbels are machine-gunned to death in a burning theater along with the entire Nazi high command, has thus far generated neither historiographical outrage nor the kind of recuperative reading that Rosenstone brought to *Walker*.[7] For more consistently provocative experiments with cinematic historiography, we must turn to the margins of both "history" and cinema. This chapter focuses on two remarkable bodies of film in which issues of textuality, politics, and materialism are played out with unusual rigor and sophistication: the work of Straub/Huillet and Benning. Although they differ in many important respects, Benning's and Straub/Huillet's work is also uncannily marked by significant points of convergence in terms of form, content, and commitment to a radical political agenda.

The Historiographical Films of Jean-Marie Straub and Danièle Huillet

Since the early 1960s, Huillet and Straub have created a large and diverse body of film work devoted to expanding the aesthetic, political, and historiographical potentials of cinema. Although Straub/Huillet's[8] importance to cinematic historiography has not been neglected entirely, far more critical attention has been paid to the operation of formal interventions in relation to their avowedly radical politics. Even some of their most appreciative critics have declined to engage with certain political dimensions of their work.[9] They are most often positioned critically in relation to Godard (whose forays into radical historiography have also been eclipsed by his formalism and cinephilia) and several German directors, including Rainer Werner Fassbinder and Alexander Kluge. Their reciprocal influences on the European new wave and post–new wave movements are undeniable, as is a dialogic relation with Hollywood cinema. However, Straub/Huillet remain distinct and somewhat enigmatic, eschewing affiliation with any recognizable movement, crossing borders to produce work in Germany, France, and Italy, and creating hybrid works that blur distinctions among narrative, fiction, essay, and documentary.

Unlike Godard and Fassbinder, the American "art house market" for Straub/Huillet has rarely supported widespread distribution or exhibition. The films, many of which require multiple viewings, are not in legal distribution on video in the United States. Certainly, factors such as their refusal to confine themselves to recognizable genres and their work in multiple languages (French, German, and Italian) create marketing difficulties. However, the most consistent charge leveled at Straub/Huillet is that it simply requires too much effort and concentration to get past the "tedium and opacity"[10] of their work. Even critics who have written about them with great insight and clarity tend to take an apologetic tone with regard to watching Straub/Huillet's films: Maureen Turim calls them "intellectual, dry, difficult,"[11] while Martin Walsh admits to finding them "rarefied, difficult,"[12] though both authors also regard their work as replete with irony, wit, and intellectual rigor. For the purposes of this discussion, however, questions of form and accessibility will be of secondary importance to Straub/Huillet's development of a unique mode of cinematic historiography that emphasizes process and (inter)textual construction.

As "difficult" as their work is purported to be, Straub/Huillet insist they are engaged in a form of political praxis that is fundamentally popular. However, it is also fundamentally controversial. Their 1992 film, *Antigone*, for example, was dedicated to the Iraqi dead whom the audiovisual media denied in its coverage of the Gulf War. Similarly, in 1968, Straub proclaimed that their film *The Chronicle of Anna Magdalena Bach*, a meticulously costumed period biography of the composer told through the eyes of his wife, constituted a gesture of support for the Viet Cong in its opposition to American imperialism. For Straub/Huillet, such claims are meant to be provocative, not merely hyperbolic. Their project is self-consciously coextensive with a definition of artistic and political praxis that resists both marginalization and institutionalization.

For Straub/Huillet, artistic engagement in institutional and political critique is linked to the dismantling of not only the existing aesthetic practices of bourgeois cinema but also the very foundations of industrial capitalism that give rise to them. Taking sociopolitical revolutions—both in theory and practice—as the explicit subjects of at least two of their films (*Too Early, Too Late* and *Every Revolution Is a Throw of the Dice*), Straub and Huillet set out on a parallel trajectory with Godard to create a genuinely Marxist cinema, shaped theoretically and in varying ways by the work of Theodor Adorno, Bertolt Brecht, and Walter Benjamin. However, even more so than Godard, the key to their project has been the systematic rethinking of historical construction.[13]

According to Barton Byg, "Straub/Huillet insist on a documentary accuracy, resolute commitment to a redemptive view of 'history,' and a search for a liberated spectator who could become the historical subject that until now has been obliterated by various modes of oppression."[14] It is toward the construction of this "liberated spectator"—which Byg finds in the reciprocity between text and viewer—that Straub/Huillet's aesthetic interventions are directed. Straub/Huillet's work is exemplary in its commitment to defining the origins of political praxis through a reciprocal relation between artist and audience. Far from conceiving filmmaking as a medium for delivering images or even ideology, Straub/Huillet present a cinema that requires viewers to construct meaning through a combination of prior, extratextual knowledge and investment in the materiality of film language as a system of representation.

This emphasis on a systemic understanding of filmic representation bears an analogic relation to Straub/Huillet's construction of history. Viewers, who are invited to participate actively in the construction of the film, are required (or presumed) to bring a certain degree of historical knowledge and sophistication to the screen. The absence of an authorized historical voice doubtless renders certain elements of each film opaque to viewers who lack the requisite historical knowledge. However, this use of controlled ignorance may be viewed as a strategy rather than a deficiency, serving to throw into relief the impossibility of omniscient, objective, or comprehensive knowledge of "history." The historiography into which viewers are invited is thus always contingent, partial, and open to subsequent textual reinterpretation. This serves to undermine any sense of historical omniscience or closure, while mapping out the political grounds on which any future transformation of society will be possible.

A key strategy for achieving the "documentary accuracy" to which Byg alludes is Straub/Huillet's exclusive use of directional, synchronized sound and hard audio cuts corresponding to each picture cut.[15] The result of this practice is to emphasize the shift in audio perspective and the rupture of temporal continuity that accompanies even continuity editing.[16] Their use of "direct" audio suggests an ontological imperative that has been taken up with varying results by film movements as diverse as the cinema verité and "direct cinema" movements of the 1960s and the group of filmmakers subscribing to Danish filmmakers Lars von Trier and Thomas Vinterberg's Dogme 95 "Vow of Chastity."[17] Straub/Huillet's deployment of synchronous sound aligns their work with a privileged moment in cinema history. As Donald Crafton has argued, it was synchronously *recorded* sound (not merely synchronized sound) that revolutionized film production in the late 1920s.[18] Lip synch also carries particular connotations within the European film industry where postsynchronization and dubbing of character voices (practices that, although common, are pathologically concealed in Hollywood) are the norm rather than the exception. Straub/Huillet's insistence on recorded synch is both historically and geographically specific, defining their work as a representational system with a clearly defined ontological relation to the world and film history.

The relationship of Straub/Huillet's films to the representational codes of classical cinema may be described as dialogical rather than oppositional. With certain exceptions, factors such as focus, exposure, and frame rate, as well as manipulations of the photochemical process—regarded by some sectors of avant-garde filmmaking as creative variables—approximate the technical standards of Hollywood cinema. Their legendary precision and attention to formal structures result in a distinct formal quality. Conventions such as shot-reverse-shot and eyeline matching are eschewed in favor of systematic articulations of filmic space.[19] One interview sequence in *History Lessons* (1972), for example, is constituted through a series of static shots in which each camera angle is unique and unrepeated, moving in fixed increments of approximately twenty-five degrees around a semicircular arc.[20] The result is spatially disorienting only by comparison with the codes of classical cinema and expectations of suture and continuity. The articulation of the space of the interview is arguably more "complete" than that of a conventionally photographed sequence, as each character is shown from seven angles around a 180-degree arc instead of the usual progression from establishing to point of view (POV) shots, all located on one side of an imaginary line. Although the camera angles clearly change according to a regular and predetermined plan, the effect differs from that of a structural film in which discovery of the plan is a primary part of the experience of watching the film.

Although this scene from *History Lessons* was clearly constructed according to a deliberately executed system, it is not a formal gesture for its own sake. The spatial recomposition of this scene is consistent with Straub/Huillet's both formal and historiographical attitude toward the past. Their goal is to defamiliarize rather than to negate, to systematize rather than to regulate, and to employ formal interventions only in service to a political or historiographical function. A related strategy in Straub/Huillet's films is the use of nonnaturalistic acting and patterns of speech. Derived from Brecht, this technique seeks to emphasize the materiality of the words being spoken and their ontological status as uttered sounds that have been assigned meaning based on arbitrary linguistic conventions.

Lines are delivered as if they are being quoted,[21] or they may be spoken with a foreign accent by nonnative speakers of the film's primary language. Because such distinctions are most evident to viewers fluent in the primary language of the film, Straub/Huillet create an analogous effect in the way they render the subtitles for foreign audiences. In an effort to draw attention to the rhythms and aural quality of spoken language, subtitles are omitted from selected segments of each foreign release. In addition to highlighting the qualities of the spoken language, this omission prevents the impression of linguistic omnipotence afforded by conventional foreign distribution practices (i.e., dubbing and subtitling).[22]

This refusal to transcend the limitations of language is paralleled in Straub/Huillet's resistance to creating a sense of historiographical mastery through the detailed set and costume design that characterizes most historical filmmaking. Straub/Huillet's radical departure from convention may be seen clearly in the seemingly perfunctory costuming of *Othon*. Ostensibly set in ancient Rome, all actors appear plausibly garbed in togas, with the vast majority of their interactions taking place in temporally indeterminate exterior landscapes. Unlike the carefully presented interiors of *The Chronicle of Anna Magdalena Bach*, few scenes in *Othon* allow for a sense of immersion in three-dimensional film space.[23] Actors' movements are orchestrated to emphasize the flatness and artificiality of each scene, while the near total absence of props and conventional signifiers of ancient Rome works against the creation of a historically convincing diegesis. *Othon*'s historical events and figures are constructed through a range of textual processing and opening up of discursive fissures, resulting—in Jacques Derrida's terms—"in not one single history, a general history, but rather histories different in their type, rhythm, mode of inscription—intervallic, differentiated histories."[24] Cumulatively, their work develops a diverse and sophisticated vocabulary of cinematic historiography.

Straub/Huillet's mobilization of conventional historical signifiers ranges from the inescapable artifice of *History Lessons* (in which the toga-clad characters compete with traffic noises) to the deep focus and long takes of *The Chronicle of Anna Magdalena Bach*. Although the Bach film is uniquely concerned with accuracy in costuming, props, and performances, it also includes striking moments of deliberate artificiality. In one particularly memorable scene, the actor (Gustav Leonhardt) portraying Johann Sebastian Bach is garishly illuminated by torchlight while conducting an unseen orchestra in front of a canted, rear projection image of an opera house destroyed in World War II. Rather than re-create this location as an interior set or disguise the fact of the building's historical destruction,

Gustav Leonhardt as Johann Sebastian Bach in Straub/Huillet's *The Chronicle of Anna Magdalena Bach.* (Franz Seitz Filmproduktion, 1968)

Straub/Huillet create a striking metaphor for their historiographical practice. The torchlight, like the landscapes that dominate their later history films, signifies timelessness and historical persistence (a burning stick in the eighteenth century is indistinguishable from a burning stick in the twentieth), while the rakish slant of the camera and the rudimentary rear projection warn against the potential mendaciousness of even their own careful efforts at historical re-creation.

Rather than constructing themselves as self-contained and comprehensive visions of the past, virtually all of Straub/Huillet's historical films foreground their textual origins. The films thus highlight their construction through a process of textual layering and their insertion in ongoing discourses of history writing. For Straub/Huillet, historiography is constituted through a process of rewriting the past in which all previous histories are implicated. The palimpsestic nature of their work is underlined through the practice of assigning lengthy or extremely precise titles to the films. For example, the full title of the film known as *Antigone* is "*Antigone des Sophokles nach der holderlinschen Ubertragung fur die Buhne bearbeitet von Brecht 1948 (Suhrkamp Verlag)*," which literally translates as "Sophocles' Antigone from Holderlin's Translation Adapted for the Stage by Brecht 1948 (Suhrkamp Publishing)." In addition to calling attention to the textualized nature of the historical record, certain of their films deal with the multiple representational systems through which filmic records are produced and conveyed from past to present. The layering of representational systems is apparent in the recurrent *mise en abyme* structure of several works, most notably *Moses and Aaron* (opera), *The Bridegroom, The Actress and the Pimp* (theater), *The Chronicle of Anna Magdalena Bach* (music), and *Fortini/Cani* (literature). These structures are undeniably self-reflexive, but the goal is a rethinking of historiographical construction rather than merely the cinematic form. By implication, we must be equally attentive to questions of historical detail and the conventions by which particular histories become a part of cultural discourse.

The question of what is left out of these cultural discourses is raised with particular eloquence in two films: *Othon* (aka *Eyes Do Not Want to Close at All Times or Perhaps One Day Rome Will Choose in Her Turn*, 1969) and *History Lessons* (1972). Both films are based on obscure literary works: *History Lessons* on Brecht's unfinished novel *The Business Affairs of Mr. Julius Caesar* and *Othon* on a little-known seventeenth-century play by Pierre Corneille (which in turn is derived from an account written by the ancient historian Tacitus). Both films address the relationship between modern and ancient Rome through the use of striking juxtapositions. In addition to originating in different periods in Roman history, the subject of both films may be said to be the impossibility of representing ancient history outside the context of a contemporary perspective. Although these two films were made consecutively, they represent two divergent trajectories in Straub/Huillet's work.

Whereas *Othon* presents the uninterrupted enactment of Corneille's text by actors in period costume in a rural setting (a strategy repeated in *Moses and Aaron* and *The Death of Empedocles*), *History Lessons* places four purportive historical figures in the center of urban Rome, a deliberately anachronistic gesture that resonates in the structure of films such as *Too Early/Too Late* and *Fortini/Cani*. Its pedagogical pretensions made explicit in its title, *History Lessons* is structured as a series of interviews between a young man in contemporary clothing and four men who are dressed in togas. Each interview is separated by a lengthy, single shot sequence of the interviewer driving through the crowded streets of Rome. The first driving sequence commences immediately following three quick cut shots of maps depicting the loss of territory during the fall of the Roman Empire followed by a similarly fleeting shot of a statue of Julius Caesar (four shots in approximately eight seconds). The driving sequence simply begins— without explanation or hint of a destination—following an unpredictable trajectory through the crowded streets of Rome in a small car with an opening in the roof. This sequence is ingeniously allegorized by Walsh as being "like history," a seemingly chaotic, incomprehensible flow from which we try desperately to derive some sense of meaning or pattern.[25]

In their discussions of the film, both Turim and Walsh emphasize the division of the film frame into a cluster of subframes: windshield, side windows, sunroof, and rear view mirror. These subframes may again be allegorically conceived as a setup for the multiple perspectives that will be provided by the various interview subjects (banker, poet, peasant, and lawyer) who appear at the end of each driving sequence. Structurally, the interviews highlight the conflict between ancient and modern through the juxtaposition of a contemporary interviewer with subjects who purport to speak from firsthand knowledge about the historical figure of Julius Caesar. Significantly, in the course of this interrogation, Straub/Huillet neither show nor allow Caesar to speak for himself. The statue of Caesar that appears briefly in the opening montage functions not so much to give us a mental image of Caesar the man as to implicate his body in the process of historical textualization to which the rest of the film will be devoted. The statue, which was erected by Mussolini, stands as a monument to not only the historical instrumentalization of the fascist state but also the many layers and valences that are possible in the realm of historical textualization. As Turim notes, "Words no longer present us with the illusion of reconstituting the past. Instead, they are themselves reconstituted as textual 'traces' from the vantage point of our current position in history and theory; traces are presences that hide absences."[26]

Straub/Huillet's obsession with textuality may be seen in the layering of texts that occurs both explicitly (e.g., in the use of written or spoken texts on screen) and implicitly (e.g., in *Moses and Aaron*, the filming of an opera that is in turn based on a biblical story). In both *Moses and Aaron* and *The Death of Empedocles*, the existence of a written text that underlies the filmed performances is emphasized by the delivery of lines in a rapid-fire monotone and the selection of actors who are nonnative speakers of German. Textual layering is also apparent in *Fortini/Cani*, which opens with Franco Fortini, the author of the decade-old novel *I Cani del Sinai*, on which the film is based, reading aloud from his own book. Here again, the title of the film is meant to call attention to not its subject matter but rather one aspect of the textual relations by which it was constructed, namely, the relationship between author and text. As Peter Wollen notes, "The films of Straub/Huillet are almost all 'layered' like a palimpsest—in this case, the space between texts is not only semantic but historical too, the different textual strata being the residues of different epochs and cultures."[27] The result of this near overproliferation of textual references is to emphasize Straub/Huillet's engagement with systems of textual practice and mediation. It is only through the aggregation and negotiation of multiple layers that any sense of closure may be realized. In an unusually direct but characteristically provisional statement in *Fortini/Cani*, Straub/Huillet's epistemological commitment is put bluntly: "The truth exists, absolute in its relativity."

Visions of Utopia: James Benning's Southwest History Trilogy

In his 1984 article "An Avant-Garde for the Eighties," Paul Willemen described the goal of the avant-garde in the 1980s (paraphrasing Godard) as "cinema which doesn't just ask the questions of cinema historically, but asks the questions of history cinematically."[28] A few years later, Paul Arthur concurred, noting that, since the 1970s, the American avant-garde had been "increasingly infused with a historicizing energy" that represented a break with the previous thirty years of deliberate and insistent ahistoricism.[29] Both Willemen and Arthur viewed this "turn to history" in conjunction with a revitalized sense of political relevance in avant-garde filmmaking. Willemen claims that this reorientation is reflected in the shift in importance within the European avant-garde from Godard to Straub/Huillet, arguing that, while Godard's primary intervention in film history failed to expand beyond the formal and aesthetic properties of cinema, Straub and Huillet have been more successful at integrating their aesthetic practices into a political agenda.[30] Arthur's exemplar is Benning's *American Dreams* (1984), a rigorously structured film that brings together competing visions of America focused around Babe Ruth's capturing of the home run record and Arthur Bremer's attempted assassination of George Wallace. For Arthur, Benning's film is emblematic of a larger shift within the American avant-garde away from strictly formalist concerns toward a more substantive engagement with both historiography and politics.

The aspirations of the following treatment of Benning's historiographi-cal work are somewhat more modest. From the perspective of the early twenty-first century, it is not clear that a dominant set of concerns of any kind has emerged within the American avant-garde, a field of practice so widely diversified as to resist generalization. Additionally, the turn to history that Willemen and Arthur associate with the 1980s has shifted significantly in both form and function in the new millennium. To follow up on Willemen and Arthur, I see a proliferation of experimental films dealing with historical subject matter in the past three decades that may be roughly divided into two areas: those that explore issues of historical authority and textuality and those invested in the expression of personal histories and memory. Whereas Straub/Huillet's *ouevre* includes several films on the subject of postwar German cultural memories (including *Machorka Muff* and *Not Reconciled*) Benning's engagement with memory is largely limited to individual memories of events that are of a personal rather than a historical character.[31]

In Benning's films, "history" is constituted through relations between texts, places, artifacts, and figures that are linked through a series of textual contingencies. The work of the films is not merely to draw the fragments together but rather to position them in relation to historiographical and po-litical questions. In the rare cases when his films focus on historical figures (e.g., Che Guevara, Hank Aaron, and Arthur Bremer), the stories they tell are fragmented and dispersed, constructed through overlapping layers of texts, images, and minifictions. However, it is insufficient simply to argue that, because certain films resist narrative coherence, causality, or charac-terization, the historiography they practice is inherently politicized. The politics of Benning's work (again, like Straub/Huillet) is reinforced through the selection of historical moments and figures in which events and issues such as revolution, the creation or destruction of empires, and the playing out of political and economic struggles are foregrounded. Implicit in this strategy is an argument about the contents of "history," which will become clear when considered in relation to specific films and their contexts.

Landscape Historicide

Before he began making films, Benning taught mathematics in the Midwest, worked as a political organizer in the South and a farm laborer in Colorado, and achieved some success as a studio artist in New York in the 1960s, turning to filmmaking around the time of the peak and decline of the structural film movement in the early 1970s. Although he was clearly influenced by this work, Benning's earliest films departed significantly from the narrowly defined concerns of structural film, incorporating issues of narrative, space, landscape, and time. Throughout his career, Benning has functioned as a transitional figure within the American avant-garde, combining formal and narrative experimentation with a series of thematic concerns. A central figure of the new narrative movement of the 1980s, he was also influential on the burgeoning independent film movement in the United States, which found its commercial terminus in the work of filmmakers such as Jim Jarmusch.

Beginning in the 1990s and continuing to the present, Benning has created a remarkable series of feature-length historiographical documentaries, each of which explores some aspect of the history of the American Southwest: *Deseret* (1995), *Four Corners* (1997), *Utopia* (1998), and a trilogy devoted to land use and ownership in California consisting of *El Valley Centro* (2000),[32] *Sogobi* (2001), and *Los* (2001). Traces of the dominant themes—both formal and historiographic—of all these films may be seen in earlier works such as *Landscape Suicide* (1986), *American Dreams* (1984), and *North on Evers* (1992). Taken as a whole, Benning's body of work is remarkably coherent in terms of both form and content. His interest in structural devices has persisted more than two decades after its functional disappearance from experimental film practice,[33] while themes of violence, social and economic discrimination, and historiography continue to motivate his most compelling work.

In the 1990s, Benning's films have demonstrated an unusually subtle attention to the material and textual nature of motion pictures and the inevitable processing of historical "evidence" through systems of representation. Most interestingly in this work, his attention to the material contents of "history" is realized largely without deploying the conventions of filmic reflexivity.[34] Rather than turning inward to reveal his process of construction and representation—a strategy that so thoroughly permeates postmodern culture as to have lost much of its political vitality—Benning creates a poetics of visual historiography to exceed the constraints of the factual and historical world. In other words, he makes it possible to challenge the idea of "factuality" even though the historical construction he performs relies overwhelmingly on the exact resources favored by historians: documents, artifacts, and physical evidence. While the examination of historical process seldom occurs in conjunction with actual historical research, Benning's work is exemplary of a mode of historiography that mixes visual investigations of the past with epistemology and politics.

Although not explicitly self-reflexive, Benning's historical films do engage in a kind of dual mirroring of their historical "contents" and the processes by which historical traces, evidence, and documents are pretextualized. In short, Benning's films ask the question, "What is history made of?" The answer lies at the intersection of concrete visual elements—the glacial perseverance of the landscape and the codified human texts superimposed (both literally and figuratively) upon them. Benning's films investigate both sequences of historical events as well as the larger framework of historical writing. Within this construct, the southwestern landscape functions as both a foil and a vehicle for historical argumentation. Contrary to what the subheading of this section might suggest, the landscapes in Benning's films do not bring about the death of history. Indeed, the extreme specificity of Benning's landscape photography reveals the deficiencies of conventional historiography with regard to the concept of place. Unlike individual memories that are frequently linked to the place or situation in which an event is witnessed, the context for historiographical construction has a more complicated relationship to geography. In most historiographical films, landscapes remain largely interchangeable, mere stages for the human activity through which "history" is constituted.[35]

However, for both Straub/Huillet and Benning, the specificity of the landscape provides a primary point of historiographical entry and provocation. Implicitly, images of geographic contours and the traces fixed on the landscape provide a form of visual testimony to the concreteness and materiality of historiography. Straub/Huillet's 360-degree pans and Benning's cartographically programmed movements across geographic spaces (e.g., in *Deseret* and *Utopia*) describes a historiographical correlate of cognitive mapping. In *Utopia*, Benning's visual maps of desert landscapes in California's Imperial Valley are continually overlaid with analytical and historical details that are slanted toward revealing the exploitive practices of agribusiness and the environmental and human destruction that result from corporate farming. In *El Valley Centro*, these relationships are articulated in a minimalist style that relies on a protracted credit sequence at the end of the film that simply names each shot and notes the legal owner of the land and the town where it was shot. The landscapes through which these films travel appear at once familiar and remote, specific and general. Few residents of these areas (whose population is concentrated in a handful of urban centers and military bases), bother to travel on Benning's back roads, much less delve into the region's past.

What separates Benning's work from the historical travelogue is precisely its insistence on the conjunction of "history" and politics and the implication of prosaic, geological details in relationships of historical interdependence. If there is a death constituted through Benning's work, it is the death of a "history" that his films are working to render inadequate, that is, orderly, rational, present-effacing narrative histories that converge upon and naturalize the present. Benning's work implicitly argues that such histories are historically and politically facile if not ideologically dishonest. Appropriately enough, Benning's work poses its greatest challenge to conventions of historical narrative. Although both *Deseret* and *Utopia* allow for a sense of temporal and geographical progression, the elements that ordinarily comprise a historical narrative are almost entirely absent. Much like Benning's experiments with new narrative forms in the 1980s—in which, for example, the two main characters in a story are momentarily brought together within the space of the film frame but never meet or acknowledge each other's presence (*8½ x 11*)—the progression of the narrative in *Deseret* must be constructed in the mind of the viewer. The narration contains threads of continuity, both thematic and specific, which must be recalled and reconstructed throughout the film. Ironically, conventional wisdom regarding historical filmmaking holds that the strength of cinematic historiography lies in its ability to evoke emotions and promote viewer identification with historical characters. However, Hollywood films began training their audiences to expect narrative pleasure and resolution long before Hayden White's late-seventies diagnosis that all "history is constructed and understood through narrative tropes and conventions."[36]

In *Deseret*, narrative achieves its greatest strength in brief moments of connection. What may be considered "history" must be drawn gently from the landscape, unraveled as though from a matrix of buried threads rather than excavated from a fixed site that has been divided into numbered quadrants. The film resists narrative linearity but not the pleasure that comes from drawing associations between seemingly disparate elements. When it comes to experimental filmmaking, even White reverses his emphasis on narrative. "Too often, discussions of the irredeemably fictional nature of historical films fail to take account of the work of experimental or avant-garde filmmakers for whom the analytic function of their discourse tends to predominate over the exigencies of storytelling."[37] The "analytic function" referred to by White is pursued by both Benning and Straub/Huillet via an immersion in historical details that are accessible only through the mediation of texts. Benning's historical films signify their own rewriting through the layering of their historical subject matter in images, words, and texts. His subject thus becomes both an investigation of a particular moment of regional history in conjunction with the diverse processes of historical writing. It is worth noting that, in all his experiments with textual layering and displaced authorship, Benning has never employed found footage of any kind. Although his work occasionally incorporates sounds—including music, political speeches, radio broadcasts, even an entire film soundtrack—virtually every frame of every James Benning film was shot by Benning himself. One way to understand this refusal is that, while the revision and recontextualization of found footage discussed in chapter 3 brings a temporary measure of control, it also invokes a rhetoric of authenticity and originality that is antithetical to the constructionist view of "history." For both Benning and Straub/Huillet (whose use of found footage is extremely rare),[38] this strategy implies that, in order to see or think clearly about the past. We must first construct images of it that are inescapably linked to our present moment and, as such, always already politicized.[39] Benning's films—like all historical films—may be read in relation to a dual historical narrative, one that accounts for the continual shifts and movement within film history and another that develops the historical themes and contents of their subject. Benning's work is thus that of both a historian and a metahistorian, and as such, it responds to an otherwise unresolvable conflict between the desire for a knowable "history" and the impossibility of unproblematic historical representation. Although his work has been mostly backward looking for the past two decades, Benning's political concerns clearly reside in the present.

Landscape as Text: Deseret

In *Deseret*, Benning explores the textualization of the Utah landscape from the cave paintings of its ancient inhabitants, the Anasazi Indians, and the written accounts of explorers to the institutional histories published in the *New York Times* dating back to its founding in 1852. The film is composed entirely of static shots of the landscape, with occasional structures, animals, and artifacts of past civilizations. On the rare occasions when human figures appear in the frame, they hold still for the duration of the shot as if posing for a portrait. Benning's camera traverses the landscape from north to south, a progression that may be intuited by the viewer but is only ascertained with certainty with the aid of extratextual knowledge of the geographic region. Though often beautiful to look at, the film also evokes codes of cadastral photography—including flat, symmetrical compositions and even lighting—which suggest a connection with forensic or scientific modes of representation. The history of these regions is thus constructed through the interplay of the technical and the poetic, the sublime and the mundane.[40]

Deseret's retelling of Western expansion through *New York Times* reportage inscribes the voice of "official history" in narratives of Euro-American domination and colonialism. The film presents quotations from articles in the *Times* related to the Utah territories, ranging from Indian attacks to scientific discoveries made in the area. The quotations are read in a deadpan voice-over beginning in the 1850s and moving forward into the present. The narration is spoken over landscape shots photographed by Benning that only occasionally bear discernable correlation with the newspaper reports. The result is a continual movement between desire and frustration, as the promise of a cohesive historical narrative and synchronization of text and image is repeatedly suggested but never quite delivered. The disjunctive and often trivial contents of the newspaper articles resist narrative coherence, resulting in a focus on the style rather than the contents of the writing. This pattern, too, is disrupted at times, as the contents of the articles form an intricate web of interconnections in mapping the region's past. The style of writing in the articles calls attention to the subjectivity and idiosyncrasy of even these supposedly objective journalistic accounts, thereby implicating them in the ideological and discursive systems of their time.

The progression through nearly 150 years of newspaper articles in only ninety minutes draws attention to subtle changes in the journalistic voice of the *New York Times*. As the articles approach the present day, the reportage becomes gradually more technocratic and familiar to contemporary viewers, while the ideology underpinning it grows increasingly naturalized and transparent. This process of domesticating the exoticized extremes of the newspaper's nineteenth-century prose is mirrored in images of the landscape transformed through industrialization and militarization. However, *Deseret* also highlights the ways in which the landscape remains unchanged in spite of technological and political shifts. The Manifest Destiny that propelled Western expansion, for example, is linked to the desire for scientific and technological mastery of the natural world. Perhaps most importantly for Benning, this region's past is not framed as converging inexorably on the present. For the metahistorian, the past remains a construct that is open to continual rewriting and revision, with no one moment ultimately privileged over another. Like the landscape, which is open to multiple uses and modes of representation, Benning's static images and often classically composed renderings of the picturesque may one day be reappropriated as stock footage or perhaps even the pre-text of some future rephotography project.[41] The self-consciousness of Benning's images does not inoculate them from the possibility of reworking in terms of context, narrative, or meaning. While it may be impossible for any film to resist eventual rereading and recontextualization, a work that is integrated into a plan for political praxis at least offers hope for temporary resistance in the present.

Remaking Past and Present: Utopia

In *Utopia*, Benning undertakes a (nearly) shot-for-shot remake of Richard Dindo's documentary *Ernesto Che Guevara: The Bolivian Diaries*. Benning appropriates the soundtrack of Dindo's unexceptional, expository documentary in order to map Che's failed attempt at revolution in Latin America onto images of agricultural development in California's Imperial Valley. The transposition of the Bolivian and Californian landscapes asks audiences to make enormous leaps in terms of geography, historiography, and logic. The utopianism of Che's troops and Marxist movements in the Third World can, in some sense, hardly be compared to the very different utopian vision of the corporate conglomerates that dominate California agriculture, though both are constructed around particular visions of land management and distribution of wealth. As the title suggests, interrogation of notions of utopia and idealist conceptions of "history" is at the heart of the film.

Idealism, coupled with left politics, are a recurring theme of several Benning films, many of which are populated with figures or resonances of the civil rights movement (Father Jim Groppe, Medgar Evers, Martin Luther King Jr., and John F. Kennedy), Vietnam war activism (as in the fragmented radio reports included in Benning's *United States of America*), and other anticonservative rhetoric. Che, or more precisely, images of Che, hold strong allure for American leftists, along with the importance of historiography. While Dindo's film relies heavily on the reproduction of heroic images of Che, familiar from decades of circulation as a symbol of revolutionary ideals, Benning eschews all visual references to the revolutionary leader.[42] The story of Che's ideals and martyrdom persists through the soundtrack (which Benning leaves largely intact), but his focus on landscape raises a fundamental question of historiography: "How much should be invested in individuals as agents of history?"

Both *Deseret* and *Utopia* suggest that the individual actions of even a revolutionary hero like Che are outmatched by the fundamental structures and contradictions of capitalism, media, and ideology. Benning's goal of advancing awareness and transformation of these structures is an aspiration so grand and daunting that one must ask whether it is even possible to make films about such subjects without seeming merely quixotic. Benning's films respond to this challenge by addressing themselves to historiography in both global and local senses, dwelling obsessively on obscure details of the American southwest as a vehicle for asking the big questions of historiography. His work insists on a reciprocal relationship between the process and the contents of history writing as well as the simultaneously specific and general nature of historiography. The present tense in which a majority of Benning's films are set suggests a complement to the logic of Straub/Huillet's politicization of the present by obsessive attention to the past. In Benning's work, it seems the best way to engage politically with ideas about the past is through obsessive attention to the concreteness of the present.

The reciprocal relationship that exists between historiographical viewing and historiographical thinking should motivate history-conscious viewers to develop their critical and interpretive abilities to confront the most challenging and politicized forms of historiography. This chapter outlines a few models of film practice that pose the most provocative challenges to visual historiography. Remarkably, these films by Straub/Huillet and Benning consistently eschew or question the basic formal strategies of both narrative and documentary filmmaking. The result is a form of practice that invites viewers to interrogate both historiographical and cinematic systems of authority.

The films analyzed in this chapter further suggest that cinematic structures provide a metaphor for historiography itself. Whereas the illusionist strategies of Hollywood filmmaking suggest that film and television may create a more or less transparent window on the past, these "materialist" historiographies foreground the physical and ideological apparatuses of cinema as a means of engaging with the past. Both Straub/Huillet and Benning thus advocate conceptions of historiography that are constructed and accessible only by interpreting and layering textual systems. These works bring formalism into direct engagement with politics and project the stakes of historiography into the realm of political and social contestation.

6 Digital Histories

It is a truism of the post-Foucauldian world that the very existence of categories of knowledge and institutionalized disciplines shapes what and how we think. Just as the emergence of the photographic apparatus altered nineteenth-century perceptions of the world,[1] increasingly powerful digital tools for storing, retrieving, and combining historical information now impact the way the past is conceived and reconstructed.[2] The global reach and virtually limitless storage capacity of the Internet, in particular, has inspired universities, libraries, and archives to reposition themselves as producers and distributors rather than simply preservers and guarantors of information. As a result, institutional resources are increasingly redirected toward the digitizing and organizing of historical information into databases that are accessible via both public and proprietary computer networks. The growing conception of computers as offering access to a master network of interlocking databases points to a transformation of fundamental notions of the past and the nature of historical research. It is within this milieu that Hal Foster asks, "Is there a new dialectics of seeing allowed by electronic information? . . . Art as image-text, as info-pixel? An archive without museums? If so, will this database be more than a base of data, a repository of the given?"[3]

One answer may be found in the movement toward recombinant or "database histories"—that is, histories comprised of not narratives that describe an experience of the past but rather collections of infinitely retrievable fragments, situated within categories and organized according to predetermined associations. These collections in turn offer users, whether they are artists, gamers, or geeks, both the materials and structures by which the past may be conceived as fundamentally mutable and reconfigurable. Taking advantage of the logics of remix and computational culture and the kinds of repetitions and modifications built into video games, these projects rest along a continuum, moving from serious artworks to pop-culture hacks; however, they share a staunch refusal of the stability of a single "history," instead offering us a relation to the past that is always already open to continual revision and reinterpretation.

Writings in literary theory and the philosophy of history have demonstrated that the various forms that historical writing have taken are deeply entwined with the prevailing ideologies and literary conventions of their time.[4] In recent decades, similar efforts have been undertaken to theorize relations between motion pictures and "history." With the provisional incorporation of cinematic and televisual histories into academic curricula, historians have begun to recognize the unique power of media to bring the past "to life," promoting public interest in and—with some caveats—knowledge of historical events. A degree of experimentation with form, telescoping of temporality, and character compositing is even tolerated in the interests of pursuing "serious engagement" with the past.[5] Although much that is written about film and history remains devoted to correcting the media industries' more flagrant departures from fact, larger questions pertaining to the impact of visual media on fundamental conceptions of the past lie just beneath the surface.

When the perceived reality of the cinematic spectacle is mobilized against, rather than in service to, the interests of a consensual historical narrative, strategies of historical construction and rhetorics of authenticity are brought to light. This is particularly important within the realm of digital historiography, where the already problematic ontological status of photographic realism confronts even greater challenges. However, rather than focusing on the potential for artifice, the majority of public discourse surrounding the move to digital image acquisition has focused on the ability of digital video to capture or emulate the real world beyond the capabilities of conventional cinema. Returning to cinema verité's long outworn association of authenticity with the immediacy of a newly mobilized cinematic apparatus, the Danish Dogme 95 movement, for example, eschewed all forms of Hollywood artifice, gratuitous action, and generic convention. Directly inaugurated by the high-quality images captured by small, consumer-grade mini-DV cameras, Dogme 95's "Vow of Chastity" required its signatories to declare, "My supreme goal is to force the truth out of my characters and the frame of the action."

Considerations of the role of digital image processing in Hollywood have likewise tended to emphasize the potential for verisimilitude. Historians have approvingly noted Ridley Scott's elaborate reconstructions of ancient Rome in *Gladiator* (2000) and Steven Spielberg's meticulously researched, prehistoric microcosms created for the *Jurassic Park* trilogy (1993, 1997, and 2001). Computer-generated imagery, thus deployed, reinscribes these cinematic visions of the past within a narrative realist tradition that is coextensive with the type of literary history theorized by Hayden White in the 1970s. In spite of its potential for radical experimentation with eccentric forms of historiography, digital media's potential to construct willfully counterfactual histories—for example, the compositing of Tom

Hanks into archival footage in *Forrest Gump*—has been largely written off as a symptomatic excess of postmodern culture.[6]

In practical terms, the implications of digital technology for archiving have largely focused on technical questions of how best to preserve and disseminate historical data using rapidly expanding networks, notoriously transient file formats, and unstable storage media. Equally important debates have emerged around questions of intellectual property and the control of archival images, film, video, and sound recordings.[7] With the concentration of image and sound archives in the hands of a decreasing number of media conglomerates, the ability to construct widely distributable visual histories increasingly necessitates cooperation with, or oversight by, corporate entities. A few organizations have been established to advocate noncorporate-dominated solutions to these problems, including the Long Now Foundation, which is devoted to long-term planning for the preservation of digital culture; the Electronic Frontier Foundation, which promotes freedom of expression in the digital domain; and the Open Video Alliance, which promotes open standards and nonproprietary tools and codecs as fundamental to the production, dissemination, and archiving of digital video. It is ironic—perhaps even tragic—that historiography, at the very moment when it is poised to reap the greatest rewards offered by digital technology, is instead faced with its greatest threats to innovation, longevity, and accessibility.[8]

Total Archives

Well before the advent of the computer age, the analytical philosopher Arthur Danto described the "Ideal Chronicler" in 1965, using the term to designate a hypothetical model for the ultimate form of history writing.[9] For Danto, the ultimate historian would be one who could produce a complete record of all historical events—including analyses of their significance from multiple perspectives—at the same moment they are happening. Although originally postulated in order to demonstrate the impossibility of an objectively perfect form of historiography, the values reflected in Danto's ideal—comprehensiveness, multiple perspectives, and immediacy—resonate with those promised by the proliferation of today's searchable databases and digital distribution networks. Like the map described by Jorge Luis Borges in "On Exactitude in Science," in which the map of a territory becomes so detailed that it replicates the territory itself, Danto's ideal chronicler is symptomatic of a view of historiography as a totalizing process rather than one that is necessarily fragmented, indeterminate, and partial.[10] Setting aside for a moment those euphoric expectations of the wholesale transformation of culture that was supposed to accompany the digital age in the late twentieth century, information technologies—for better or worse—have undeniably altered the way historical data is captured, processed, and disseminated. Coupled with the totalizing impulse described by Danto and Borges, contemporary digital historiography seems destined to continually promise a direct and unproblematic relation to the past that awaits only the technical apparatus capable of rendering it in its totality.

But even if such a form of historiography were possible, the resulting accounts of the past would be about as useful as Borges's map. Histories that are not subject to revision and debate are also drained of dynamism and interest. More importantly, this type of "total history" is removed from the arena of social and cultural politics, where meaning is formed in relation to the needs of the present and desires to transform the future. A more valuable conception of historiography is not one that recovers or preserves an objective factual history but rather one that engages actively in the conflicts and uncertainty of the past. We are not constrained by the impossibility of total historical preservation. Rather, we are freed by it to construct a relationship with the past that is imperfect and improvisational and to understand "history" as constituted through multiple voices and cascading layers of meaning.

We may find hope in the fact that digital technologies have also enabled strategies of randomization and recombination in historical construction resulting in a profusion of increasingly volatile counternarratives and histories with multiple or uncertain endings. At the heart of these alternative visions of the past are the database and search engine, still the primary mechanisms for organizing and disseminating information within digital archives. Whereas, since the 1970s, literary tropes have been recognized as offering a foundation for much historical writing,[11] the database and search engine enable nonlinear accessing and combining of information into forms that defy both literary and historical conventions. Works of history once understood to comprise an expanding field of collective historical knowledge are thereby repositioned as raw materials in infinitely reconfigurable patterns of revision, remixing, and recontextualization. These two divergent thrusts within digital historiography represent competing conceptions of the past and give evidence of increasingly contested paradigms for historical epistemology.

An additional, a cautionary note from Borges may be found in the short story "Funes the Memorious." Also written long before the advent of digital culture, Borges's story presents a critique of the debilitating weight of the perfect recall seemingly promised by increasingly capacious digital archives. The story's eponymous character suffered a head trauma as a child, which left him with the mind-numbing ability to remember every detail (visual, emotional, and somatic) of every event he ever experienced. Overwhelmed by the continuing overaccumulation of data in his head, Funes is eventually forced to spend his days sequestered in a darkened room, avoiding all sensorial experience.

> In effect, Funes not only remembered every leaf on every tree of every wood, but even every one of the times he had perceived or imagined it. He determined to reduce all of his past experience to some seventy thousand recollections, which he would later define numerically. Two considerations dissuaded him: the thought that the task was interminable and the thought that it was useless. He knew that at the hour of his death he would scarcely have finished classifying even all the memories of his childhood.

Borges proceeds to suggest that his character's inability to forget has driven him to the brink of madness, devising ever more arcane numerical and linguistic systems in an attempt to structure and regain control over the contents of his mind. "Without effort, he had learned English, French, Portuguese, Latin. I suspect, nevertheless, that he was not very capable of thought. To think is to forget a difference, to generalize, to abstract. In the overly replete world of Funes there were nothing but details, almost contiguous details."[12]

In Borges's story, the burden of recall prematurely ages and eventually destroys Funes's body, while his mind ceases functioning except in its efforts to control the rising flood of memories, compounded by each recollection and recollection of a recollection, like the infinitely compiling data of a feedback loop. By the end of the story, Funes can neither process nor make sense of the details he holds in his mind. He can no longer think, the story's narrator notes, because thinking requires forgetting, abstracting, and generalizing. Funes is immobilized by his inability to balance the active interplay between remembering and forgetting by which meaning is constructed.

The challenge, likewise, for digital archives is their inability to forget —or rather, their inability to forget *creatively*. We are all too familiar with the capacity for digital information systems to lose or corrupt our data. But it is equally debilitating when data is inadequately tagged or organized, not just for access but also as vehicles of interpretation. Memories, then, are best understood not as data but rather as the raw materials for interpretation and transformation into vibrant, critical histories.

The Role of the Historian

Along with the shift to digital histories comes a change in perception of the role of the historian. The medieval historian, as White noted, was exemplified by the disinterested chronicler or annalist whose sole responsibility was to record the facts of the past as a realization of God's will, free of interpretation or context.[13] The historian of the modern era, in contrast, is often characterized as a detective, a lone, single-minded professional trained to seek out and judge the authenticity of historical evidence, artifacts, and testimony. These shifting conceptions of historical work and historical evidence suggest yet another model for the working historian—that of the computer hacker who is able to freely traverse computer networks and databases, discovering, reproducing, and linking data into new combinations.[14] The primacy once accorded to narrative in the structure of history writing is thus being significantly challenged by the recombinant potential of the database. The work of the historian, once understood as the "assembling of progressively larger historical truths,"[15] must now contend with the construction of open architecture databases and the accretion of huge volumes of data referencing historical events, facts, and images.

Dana Polan has noted that, in literature and film of the twentieth century, the figure of the university history professor is typically presented as an ineffectual and disconnected technician. Polan suggests that this is symptomatic of popular conceptions of the work of the historian as being the production of "reliable mimesis," citing the popularity of E. D. Hirsch's *Cultural Literacy* (1988) as a prime example of the repositioning of the past as "fixed pieces of knowledge and of history as positive retrieval."[16] With its list of five thousand references—dates, names, and facts—that "every American needs to know," Hirsch's annoying but influential book presents historical information in a database form that is structurally free of narrative and interpretation.[17] Historian Robert Rosenstone likewise notes that historians in popular culture suffer from an "image problem" exemplified by the figure of the history teacher in *All Quiet on the Western Front* (1930) who misrepresents the experience of combat in order to encourage young men to fight in World War I. Rosenstone also describes his profession's gravitational pull toward a mode of investigation that he calls "*Dragnet* history," which is characterized by the single-minded pursuit of "just the facts."[18]

Within popular culture, a few notable exceptions to these character-
izations of the professional historian have appeared, including the figure
of Spielberg's Indiana Jones.[19] Played by Harrison Ford, Jones first appeared in *Raiders of the Lost Ark* (1981), followed by *Indiana Jones and
the Temple of Doom* (1984), *Indiana Jones and the Last Crusade* (1989),[20]
and, after nearly two decades, the comeback feature *Indiana Jones and the
Kingdom of the Crystal Skull* (2008).[21] Although unforgivably anachronistic in their unproblematic resuscitation of colonialist ideology, Spielberg's
films offer a fascinating fantasy portrait of the heroic, modernist historian.
In *Raiders of the Lost Ark*, Jones is a mild-mannered history professor
who turns into a whip-cracking adventurer in order to rescue a biblical
artifact from the Nazis. At the conclusion of the film, Jones has success-
fully subdued the natives on multiple continents, defeated the Nazis, and
transported the "ark of the covenant"[22] from Africa to the United States.
However, rather than being received as a world-changing historical relic,
the ark is packed into a numbered crate and deposited in a massive government archive.[23] The film ends bitterly, with a crane shot that pulls
back to reveal thousands, perhaps millions, of similar crates stacked floor
to ceiling in a warehouse-like archive from which, it is clear, retrieval
would be next to impossible.[24] For all his daring and selfless courage,
Indiana Jones is, in the end, defeated by not the forces of evil or the supernatural but rather the implacable bureaucracy of a federal government
archive.

More than a decade later, Spielberg would offer his own response to
the irrelevance and obscurity of the total physical archive. During the
production of *Schindler's List* (1993), Spielberg was reputedly so moved
by hearing spontaneous testimonies of Holocaust survivors who came to
witness the shooting of the film on location in Poland that he decided
to begin recording survivor testimonies on video. Following the success
of *Schindler's List*, which earned seven Academy Awards including Best
Picture and Best Director, Spielberg established the Survivors of the
Shoah Visual History Foundation. The foundation was charged with the
Sisyphean task of videotaping testimonies by every living survivor of
the Holocaust. Part of the goal was to create an undeniable mountain of
evidence that would have a continuing presence generations after the last
survivor has died. The Survivors Project resulted in interviews with over
fifty thousand Holocaust survivors from fifty-seven countries, conducted
in thirty-two languages, and compiled on over one hundred thousand
hours of digital videotape.[25]

Faced with the overwhelming challenge of making this body of material accessible, the foundation began work on a proprietary, high-speed delivery network capable of providing access to all one hundred thousand hours of testimony at selected sites—mainly Holocaust museums and educational institutions—around the world. The interviews now reside in a system that allows viewers at multiple locations to retrieve full resolution video and sound over a fiber-optic network via a searchable, cross-referenced database.[26] The foundation has experimented with numerous systems for making this overwhelming array of video information accessible and usable, including a system for automatically generating montage sequences by tying a database of archival film images to an index of approximately eighteen thousand keywords associated with the spoken testimonies. The project databases were configured for dynamic combination so that, if a survivor referred, for example, to riding on a train, the video automatically cut to an image of a train while the audio continued in voice-over. In addition to adding somewhat generic visual variation to the interviews, this practice served to authenticate the memories of the survivors as direct historical evidence, a strategy in keeping with long-standing traditions of oral history and documentary filmmaking.[27] Innovative efforts to maximize the impact and relevance of the collection continue, and in 2007, the entire Shoah Foundation collection was relocated to the University of Southern California, where a full-time staff of researchers and archivists works to develop strategies for making the collection available for research and the production of scholarly works by students and faculty members.

The Survivors Project's singular privileging of experience in the case of Holocaust survivors may be viewed as a return to the role of the historian as an impartial chronicler and assembler of evidence. Due to the explicit preservationist motivations of the foundation, questions regarding the accuracy or verifiability of the oral histories captured on tape are elided entirely. The need to establish a primary record of these vanishing accounts in the face of historical revision and widely perceived tendencies toward cultural amnesia superseded the historian's conventional need for verification and cross-referencing of testimonial claims. In addition to the stated goals of the foundation, this vast archive, the overwhelming size of which renders its contents inseparable from its systems of access, may offer its greatest potential as not a total archive but rather a basis for subsequent interpretations and recombinations—a resource for future historical discourse as much as an end in itself.

The History You Deserve: Terminal Time

How can historiography be reconsidered not in terms of factual reclamation but instead as an active process of construction, animation, and
recombination? The radical potential of the open architecture historical
database lies in the prospect of reconfiguring the categories of knowledge
on which our understanding of "history" is based. Much has been written about the complicity of technology in developing systems of social
control and instruments of surveillance—both corporate and governmental. However, as Michel Foucault reminds us, the specific apparatuses of
information storage and retrieval can also be tactically redeployed against
constraining fields of knowledge. Foucault critiques the archive not simply because its structure conceals the networks of power from which it
derives its authority but also because it creates static, categorical divisions
of knowledge, obscuring how knowledge is acquired and deployed. As a
repository of historical knowledge, the archive further promotes an image
of unity and stability that belies the discontinuity of "history." Above all,
Foucault argues, knowledge does not form itself into discrete unities. Like
the past, it is discontinuous, disjunctive, and chaotic.

In *The Archaeology of Knowledge*, Foucault describes his own historical practice as marking a shift from viewing "history" as a grand, totalizing
narrative to a splintered conglomeration of subdisciplinary investigations,
each emerging from, and self-consciously subjected to, their own rules of
formation. Foucault notes this movement away from a single "history"
toward fragmentary histories as an important step toward acknowledging
the chaos of the past and the unruliness of human thought. Discrete statements, he argued, must always be analyzed within a field of discourse and
considered in relation to disruptions, discontinuities, thresholds, muta-
tions, and limits.[28] Within the realm of visual historiography, one of the
most provocative examples of this critical redeployment may be found in
a project known as Terminal Time.

Created in 2000 by a group of artists, computer scientists, and filmmakers calling themselves the "Recombinant History Project," Terminal
Time is an artificial intelligence-based interactive multimedia apparatus
that constructs real-time historical documentaries covering the past one
thousand years of human history. The creators of Terminal Time describe
it as "a history engine: a machine which combines historical events, ideological rhetoric, familiar forms of TV documentary, consumer polls and
artificial intelligence algorithms to create hybrid cinematic experiences
for mass audiences that are different every single time."[29] Utilizing an

applause meter to gauge audience responses to a series of questions regarding values and beliefs, Terminal Time bases its historical narratives on a database containing thousands of still images, video clips, and written commentaries, which are rendered through a text-to-speech program. Each "history lesson" deploys the characteristic strategies of a conventional historical documentary—omniscient narration, reenactment, archival images and film clips, documents, artifacts, testimony, and so forth. The resulting minidocumentaries are broken down into three parts representing the time periods 1000–1750, 1750–1950, and 1950–2000. Following each narrative, the audience is asked a series of questions intended to refine and focus their attitudes toward ideologies of race, gender, colonialism, technological positivism, and so on. The content of the documentaries reflects a slightly exaggerated version of audiences' stated values, often making humorous associations and carrying historical ideologies to hyperbolic extremes.

Terminal Time's ironic appropriation of the audience-survey format critiques individuals' complicity in electronic data-gathering technologies used to create marketing profiles. As Terminal Time's creators note, "Especially as more computer-mediated interaction moves into networked environments (e.g., the Web), the very acts of user intentionality, those manifestations of the power of free choice lauded by information technology enthusiasts, have become the raw material for corporate data collection."

The questions asked by the Terminal Time apparatus self-consciously mimic the demographic sampling strategies of the consumer survey. Part performance, part installation, and part cinematic spectacle, the project's tag line is, "At long last, Terminal Time gives you the history you deserve!" The introduction to the Terminal Time apparatus clarifies its operating premises for the audience with the following tongue-in-cheek affirmation of Enlightenment rationality and order.

With every new day, a new chronicle of history is born, arising from the ultimate design of the universe. Yet there is not the slightest theoretical importance in a collection of facts or sequence of facts unless they mean something in terms of reason—unless we can hope to determine their vital connection within the whole system of reality. We, as citizens of history are obliged to make and to be made by this system of reality since the beginning, and until the end, of time.

At a typical performance of Terminal Time, the apparatus is presented twice to a single audience. During the first presentation, the audience is encouraged to respond genuinely to the survey questions, expressing actual biases and opinions. The second time, however, audiences are encouraged to elicit different responses from the apparatus in order to demonstrate its ability to respond to varying ideological beliefs.[30]

In one Terminal Time presentation, for example, an audience whose members first described themselves as optimistic, white liberals who were committed to technological progress chose, in the second presentation, to describe themselves as African Americans who believed that the greatest problem facing society was that people were forgetting their ethnic heritage. They also claimed to be in favor of legalizing drugs and continuing the decolonization of the Third World. The resulting "history lesson" portrayed Rastafarians as the central historical players with the main threat of globalization characterized as the breakdown of ethnic divisions. When the "documentary" reached the twentieth century, Nazi Germany was described as having the right idea about racial purity but being misguided in believing that the European races were superior to Africans. And in a subliminal flourish, each historical segment was accompanied by a reggae musical score. The stark contrast between these two visions of the past resulted in precisely the kind of humorous, yet critical, juxtaposition Terminal Time's creators intend.

Of greatest interest is not simply Terminal Time's illustration of the fairly commonplace assertion that "history" is open to multiple meanings that are dependent on ideology and preconception. A more provocative historiographical argument is posited in the premise of the apparatus that encourages audience members to lie—to pose as someone other than themselves—in order to generate alternate histories. In Terminal Time, historical truth and insight into the past are rendered accessible not through the conventions of academic historiography—exhaustive research or the careful treatment of facts—but rather through the dynamic interplay of truth and lie. Arguably, Terminal Time fails to pursue its own logic much beyond this observation, but in light of the remarkable persistence of positivist history, there is much to be gained from work that dissolves the binaries dominating discourses of film and history—fact/fiction; history/memory; and real past/invented fiction—and demythologizes the ideological investment of historical documentaries.

In another presentation of Terminal Time, the audience activated the antitheological "rationalist" historical narrative via the applause meter. The resulting historical narrative embraced and hyperbolized the premises of Enlightenment rationality: "Amazing technological advances flowed from the minds of the scientists. In England one of the first computers was built to crack the military codes. At the radiation lab at MIT, radar was developed, allowing ships and planes to see through night and fog." The proscience narrative voice-over proceeded with its celebration of the advancement of science, accompanied by images of scientists and industrial manufacturing. In a voice-over, linked to images of atomic explosions, the narrative concluded, "And some of the greatest physicists in the world developed the atomic bomb, perhaps the ultimate symbol of science and progress. When the atomic bomb shined the light of reason on Japan, the war was over." This final, horrific line is delivered—without emotion—by the digitally synthesized voice of the Macintosh voice synthesis program. The impassiveness of the artificial voice adds to the chilling impact of the statement and, by extension, poses a critique of the omniscient narrator's voice in conventional, expository documentary films. The detachment of Terminal Time's narrative voice also invites an ironic critique of the artificial intelligence apparatus as a means of transforming and recombining historical information. The computer faithfully delivers its programmed narrative without regard for the content of the story it tells. In light of the surfeit of computer data, artificial intelligence represents the most likely hope for traversing and channeling the networks of databases promised by information industries. Terminal Time thus offers yet another—increasingly problematic—model for the "historian" as an artificial intelligence apparatus that dispassionately traces associative threads within predetermined fields of possibility.

Overall, then, Terminal Time presents a three-pronged critique of documentary conventions, historical authorship, and utopian discourses of interactivity. Terminal Time further suggests a radical conception of historiography as enabled by digital technology and the proliferation of narratives driven by the logic of databases and search engines rather than the codified conflict-resolution structure of most commercial cinema and mainstream documentary filmmaking. The possibilities for permutation and recombination of historical information created by the Terminal Time apparatus guide viewers to embrace a mode of historiography that thrives on mutability, multiplicity, and lies. At their best, these technologies may give rise to a profusion of counternarratives and alternative histories constructed from the point of view of traditionally disenfranchised or voiceless peoples. However, the question of whether these works undermine fundamental conceptions of historical meaning remains open. Even in the midst of a culture of paranoia, the desire for coherent, historical narratives that rationalize the present remains powerfully seductive.

Nonetheless, the ease with which Terminal Time mobilizes historiographical and documentary conventions in the interests of ideology and exploits the digital archive's capacity for repetition and recombination usefully calls into question the epistemological premises that have guided debates over media and history during the past three decades. Significantly, Terminal Time offers a form of participatory history in which individuals and groups are positioned as possessing the potential to radically alter conceptions of the past. In addition to highlighting the inherently ideological and mutable nature of "history," Terminal Time constitutes an unusually elaborate joke at the expense of historical documentary conventions. But it also poses a serious intervention in an entangled array of cultural discourses related to technology, corporatism, and historiography. Although Terminal Time represents a much-needed provocation and a rare exception to the rule, the goal of thinking about historiography in terms of not accuracy and factuality but rather recombinant multiplicity remains a faint glimmer on the horizon of mainstream studies of media and history.

The JFK Assassination in Digital Space

It is difficult to imagine a more thoroughly mediated historical event than the assassination of John F. Kennedy in Dallas, Texas, on November 22, 1963. The American cultural obsession with the assassination is well known, and I will not attempt to summarize it here.[31] Instead, I would like to focus on some of the ways the assassination has been textualized via digital media and technology. The body of media "evidence" surrounding the JFK assassination has continued to grow, ranging from the sober re-enactments filmed by the Secret Service just days after the assassination, to the video art collective Ant Farm's ironically embodied performances documented in *The Eternal Frame* (1975), and to cinematic and televisual treatments such as Oliver Stone's *JFK* (1991) and *Quantum Leap* ("Lee Harvey Oswald," 1992). More recently, the proliferation of increasingly accessible 3-D models, digital reconstructions, and hybrids of photographic and computer-generated imagery have opened additional avenues of historiographical potential. As with the totalizing archival impulse of the database histories described above, this proliferation of "secondary" evidence yields a paradox: the combination of more information and increasingly powerful tools for organizing and accessing that information does not necessarily lead to greater certainty regarding the assassination itself. Indeed, these tools and their associated historical data make it possible to imagine a vast range of histories that do not necessarily move toward more accurate visions of the past.

Lee Harvey Oswald reenactments clockwise from top left: Sam Bakula in *Quantum Leap* (1992); Kevin Costner in *JFK* (1991); U.S. Secret Service, *The Assassination of President John F. Kennedy* (1963); and *JFK Reloaded* (2004).

The transition to digital imaging that occurred in the 1990s had both technical and epistemological implications for cultural discourse surrounding the assassination and its media records.[32] On one level, the "digital remastering" of documents such as the 8 mm movie film taken by Abraham Zapruder is coextensive with previous, photochemical processes to stabilize and clarify the film's grainy imagery.[33] And while both restoration efforts resulted in improved image quality, no definitive transformation of the film's interpretation has been forthcoming. Numerous attempts have also been made to use 3-D modeling to replicate the space of Dealey Plaza where the assassination took place. In 2003, for example, the Discovery Channel commissioned a comprehensive digital reconstruction of the plaza and produced an episode of the *Unsolved History* series called "JFK—Death in Dealey Plaza." This hour-long TV documentary proposed to bring together all known physical documentary evidence of the assassination (as well as filmed and photographed reenactments of their own) with the 3-D model in order to reexamine prevailing theories about the assassination. The emphasis, in these re-creations, was on establishing continuity and visualizing the physical spaces that were captured on camera, in essence, using digital models to create a spatialized context for a still primary set of *photographic* documents.

As the tools needed to create correctly scaled 3-D models of real spaces have become more readily available, a number of virtual Dealey Plazas have appeared, each with varying investments in exploring the forensic aspects of the assassination. Perhaps the most controversial of these is the online video game *JFK Reloaded*, by the Scottish game design company Traffic, which was released on November 22, 2004, the date of the forty-first anniversary of the assassination. The premise of the game was determinedly minimal, presenting an opening screen that stated simply,

> Dallas Texas
> 12:30PM November 22nd, 1963
> The Texas Schoolbook Depository, sixth floor
> The weather is fine
> You have a rifle

The stated challenge of *JFK Reloaded* was simple: the player who most closely approximated the timing and trajectory of the three shots recognized by the Warren Commission's report on the assassination could win a cash prize of "up to $100,000." The competition lasted only three months, and the game went offline in August 2005 amid widespread controversy.[34]

The condemnation of *JFK Reloaded* in the press was nearly unanimous, with public figures including Senator Edward Kennedy coming forward to denounce the game. I am not interested in adding to the chorus of moral condemnations of the game, or even in decrying its uncritical reification of the Warren Commission report. What interests me instead is the way the game has continued to live on, not in interactive form, but rather in the form of video documents of player interactions. With the game's official Web site offline, the closest thing to experiencing *JFK Reloaded* is through machinima[35] video recordings of playthroughs of the game, dozens of which are readily viewable via online video sharing services such as YouTube. Even a cursory survey of these videos reveals a remarkable array of the divergent trajectories of digital historiography outlined above. Although they are in the minority numerically, a significant number of the videos are posted by players who have attempted to adhere rigidly to the game's rules and have documented their highest-scoring playthroughs. The game encourages this type of reflection by offering postmortem repetitions of the gameplay viewable from multiple perspectives, including a ballistics report showing the impact points of each shot and a view from the virtual viewpoint of Zapruder. Players are thus invited not only to "make history" by playing the role of Lee Harvey Oswald as scripted by the Warren Commission but also to create their own Zapruder film—

complete with image quality that is processed to resemble early 1960s Kodachrome—as a memento of their marksmanship.

A far greater number of *JFK Reloaded* machinima videos, however, take a different approach, exploiting the potential for the game engine to depart radically from not only the historical record but also the laws of physics. For example, a player choosing to shoot not at the president but rather at the drivers in the motorcade can create multiple car crashes resulting in extreme carnage in the plaza. Carefully placed shots can even result in a pileup of cars in the motorcade, causing vehicles to be propelled high into the air. Still other videos reveal more perverse targeting strategies such as one titled "LBJ Reloaded," in which the vice president riding in the second car is assassinated, and another titled "Historical Inaccuracies" that focuses on car crashes, while other videos target the president's wife, the motorcycle escorts, Secret Service agents, and so on.

Only a few critical treatments of *JFK Reloaded* have bothered to look beyond the ethical aspects of the game and its repeated citations by politicians and anti-video-game-violence pundits for whom *JFK Reloaded* makes a convenient scapegoat. Among these is a commentary by designer-theorist Tracy Fullerton, who considers the game in terms of its place in an emerging "documentary" tradition in video games. Fullerton correctly views *JFK Reloaded* as part of a continuum in documentary film production that expands the purview of the documentary mode into such nonobjectivist forms as essayistic or performative representation.[36] Likewise, Gareth Schott and Bevin Yeatman, in an article titled "Subverting Game-Play: *JFK Reloaded* as Performative Space," discuss the game in terms of its deployment of the qualities of "ludus" (game) and "paideia" (play), or the extent to which a game rewards adherence to rules and intended uses, compared with a more free-form approach to appropriating the possibilities of play.[37] However, neither of these accounts of the game focus on the assassination as a historical event or its implications as a form of historical re-creation.

Taken in isolation, *JFK Reloaded* might seem like an inconsequential aberration, but as a limit case, it exemplifies the two extremes (total order versus total chaos) enabled by digital re-creations. In between these two extremes, users of the multiuser virtual environment Second Life (SL) can visit a region called Dealey Plaza Dallas, created by a designer called TheHino Merlin for the SL-based advertising agency Avatar Promotions.[38] The Dealey Plaza simulator features an empty convertible that makes continual circuits of the plaza, while rifle shots are heard each time the car passes through the stretch of road where the assassination took place. Signs placed in the center of the plaza invite prospective advertisers to

buy space in the plaza, but as of this writing, no contemporary advertising may be seen, although a large-scale billboard for Hertz Rent-a-Car
appears on the roof of the book depository, as it did in 1963. At the base
of the Hertz sign, one of the few indicators of the use to which the space
is put is an announcement of the meeting of a virtual T-birds car club
every Tuesday. Periodically, Avatar Promotions also holds more complete
re-creations of the assassination that are closed to public view, and the
company promises that future iterations of the space will allow partial
re-creations in which visitors may bring guns to the space and shoot at
other avatars, though the convertible is designed to prevent avatars from
occupying Kennedy's seat in the vehicle.[39]

As tools for representing surfaces of the earth continue to multiply, a
useful comparison with the SL environment may be found in the Google
Earth location corresponding with Dealey Plaza. Like most spaces in
Google Earth, the rendering of Dealey Plaza allows access to multiple
layers of information from widely varying sources. These include an as-
sortment of commercial business listings and reviews, traffic and weather
patterns in the area, embedded tourist photographs and videos, as well as
reproductions of the Zapruder film and excerpts from various documentary accounts representing both sides of the conspiracy debate. There are
also links to high-resolution "Panoramio" images of the plaza, Wikipedia
entries, and so on. Perhaps most interesting are the community-contrib-
uted information placemarks, which articulate various narratives, some of
which are interpretive or speculative, but the majority of which recapitulate versions of historical events from predictable perspectives. Beyond
these publicly accessible information nodes, Google Earth allows for a
virtually limitless array of privately interpretive data sets to be embedded
in a Google-owned database. Taking the form of extremely compact KML
files, competing histories of the assassination may be articulated, visual-
ized, stored, and distributed via a single interface.

Google Earth, along with parallel efforts such as Microsoft's Virtual
Earth project, is indicative of the movement toward increasingly hybrid
online representations of physical spaces. Although somewhat tangential
to the focus of this chapter, these systems for capturing and representing
the world have historiographical implications. The long-term vision of
these projects seeks a thorough integration of the physical world with the
data world—or, more precisely, the linkage of photographic representations of the physical world with data *about* the physical world. As tools
for mapping photographs onto 3-D models—such as Michael Naimark's
Viewfinder project for Google Earth and Microsoft's Photosynth for Virtual

Earth—seek to seamlessly merge these two representational paradigms, the power of combining the efforts of distributed communities of users with centralized computational systems becomes apparent. Increasingly, the structural capacity of these tools for including annotations (text, photographs, audio, and video) in conjunction with map coordinates suggests a provocative merging of geospatial and historiographical documentation. The evolving transformation of conceptions about space occasioned by this combination of tools and social practices thus also has implications for our ever-changing relations to the construction of history.

Visualizing Histories

Visualization has emerged as one of the most powerful modes of digital historiography of the past decade. Tools for automating and customizing the display of historical information have proliferated in parallel with the evolution of the dynamic Web and protocols such as XML, RSS, and APIs that facilitate the circulation and recombination of data from multiple sources. As with other tools for digital historiography, the current and ever-changing slate of timeline visualization tools has the potential to faithfully present consensual visions of the past as well as more contentious or discontinuous forms of historiography. Without exception, however, these tools are conceived and presented as powerful tools in the service of making accepted histories broadly legible and encouraging the curation of specialized collections of events by historians and amateurs alike.

One example is TimeGlider, a free, online tool formerly known as Mnemograph, which offers this summary of its capabilities:

> There is a wealth of historical information available on-line today, but much of it is organized in long web-page tables so that the information is there, but much of the meaning is held captive. The time has come for a new way to visualize and share historical information. TimeGlider is a free web-based timeline application. Already used by academics and amateur historians around the world, it represents a new and intuitive way of visualizing historical information. An interactive axis of time runs across the screen around which you create, import, and categorize events. A canvas stretching from the big-bang to any point in the future, it lets you zoom out to see millennia and zoom in to see details down to the minute.[40]

TimeGlider also includes a tool for analyzing the frequency of keywords appearing in the *New York Times* and is architected to accommodate similar data streams from other sources. In its API documentation, the *New York Times* Web site marks an interesting distinction between the digested news offered in its print and online editions and the raw data by which the contents of the paper may be reconfigured. "You already know that NYTimes.com is an unparalleled source of news and information. But now it's a premier source of data, too—why just read the news when you can hack it?"[41] The ability to scrape parsed text data from the *New York Times* has given rise to numerous projects that take the *Times* up on their offer to "hack" the paper's contents, but few of these efforts attempt to genuinely revise the dominant narratives of this mainstream news source, instead serving to reify the authority of a corporate entity as a primary arbiter of historical information.

The Massachusetts Institute of Technology's (MIT) open source Simile project offers another example of the dynamic Web being mobilized for a range of data visualizations and reconfigurations. Two of the group's earliest efforts include Timeline and Timeplot, widgets for capturing time-based data from Web sources and visualizing them in a customizable, extensible, interactive interface. Interestingly, the first public sample of Timeline maps the events of the JFK assassination into a scrollable interface, drawing information from multiple sources and offering users the ability to add commentary or annotation to each item in the timeline. Based on the same underlying Simile architecture, Timeplot adds the ability to plot quantitative information onto a timeline, allowing users to visualize statistical changes (e.g., energy prices, presidential approval ratings, and immigration patterns) over time. Commercial software for creating timeline-based visualizations such as Beedocs have also appeared in recent years, encouraging the creation of 3-D and graphically sophisticated timelines for presentations and online publication. Never before has the creation of visually compelling, convincing, and complete histories been so readily available to would-be visual historians. But even as content-agnostic tools continue to proliferate, we must ask whether the paradigms we have for thinking about the past have kept pace with the sophistication of such expressive platforms. The most interesting histories are not necessarily those with the greatest capacity for multiplicity, reconfigurability, or even managing quantities of diverse data.

Augmented Histories

Often cited as the first "location aware narrative," "34 North 118 West" was created by artists Jeff Knowlton, Naomi Spellman, and Jeremy Hight

in 2002, using still novel GPS tracking in conjunction with a laptop computer to embed audio files in the urban landscape of downtown Los Angeles. Users of the system were guided around the streets and open spaces
surrounding a former train depot (currently home to the Southern California Institute of Architecture). When users entered a virtual hot spot, an
audio file was triggered, conjuring a fictional audio narrative and sound
effects from the area's presumptive past. A similar project, Jan Torpus and
Nikolas Neecke's "LifeClipper," was launched in the city of Basel, Swit-
zerland, in 2004, providing a historical overlay with images and narrative
elements depicting the city's rich medieval history. Users of LifeClipper's
augmented reality system wear a head-mounted display and headphones
through which the surrounding environment is mediated, blending historical overlays with real-time video images of the spaces of the city. The
user moves through GPS-identified zones that include content pertaining
to the city's past—an eight-hundred-year-old paper mill, for example, or
the image of medieval soldiers who walk along one of the city's fortress
walls. Pressure sensors placed in the user's shoes transmit signals to a
computer system that is carried in a backpack, signaling whether the user
is walking at any given moment, which in turn affects the contents of the
video overlay.

The "blended histories" of LifeClipper are also reminiscent of the
core trope of visual historiography developed for a series of DVD ROMs
produced by Marsha Kinder's Labyrinth Project between 2000 and 2005.
Several of the Labyrinth projects, including "Bleeding Through: Layers
of Los Angeles, 1920–1986" and "Cultivating Pasadena: From Roses to
Redevelopment" feature the ability to interactively merge current and
past images of Los Angeles and Pasadena, California, respectively. The
visual trope of the "bleed-through" was initially developed by members
of the Labyrinth design team, which includes Rosemary Comella, Kristy
Kang, Andreas Kratky, and Scott Mahoy, for the digital adaptation of Norman Klein's book, *The History of Forgetting: Los Angeles and the Erasure
of Memory*. The premise underlying both Klein's book and Bleeding
Through is the instability and uncertainty of history, which is amplified
by the amnesia-inducing omnipresence of the media industries in Los
Angeles. Indeed, the central figure of both projects is described as "Molly,
a fictional character based on a real life person who may have murdered
one of her husbands."[42] Klein's book is additionally remarkable among
works of cultural history in its deliberate inclusion of fake footnotes and
references to imaginary historical events such as the emigration of Walter
Benjamin to Los Angeles in the late 1930s, making it an ideal source for

the historiographical orientation of Labyrinth. For more than a decade, Kinder's Labyrinth Project has created some of the most evocative explorations of the intersection of digital scholarship, cultural history, and personal memoir, simultaneously destabilizing the authority of archival history while reasserting the importance of histories that emerge from the conjunction of personal and culturally specific narratives.

Each of these components of historiographical augmentation comes to fruition through the capabilities of the current generation of GPS-enabled mobile devices, which obviate the need for backpacks, laptops, and head-mounted displays to incorporate historic images into the experience of real spaces. One such project is the Museum of London's augmented reality project Streetmuseum (2010). Streetmuseum allows iPhone and iPad users to access hundreds of historical images from the museum's collection, creating overlays with the physical spaces of contemporary London when accessed in conjunction with GPS coordinates from a mobile device. A free application created by Thumbspark, Ltd., Streetmuseum offers users "a window through time" with supplementary "historical facts" available at the tap of a button. The narrative of Streetmuseum positions users in the role of a tourist-detective faced with the challenge of reconciling historic evidence of "both everyday and momentous occasions in London's history, from the Great Fire of 1666 to the swinging sixties" with the reality of today's downtown London:

> Of course, with thousands of years of turbulent history, London has changed many times so some streets or buildings may not exist today. Where precise locations aren't available, relish the challenge of identifying recognisable landmarks which may offer you clues as to the current day site. A street name in the background or a church spire in the distance may be all you need to find the view. Our descriptions can also help you locate the right spot.[43]

Although Streetmuseum is far from the first to pursue the conjunction of historical materials and real-world spaces, the richness of its archive and accessibility to a growing user base make it worthy of note and a likely precursor of many similar projects to come. As GPS-driven technologies for merging real and virtual spaces become increasingly ubiquitous, we may expect that the current fixation on experimentation along the temporal axis (i.e., GPS-based positioning is still used instrumentally to achieve the "correct" registration of historic images or narrative data in contemporary spaces) will give way to explorations of the potentials of augmented history that include more complex and disruptive spatial dimensions as well.

Simulating Histories

The question of digital media's ultimate role in what we remember and how we view ourselves in relation to the past remains the subject of ongoing debate as tools for the visualization of history proliferate across platforms, networks, consoles, and screens. It is striking how readily such debates, which often purport to be specific to digital culture, precisely recapitulate the concerns voiced by previous generations of media critics and historians with regard to film, video, and television.[44] Like mainstream cinema, the commercial video-game industry is replete with examples of games that are set in the past.[45] Also like Hollywood film, this "past" readily includes both fictional and factual events, people, and places, sometimes maintaining rigid boundaries between fact and fiction, other times reveling in the conflation of the two. Often these games' past*ness* functions essentially on the level of production design for stories that are only incidentally related to a specific time period (e.g., popular games set in antiquity, such as the *Prince of Persia* or *God of War* series), while others such as the *Civilization* franchise or World War II games such as *Call of Duty* make more explicit reference to concrete historical events, staging reenactments of well-known battles and interspersing quotations by historical figures throughout the game.

A significant difference from mainstream film, however, is the possibility that game titles may be modified by communities to address historical inaccuracies. A prime example is Sega's *Total War* game engine used to create titles such as *Rome: Total War*, *Napoleon: Total War*, *Shogun: Total War*, and *Empire: Total War*, each of which has been heavily criticized for taking liberties with historical facts, ranging from the particularities of soldiers' costuming, armaments, and battle strategies to the presence of deeply anachronistic historical elements (e.g., critics of the Egyptian campaign in *Rome: Total War* pointed out that the depicted use of chariots in the game is off by nearly seven centuries. A well-known community response to *Rome: Total War* was a "mod"[46] called *Rome: Total Realism*, which sought to correct these and many other historical inaccuracies at the level of graphics, narrative, and the algorithms that drive the game's battle mechanics. According to their Web site, "The *Total Realism* community is a volunteer, not for profit team of development groups, administrators, moderators, and historical scholars working together to provide a quality range of modifications, presenting history as it should be viewed, with accuracy and an eye for realism."[47]

Like many commercial games, Ensemble Studios' historical strategy

series *Age of Empires* offers an internal "scenario editor" that allows players to customize their own battles and narratives, potentially remixing
elements from widely disparate cultures and geographies. A platoon of
American Revolutionary soldiers led by George Washington can be made
to do battle with Japanese Ronin swordsmen, for example, or Montezuma's
Aztec warriors can take on the armies of Alexander the Great. Although
internal editors make such idiosyncratic modifications readily available
to individuals (as opposed to the long-term, technically complex community effort that went into the *Rome: Total Realism* mod), the vast majority of gamers choose to spend most of their time within the prescribed
parameters of a game's core narratives and historical conventions. Unlike
the chaotic impulses evidenced in player's misappropriation of the *JFK
Reloaded* scenario, gamers' responses to the potential of even greater extremes of historical anachrony through "modding" and custom scenario
editing instead tend toward faithful reproduction and didactic recapitula-
tions of accepted historical fact.

Other examples of reality-obsessed game worlds include the stunning,
photorealistic historical models of Renaissance Florence created for Ubi-
soft's *Assassin's Creed II* and Sid Meier's real-time strategy series *Civilization*, known for its complex simulations of thousands of years of human
history. Like a majority of adventure games set in the past, the *Assassin's
Creed* series treats its historical setting as little more than a meticulously
designed backdrop, providing a thin narrative premise for the game's primary action.[48] Strategy-based simulation games such as *Civilization* have
proven more agreeable to pedagogical contexts and, like historical films,
are sometimes used in hopes of sparking student interest in temporally
or geographically remote subjects. Although positively regarded for the
complexity of the algorithms (balancing social, economic, agricultural,
political, and geographical factors) used for modeling ancient, medieval,
and modern civilizations, these simulation games are also widely criticized for lack of historical detail and emphasis on the drama of warfare. In
each segment of *Civilization*, for example, players are invited to identify
with specific civilizations and well-known leaders at crucial moments in
history, for example, Abraham Lincoln during the Civil War, the Soviet
Union's Joseph Stalin during World War II, Genghis Khan during the Mon-
gol invasions, and so on. The historiographical premise of *Civilization* is
thus more akin to historical fiction in its pedagogical applications, insofar
as its perceived value lies in its ability to bring the past "to life." *The History Channel*, in fact, has begun coproducing history-related video games,
including such titles as *Civil War: A Nation Divided* and *WWII Experience*.

With similarly explicit pedagogical intentions, the independent game company Muzzy Lane Software has developed *Making History*, a World War II strategy game that boasts Harvard historian Niall Ferguson among its advisors. Ferguson, who has long been a proponent of counterfactual history, was instrumental in the design of *Making History II* to include multiple counterfactual scenarios as a tool for thinking about twentieth-century global conflicts. As history-related games, mods, and customizable content continue to expand the range of digital historiography, it is incumbent upon critics not just to consider questions of accuracy but also to interrogate the teleological implications of algorithm-driven simulations based on known outcomes and reductive or deterministic relations of cause and effect. In spite of its vast potential, the relatively narrow range within which simulation is currently deployed places it among the least interesting and most conservative models for digital historiography. For our purposes, a more productive critical vector lies in investigating the role of interactivity in constructing a sense of engagement, possibility, and self-conscious historical agency.

Art and Politics in History Games:
From *Kuma\War* to *The Cat and the Coup*

As with commercial cinema, the majority of games set in the past conform to one of two historiographical paradigms: fictional dramas or adventures set in a generic or panhistorical past and scenarios situated in proximity to specific historical events, where characters and actions are more or less constrained to replay a known historical outcome. Also following the pattern of cinema, however, a subset of games explores questions of alternative or counterfactual history while respecting the conventions of historical linearity and causality.[49] In February 2004, an independent company called Kuma Reality Games began offering downloadable games based on contemporary U.S. military operations in Iraq and Afghanistan under the series title *Kuma\War*.[50] The goal of *Kuma\War* was to capitalize on the ongoing war in the Middle East, with titles that are produced quickly and cheaply, incorporating scant historical specificity beyond a basic narrative premise. Although it is an independent company, Kuma has close ties to the U.S. military and presents generally sympathetic and prowar scenarios.[51] The games are known for including extensive documentation of the mission scenarios, which are often drawn from Pentagon documents, and Kuma promotes them as "Real War News. Real War Games," using the tagline, "Stop watching the news and get in the game!"

Kuma\War, John Kerry's Silver Star. (Kuma Reality Games, 2004)

On October 21, 2004, shortly before the 2004 presidential election, Kuma also invited players to get in the race between Democratic nominee John Kerry and incumbent president George W. Bush with the game *John Kerry's Silver Star.* The game responded to a campaign controversy in which decorated Vietnam veteran Kerry's war record was called into question by a veterans' group called Swift Boat Veterans for Truth. One of Kuma's few explicitly "historical" titles, *John Kerry's Silver Star* invited players to reenact the mission in 1969 when Kerry won a medal for "gallant actions in combat." It is difficult to know how the game was received by subscribers to the then new *Kuma\War* franchise, but the timing of the game's release exemplifies the company's strategy of garnering media attention through controversy. Although *John Kerry's Silver Star* allows players to fail in any number of ways, the game stops short of overtly authorizing the alternative account of Kerry's actions put forward by the Swift Boat Veterans.

In her analysis of Kuma\War as part of an emerging movement of "documentary games," Fullerton notes that, although Kuma games such as *John Kerry's Silver Star* allow players the ability to decide how closely they want to adhere to the historical record, "the technological cycles that have driven the game industry to date all seem to move toward a point of convergence at which photorealistic visuals and painstakingly accurate simulations will meet."[52] For Fullerton, the value of documentary games is as an extension of the documentary genre in cinema and television that adds potentially very powerful, experiential, and participatory components. Despite numerous limitations on the contemporary cultural

Kuma\War, Iran Hostage Rescue. (Kuma Reality Games, 2004)

status of games, Fullerton argues that documentary games "add to our understanding of historical events and the situations surrounding them, rather than simply allowing us to be 'in the moment.'"[53] Venturing further into the realm of speculative history, the Kuma title *Iran Hostage Rescue Mission Parts I & II* offers players the opportunity to replay another election-sensitive event, the Carter administration's ill-fated attempt to rescue fifty-three American hostages from Tehran in 1980. Kuma describes the *Iran Hostage Rescue Mission* as follows: "You are a highly trained Delta Force operator carrying out the Pentagon's actual plan to rescue 53 Americans held hostage in Tehran. Storm the besieged American embassy, free the hostages from the radical 'students,' and make it out of Tehran—a city swarming with anti-American militants—any way you can."[54] As a historical event, the failed Iranian hostage rescue mission has rarely been the focus of historical re-creation. Instead, it is widely viewed as having cost Jimmy Carter the election and setting the stage for the victorious Ronald Reagan's success in negotiating the release of the hostages shortly after taking office. Rather than historical revision, conspiracy-oriented readings of this event have focused on the Reagan campaign's suspected backroom dealings that delayed the hostages' release until after the election was decided.

On September 30, 2005, Kuma again raised controversy by releasing a mission set in Iran amid public concerns about the Bush administration's intentions toward the country, which had been named as part of a new "axis of evil" in Bush's 2002 State of the Union speech. The game *Assault on Iran* is described by Kuma:

As a Special Forces soldier in this playable mission, you will infiltrate Iran's nuclear facility at Natanz, located 150 miles south of Iran's capital of Teheran. . . . Your team's mission: Infiltrate the base, secure evidence of illegal uranium enrichment, rescue your man on the inside, and destroy the centrifuges that promise to take Iran into the nuclear age. Never before has so much hung in the balance . . . millions of lives, and the very future of democracy could be at stake.[55]

Assault on Iran thus recuperates the Pentagon and Bush administration's specious assertions about Saddam Hussein's possession of "weapons of mass destruction" (WMD) and the threat such weapons posed as the justification for invasion in March 2003. The undisputed fact that no evidence of WMD or their manufacture was discovered in Iraq makes this one of Kuma's most irresponsible premises but one that is equally historiographically inconsequential. Of greater interest for the present discussion are titles such as *Osama Tora Bora*, which allows players to succeed where real U.S. forces failed in 2001 to capture Osama bin Laden in the mountains of Afghanistan. Departing from the pro-Bush administration agenda behind most *Kuma\War* titles, *Osama Tora Bora* implicitly suggests that the pursuit of bin Laden may have been an appropriate high-priority goal for U.S. forces in the Middle East, while military resources were instead being channeled toward Iraq. Although it is beyond the scope of the game to pose a critique of the allocation of Pentagon resources, the alternative history allowed by *Osama Tora Bora* reveals a key structural limitation of the succeed-or-fail format of the missions in nearly all Kuma games. If it is of any consequence at all, the historiography of *Kuma\War* is best understood as a symptom of historical consensus as it is constructed and consumed via commercial media. While effective for marketing purposes, the "ripped from the headlines" approach to framing its narratives is only minimally conducive to the kind of disputation of interest here.[56] Whereas foregoing the temporal distance usually reserved for historical reflection might have resulted in more fluid drafts of historical construction, *Kuma\War*, in the final analysis, offers little more than a faster-than-usual timeline for releasing games based on real-world events.

Vietnam Romance *and* Waco Resurrection

Artist and designer Eddo Stern also uses video games to interrogate the function of "history" and its eccentric potentials. For more than a decade, Stern has been a central figure among alternative and art game design-

ers and the Los Angeles–based digital art collective C-level,[57] creating a
provocative countercurrent of games and game-inspired art that draws
attention to the presumptions, styles, and experience of gameplay. In
two of his most remarkable works, *Vietnam Romance* (2003) and *Waco
Resurrection* (2004), Stern reconsiders the potential for games to engage
questions of history and memory. More than two decades after the heyday
of Vietnam films in the late 1970s and '80s, Stern's *Vietnam Romance*
mines a different archive of images and sounds not usually included in
representations of the Vietnam War. *Vietnam Romance* borrows video sequences, graphics, and music from Vietnam-based video games to create a
mashup that highlights the embeddedness of video-game technologies in
their cultural-technical moment, with imagery that move seamlessly from
the 8-bit graphics of *Platoon* (1988), often listed among the worst games
of all time, to the visually rich game *Deer Hunter* (2003).[58] By eschewing
concerns with stylistic coherence, Stern allows viewers to focus on what
is evoked by these images and challenges them to compare the iconicity
of video-game representations of the war with both cinematic and official
historical renderings.[59] *Vietnam Romance* thus rewrites the cinematic
iconography of the Vietnam War to include the game memories of a
generation who first experienced the war as not a televisual or cinematic
spectacle but rather a playable environment. Describing the project as "a
tour of nostalgia for romantics and *Deathmatch* veterans," Stern updates
the cultural discourses and long-troubling representations of Vietnam
for the digital generation. *Vietnam Romance*'s jarring strategies of remix
create unexpected resonances across films, TV, documentary, and games,
with a result that it is at once serious and playful, ironic and perversely
respectful.

Where *Vietnam Romance* merely evokes nostalgia for gameplay, *Waco
Resurrection*, created by the C-level design collective in 2003, focuses on
reenacting the 1993 massacre of Branch Davidians by federal agents at
David Koresh's cult compound in Waco, Texas. In an inspired twist on
the conventions of multiplayer gaming, every player occupies the role of
Koresh himself, making life-and-death decisions on behalf of himself and
his followers, while coming into potential conflict with the other Koresh
players in the game. Stern's multiplication of Koresh figures in the game
environment responds brilliantly to the historiographical dilemma of addressing uncertainties or conflicting versions of past events. At the same
time, players are invited to empathize with the situation of both Koresh
and his followers during the final hours of the fifty-one-day siege, during
which fire destroyed the compound, killing seventy-six Branch Davidians.

Each Koresh figure has the opportunity to focus his energies on the agents, including, bizarrely, the ability to convert agents to become cult members or to engage his rivals inside the compound. Players are therefore literally engaged in both internal and external conflicts, and playing against insurmountable odds, due to the all too well-known outcome of the siege. No matter what path a player takes, the compound will inevitably be destroyed and Koresh will die. By focusing on not outcome but instead process and experience, *Waco Resurrection* suggests a genuinely radical, alternative approach to playable historiography.

The Cat and the Coup

The Cat and the Coup is a video game created by Peter Brinson and Kurosh ValaNejad, taking as its subject the overthrow of Iran's democratically elected prime minister Mohammad Mossadegh, and the United States' role in returning the country to monarchist rule under the shah in 1953. On one level, *The Cat and the Coup* could be understood as a microhistory, focusing on a specific, historical incident, using factually grounded sources such as *New York Times* headlines to recapitulate a once-contested but now largely consensual history. Indeed, the game focuses on revisionist accounts of Mossadegh's overthrow that admit to the central role played by the United States. This aspect of the narrative is introduced as neither controversy nor correction but rather a taken-for-granted and by now all too familiar pattern of foreign interventionism by the postwar United States. What makes *The Cat and the Coup* remarkable is its entirely novel positioning of the player. He or she does not play Mossadegh or any of the key historical figures, and indeed, Truman, Churchill, and the shah are all presented as background figures with animal heads (a bunny, a bulldog, and a peacock, respectively). Instead, the player adopts the role of Mossadegh's cat.

The game's interface is deceptively simple, using only arrow keys to control the movement of the cat through a meticulously designed 2-D space, art directed by ValaNejad in the style of intricately crafted Persian miniatures. The game mechanics are likewise deliberately stripped down, allowing for severely limited intervention as the story unfolds, at first backward through time beginning with Mossadegh's death in 1967 to his rise to power in 1951; then the game switches direction to move forward, allowing us to reexperience the coup and revelations of U.S. involvement, proceeding through to his death. Thus, player agency is also limited to only the first half of the game, via a series of puzzles that must be solved

Iranian prime minister Mohammad Mossadegh and his cat plummet through history in *The Cat and the Coup*. (Brinson and ValaNejad, 2010)

through indirect actions by the cat, each of which results in Mossadegh falling downward into the next level of the game. The player must then choose to follow Mossadegh on his downward plunge by leaping into the unknown, a metaphor for the uncertainty of historical outcomes, but as a cat, the player is assured of landing on his or her feet, unlike Mossadegh. This serial descent is ultimately followed by a protracted scene in which Mossadegh floats on a rising tide of oil back through the game space, now clarified with historical photographs and newspaper headlines, ultimately returning to his deathbed, perhaps realizing for the first time the extent of his betrayal by his allies in the West.

The stylistic choices of *The Cat and the Coup* deliberately avoid the conventions (cuts, fades, and dissolves) of cinema, opting instead for a contiguous spatial aesthetic and visual iconography that is part photographic and part illustration, coupling ValaNejad's painstakingly crafted backgrounds and textures with simple line drawings for Mossadegh and the cat. Brinson, who is a former member of C-level and a cocreator of *Waco Resurrection*, conceptualized *The Cat and the Coup* as an opportunity to create a connection between players and what is for many a remote and idiosyncratic historical moment. Players are limited to solving short-term puzzles that have uncertain outcomes, a metaphor that Brinson likens to historical agency itself, noting that "historical figures don't always know what they're doing and what the consequences of their actions will be. The inability to concoct long-term strategies or predictable outcomes is emblematic of American foreign policy that focuses on short-term solutions."[60]

What makes *The Cat and the Coup* exemplary from a historiographical perspective is its striking adherence to, and departures from, the historical record. We have no reason to believe, for example, that Mossadegh had a cat or indeed a domestic pet of any kind—nor is the cat intended as a surrogate for a historical figure or even the whim of historical chance. While it is tempting to read the cat as a metaphor for Western meddling in Iranian affairs of state, the cat's inability to bring about direct consequences suggests the need for a more nuanced reading. The cat is simply the vehicle for our engagement with this particular historical narrative, and like historical agents, our role wavers between seemingly arbitrary constraints and actions with uncertain outcomes.

Each of these examples—*JFK Reloaded, Kuma\War, Vietnam Romance, Waco Resurrection,* and *The Cat and the Coup*—represents a variant on the potential conjunction of games and history, ranging from procedural mayhem and designed uncertainty to a wholly conservative recapitulation of cause-effect gameplay with a historical veneer. Like other forms of popular culture-based historiography, the commercial gaming industry has both great potential and limited wherewithal to make significant contributions to the cultural discourses of history. For every art game that achieves the level of thoughtful experimentation seen in *Waco Resurrection* or *The Cat and the Coup*, the industry markets a dozen games with premises no more sophisticated than the plethora of alternative histories focusing on World War II or Cold War reversals of fortune. Indeed the default preoccupation of commercial history games precisely mirrors that of commercial cinema by presenting a recognizable set of historical *or* counterfactual circumstances within which a player may exercise varying degrees of agency in affecting a sequence of events. In theory, computational histories should rival and surpass linear histories for their potential impact on creative reinterpretations of the past, but it is a rare work of experimental history that takes full advantage of this capability.

Remixing Katrina: Internet as Public Memorial

If video games offer a foundation for one platform of unorthodox digital historiography, the amateur music video offers yet another. Some of the most vibrant examples occurred in response to Hurricane Katrina, which hit New Orleans in August 2005. For a brief moment, in response to the devastation, the Internet seemed to live up to its promise of offering an alternative public sphere, a participatory space where individuals could contribute to the cultural processing of a national tragedy. As the disaster in the Gulf region unfolded, a remarkable profusion of image, sound, and video files sampled from both mainstream and independent news sources began circulating over the Internet. While cable news channels broadcast twenty-four-hour coverage of the disaster and its relief efforts, the Internet began to function as a dynamic archive—a kind of communally programmed digital video recorder—for the selection and redistribution of key images, audio, and video clips. This process of digestion gravitated toward not a synthetic overview of events or analysis about the disaster but rather idiosyncratic samplings of moments of transgression, intensity, or excess that came to symbolize the news coverage of Katrina. Arguably, it is by these exceptions to the various rules of broadcast journalism that media coverage of Katrina will be remembered—racist comments, breaches of journalistic protocol, and displays of extreme emotion—all of which remain easily accessible on the Web via simple keyword searches, while the vast majority of news as usual is consigned to the restricted access broadcast archives of history. The Internet also provided a forum for unprecedented numbers of amateur-produced Katrina video memorials, which began appearing within days of the disaster via the then novel phenomenon of free, online video distribution channels such as YouTube and Vimeo. The majority of these were remixes of still and moving images drawn from broadcast and Internet-based news sources, accompanied by popular songs, and nearly all included an exhortation to contribute relief funds to the Red Cross.

The online video memorial emerged as a well-established genre shortly after the 2001 attacks on the World Trade Center and Pentagon by members of bin Laden's al Qaeda network. These, in turn, continue a much longer history of personal memorialization undertaken in less public contexts such as scrapbooks and photo albums, as well as the ritualized leaving of objects at public memorial sites such as the Vietnam Veterans Memorial in Washington, D.C., or the Federal Building in Oklahoma City. In contrast to these site-specific practices, the online memorial may be constructed and accessed regardless of geographic location. Indeed, many Katrina memorials were created by individuals whose primary emotional connection to the Gulf region developed while viewing apocalyptic imagery on television and computer screens. Additional continuities between the World Trade Center attacks and Katrina are evident in the number of sites that host both Katrina and "9/11" memorials, sometimes posted side by side or with identical design layouts.[61] The close interconnection of Katrina and "9/11" memorials has also resulted in a regrettable tendency to frame these two very different national tragedies in similar terms, the effect of which is a simultaneous politicization and depoliticization of the memorial narratives accompanying these two events. Conflating America's innocent victim status in these two events suggests a lack of culpability not entirely applicable to either. Certainly, America's dependence on Middle Eastern oil reserves and its resulting interventionist foreign policy contributed to al Qaeda targeting it; while the lack of infrastructural investment in the levees around New Orleans clearly transformed the flooding of the Gulf region into as much a "man-made" as a "natural" disaster.

Unlike past memorials that have taken years or decades to conceive and build, the possibility of "virtual memorials" has radically accelerated the process of memorialization in the United States. The U.S. Holocaust Memorial Museum in Washington, D.C., took nearly a half-century to build, while the Vietnam Veterans Memorial and Oklahoma City memorials took seven and five years, respectively. As Marita Sturken has noted, efforts to memorialize the 2001 World Trade Center attacks were almost instantaneous, emerging organically from the practice of posting images on walls and electronic bulletin boards in an effort to find missing family members.

> In the face of absence, especially an absence so violently and tragically wrought at the cost of so many lives, people feel a need to create a presence of some kind, and it may be for this reason that questions of memorialization have so quickly followed this event. It seemed as if people were already talking of memorials the day after, when the numbers and names of the missing were unknown and the search for survivors still the focus of national attention. What, we might ask, is behind this rush to memorialize and to speak of memorials? Could we imagine people talking of memorialization after the destruction of the Warsaw Ghetto, or the bombing of Hiroshima?[62]

Following Katrina, the floodwaters had barely retreated when debates about whether and how to rebuild New Orleans began. Some worried that a Disneyfied version of the city would be hastily constructed like a film set for tourists, freed at last from the racial and economic realities of the city's previous inhabitants. The "real" New Orleans would at least be memorialized through the photographs and video collages created by amateur auteurs, some of whom did not hesitate to admit they have never actually visited the region. Part of what makes this remarkable is the shift from regarding the practice of memorialization as a matter entrusted to government officials and organizations to something that may be meaningfully and publicly practiced by individuals.

In part, I believe this reflects public outrage at the inadequate federal response to the hurricane, a sentiment that was almost certainly catalyzed by frustrations with the war in Iraq that were already heating up in 2005. Occasionally, television commentators made these connections explicit, wondering aloud whether the National Guard would have been so slow and ineffectual if it were not already burdened by deployment in that "other" Gulf region. More common, though, was the sentiment—posed as part speculation, part obvious statement of fact—that the determining factor with regard to government response was the race and economic status of the communities—poor, African American neighborhoods—most devastated by the hurricane and floodwaters. Given the lack of initiative taken by the federal government to help victims of the disaster, why would a traumatized public even consider relying on those same government officials to address their need for mourning?[63]

It would be all too easy to find ourselves sliding toward a characterization of the Internet as offering an alternative public sphere that is somehow inherently progressive. Tara McPherson's chapter "I'll Take My Stand in Dixie-Net: White Guys, the South, and Cyberspace"—originally published in 2000—represents a rare attempt to challenge some of the euphoric rhetoric about the possibilities for dispersed subjectivity on the Web and the idea that we all have multiple, deracialized, degendered identities when we go online.[64] In this article, McPherson argued that the Internet is at best agnostic with regard to the kinds of ideologies and subcultural movements it supports, citing as a primary example the Dixienet Web site, created and maintained by Michael Hill, a white professor at Stillman College in Alabama. McPherson positions Dixienet as part of a pro-Southern heritage movement that may be understood as promoting "traditional" (read "white supremacist") Southern values. Following the hurricane, the Dixienet Web site prominently featured a Katrina relief effort on its splash page, along with a statement denying reports that the organization was supporting a whites-only relief effort in the Gulf region.

As Michael Warner has argued, events of mass injury are frequently renarrativized in terms of violence done to an "abstracted body" that is symbolically represented as a singular entity.[65] In the case of Katrina, the bodies of the victims were largely poor and black—the type of body that is rarely seen on television outside the context of reports on urban crime. Media coverage of Katrina brought these bodies to national attention, asserting the undeniable linkage of poverty and race in the Gulf states and the seeming lack of government responsiveness to a tragedy whose primary victims were both poor and black. If we are to think clearly about the role of networks and emerging technologies on social groups and historical construction, it is imperative that we avoid specious assumptions about how these technologies function—and in whose interests. The still emerging practice of subindependent, do-it-yourself video production and distribution offers a fascinating case study for thinking in concrete terms about the sphere of amateur, peer-to-peer, and viral media distribution via the Internet and its implications for the nascent historiography of the digital era.

Twitter and History

Another symptom of the ongoing cultural desire to repurpose digital media for well-worn cultural practices related to history and memory may be found in the recent proliferation of historical reenactments using platforms such as Twitter, the online microblogging platform that allows users to post messages of up to 140 characters to the Internet. One such project, Twhistory, offers the witty tagline, "Those who forget history are doomed to retweet it." The project was created by two graduate students at Utah State University, Marion Jensen and Tom Caswell, who undertook a Twitter-based reenactment of the Battle of Gettysburg, concluding with Abraham Lincoln's famously terse (though not exactly Twitter-like) memorial address. The resulting multiple streams of tweets is interesting in its appropriation of a Ken Burns–style heteroglossic history from below. The emphasis on contents of the textual narratives is placed on quotations drawn from authenticated historical sources but rendered in a contemporary vernacular, while retaining historical justification, based on its adherence to verifiable details. Twhistory now serves as a clearinghouse and catalyst for others seeking to stage reenactments using Twitter, such as a high school class in St. Louis, Missouri, that organized a reenactment of the Cuban missile crisis of 1962. Another ongoing project, PatriotCast, created by Jason Phelan, offers an eight-year reenactment of the American

Revolution spanning the years 1775 to 1783. Billing itself as "A Revolutionary Way to Experience the American Revolution," PatriotCast sends multiple updates each day, detailing the minutiae of the war and linking to contemporary images of historic sites. Given the scope and duration of the project, PatriotCast opts for an omniscient, historical perspective rather than attempting to locate the source of the updates in specific historical figures. In contrast, in October 2009, former House speaker Newt Gingrich orchestrated a historical reenactment of the Battle of Trenton on his Twitter account, generating feeds to more than one million subscribers. This historical "Twitternactment," as Gingrich called it, was intended to promote the launch of his book *To Try Men's Souls*, a work of historical fiction about George Washington. Gingrich, a former professor of history and best-selling novelist of historical fiction and alternate histories of the Civil War and World War II, presents General Washington (username @GenWashington76) in the midst of the famed battle urging his men forward with under-140-word exhortations such as "Forward men, forward! Victory or death. Now forward!" and "Column has stopped! What is going on? Why the holdup?"

We may expect that historical experiments using platforms such as Twitter will continue to manifest in each successive generation of technology in an ongoing process of historiographical remediation. The Library of Congress's decision to archive Twitter feeds for the historical record marks a revealing acknowledgment of the importance of these platforms for the generation of future historical evidence, even as the discursive limitations of the form enforce its marginalization relative to "official history." The extent to which such archival efforts are predicated on curating as a manifestation of explicit historiographical intent as opposed to scale-driven acquisition is a question worth considering seriously.

The proliferation of large-scale digitizing and archiving efforts presumes that the resulting mass of raw data yielded by such efforts will be more intelligible to future generations, perhaps with access to more efficient data-parsing solutions than are currently available. It seems clear that the impulse to simply "digitize everything" dwells more in the realm of the archival than the historiographical. As this book has been at some pains to argue, the ability of future generations to make sense of such masses of data depends upon developing historiographical sensibilities and models that allow for idiosyncrasy, experimentation, and eccentricity. As we have seen, much digital historiography retains an emphasis on traditional narrative and historical tropes that regrettably fail to develop a specifically digital historiographic ethos. Historians who are more attuned to the full range of potential for digital history might function more like systems designers for the development of new tropes and tools for rendering the past. The goal of such systems could plausibly surpass the mere capturing, preserving, and accessing of digital information in favor of articulating a combined ethics and poetics of historical expression. Simply put, a database is not a "history." However, by the logic of this chapter, *the information architecture that defines a database and its underlying structures is fundamentally and fascinatingly historical.* We would do well to ask, what histories are rendered possible by such platforms? Do such experiments with digital historiography result in previously unspoken or unthought histories, or merely an updating and remixing of accepted renderings of the past? I will say it bluntly: the past deserves to be rendered, complete with its complexities, contradictions, and potentials for disruption, and such histories can and should pose threats to the political, cultural, and epistemological status quo.

Vectors of History

A number of promising experiments with the conjunction of historical research and database-driven interactive interfaces may be found in the online electronic journal *Vectors Journal of Culture and Technology in a Dynamic Vernacular*, which I coedit with Tara McPherson at the University of Southern California. Although not all projects published in *Vectors* are historical in nature, a significant number have sought to exploit the potentials of database histories, along with a richly mediated interface design. For example, Melanie Swalwell's "Cast-Offs from the Golden Age" presents a historiography of the video-game industry in New Zealand using a gamelike mechanic that invites users to unlock levels of historical information about this largely unrecognized and unwritten history. Designed by *Vectors*' creative director Erik Loyer, the project includes multiple voices across a broad spectrum of historical authority ranging from academic historians to fans, gamers, and collectors of the physical and software artifacts generated by this industry. In Cast-Offs, a player/user moves through a simulated 3-D environment populated only with paths and silhouetted avatars and objects, each of which is a portal for accessing historical information. The nature of this information ranges form Swalwell's own historical analysis to raw data including e-mail exchanges with collectors and archives. The player/user becomes a gamer/researcher who is situated as a surrogate for Swalwell herself, embroiled in a process of investigation, attempting to discover and piece together a fragmented history that insistently resists closure and comfortable teleological trajectories. This history, which is interwoven with the more well-known histories of U.S. and Asian game industries, lends itself to more discontinuous and sometimes contradictory historical narratives. It is up to the gamer/researcher to piece together historical elements to create his or her own collection of objects, stories, and people. Swalwell's project is also an open architecture database allowing for expansion to include the voices of users and the virtually limitless expansion of the fragments, narratives, and artifacts contained in the system. The explicit game mechanic contained in this project both references the fundamental historiographical paradigm of unlocking clues and levels and resonates with the project's historiographical and ethical commitments.

Swalwell's project is particularly disruptive of the preferred histories of the entertainment and technology industries, which are relentlessly framed as a series of creative and technological triumphs, moving inexorably toward faster processing, increasingly realistic graphics, and more engaging forms of interactivity. Like the film industry, game companies would probably prefer we didn't think about them historically at all, choosing instead to situate themselves on the brink of a perpetual future, looking forward to their next commercial success rather than contemplating the past and its legacies. Rather than seeking to map a comprehensive history of progress toward the present, historians such as Swalwell speak about the past as inextricably entangled with their own personality quirks and idiosyncratic obsessions. If we are honest about it, the narratives we pursue when "doing history" probably consist of as many dead ends, digressions, and anachronies as neatly packaged elements of a grand historical narrative. It is a rare work of historiography that not only acknowledges this but also seeks to weave it into the fabric of the historical work itself, becoming a strength rather than a liability.

In order to experience the largely unexamined history of video games in New Zealand, Swalwell asks us to retrace some of her steps—and occasional missteps—in seeking to discover this arcane and fragmented past. Swalwell's project refuses to deliver a comprehensive history, choosing instead to allegorize the research process by embedding bits of information within an information space. The implication is that, following Foucault, all historiography is rightly conceived of in terms of fragmentation and partiality. The seductive narrative of the definitive, totalizing history is both mendacious and misleading, and Swalwell argues implicitly that these are particularly counterproductive to the topic at hand. Swalwell's investigation is thus part exploration and part role-playing game, as different facts reveal themselves with each traversal of the research space. Without fetishizing the novelty of this spatialized and embodied interface, Cast-Offs from the Golden Age models an extremely compelling mode of historiographical investigation.

My own project for *Vectors*, also designed by Loyer and titled "Technologies of History Interactive," attempts to make explicit the challenges of writing a historical moment through the conjunction of media artifacts and textual or verbal discourse, taking as its object of study the broad and eclectic range of textualizations of the JFK assassination. This project exposes the process by which historical imagery comes to stand in for our thinking about a historical event. The project is a case study, an opportunity to put into practice some of the arguments made in this book pertaining to the entangled relations among media, history, and memory. These arguments, in fact, may only be fully articulated through media. By this I do not mean simply taking advantage of the digital format for providing media supplements or illustrations but literally aiming to think *through* the media under analysis, developing relationships among media elements themselves, rather than privileging the discursive affordances of text over images. In some ways, then, this project is not primarily *about* the JFK assassination, but the dense layers of mediation to which this historical event has been subjected provide a particularly rich set of opportunities to think about the construction of "history" itself.

Although certain aspects of the design may initially appear to resist easy navigation, the goal is neither to frustrate the user nor to indulge in aestheticized design experiments. The project presents several clearly defined modes of exploration, beginning with the "Analyzer," in which media elements are subjected to a process of tracking and fragmenting designed to simultaneously reveal and obscure the contents of a film or video clip. The user may then follow connections that are suggested by either the video segment or its accompanying text to explore further text arguments or a connection between two media clips. Each connection made is logged in the user's history and may be revisited at any time. The experience of moving through the project is therefore intended to be partly experiential and partly curatorial; users may select from categories of content that are based on genre, format, or threads of historiographical concern. The multiplicity of opportunities for revelation or chaos function as both a metaphor for history's own lack of resolution and a rhetorical strategy for resisting narrative closure.

Finally, what can we say about the collision of digital media/technology and history? In our present moment, it is still possible to speak of digital media and technology as agents of change and challenge, forces to be resisted or taken advantage of—or at the very least accommodated and responded to. In the course of this transition, we must become more sophisticated about our own practices and presumptions as historians and practitioners of culture. Some of the most productive and contentious debates over the ultimate impact of digital technology for historiography continue to arise in response to interactive digital histories, including games, networked databases, and computational systems that may or may not exploit the potentials of these platforms to pursue goals that are in any way transgressive or experimental. Part of the motivation for this chapter is to describe the continuities and coextensiveness of digital media with past forms, as well as the critical paradigms we bring to bear on them. While it's true that the affordances of digital media offer an occasion for rethinking our fundamental relations to "history," politics, and culture, we would be ill advised to frame this as a fundamentally new or exceptional circumstance.

Conclusion

Without doubt, some of the most compelling histories in technocultural studies focus on moments of a technology's emergence or its corollary evanescence.[1] Still others that are close to the heart of this project derive insight from the provocative juxtaposition of temporally disparate technologies, such as Lisa Gitelman's *Always Already New* (2006), which performs a parallel examination of early sound recording technology and contemporary digital media. A historian of technology who has turned to studying digital and electronic forms, Gitelman remarks with slightly forced hopefulness that "it is not that the Web resists history *per se*, only that electronic documents compel attention to themselves as differently—often dubiously—historical, where history always happens at the levels of—at least—data, metadata, program and platform."[2] She goes on to explain how even poorly functioning tools for historical research such as the Center for History and New Media's H-bot, which attempts to answer basic questions about historical events and people, can actually have a positive impact by virtue of drawing attention to the need for more legitimate instruments of historical provenance.[3] Basic knowledge of how digital tools function, Gitelman argues, when combined with detailed knowledge of the past can enhance our overall sense of historicity—ultimately providing a clearer sense of how historical understanding is produced.[4] In the increasingly digital decades to come, I would invert the priority ascribed by Gitelman to prior knowledge of the past to say that the best histories will be those that exhibit a sophisticated understanding of the functioning of the tools of digital historiography, coupled with the ability to effectively navigate and evaluate diverse forms of extant history.

In considering a range of media historiography from film and TV to digital platforms, we have mapped a momentarily complete spectrum of unrecognized and undertheorized forms of engagement with the past. I regret that the structure of this book has often defaulted to medium specificity as a paradigm for the works under consideration here—that is, TV shows are primarily compared to TV shows; films to films; and games to games. I hope it will be apparent that the historiographical commitments of this study are in fact more portable than these groupings suggest. True, the examples of digital historiography in the penultimate chapter, for example, thrive on the affordances of computer processors and networks, but our ability to understand what is at stake in them historiographically is deeply cathected with conceptual frames drawn from previous generations of media and technology. In all cases, my goal has been to privilege works that advocate or enable the creation of a possibility space for thinking complexly and creatively about the past in and through media. Although the focus of this book has been on works that engage the past and its construction, I hope it is also apparent that my underlying goal is to mobilize the process of historiography and historical analysis in the interests of present and future social praxis. To this end, I have included in this concluding section some models of present critique and future imagining that are not entirely "historical" but that have implications for the productive linkage of past and future.

Eccentric History as Design Fiction

The concept of "design fiction" has emerged as a rhetorical conceit among writers about contemporary technoculture. In one of his dispatches from the Near Future Laboratory, Julian Bleecker describes design fiction as working

> in the space between the arrogance of science fact, and the seriously playful imaginary of science fiction, making things that are both real and fake, but aware of the irony of the muddle—even claiming it as an advantage. It's a design practice, first of all—because it makes no authority claims on the world, has no special stake in canonical truth; because it can work comfortably with the vernacular and pragmatic; because it has as part of its vocabulary the word "people" (not "users") and all that implies; because it can operate with wit and paradox and a critical stance. It assumes nothing about the future, except that there can be simultaneous futures, and multiple futures, and simultaneous-multiple futures—even an end to everything.[5]

This description bears an uncanny resemblance to the stance this book has taken toward eccentric histories articulated across a broad array of media forms. Though not all are utopian in aspiration, these works are drawn together by a shared commitment to the possibilities of understanding in and through systems of knowledge that bear tenuous relations to what Bleecker terms "canonical truth." As we know, tightly held truths about the past are sometimes found to be in error or of limited utility as discrete objects compared to their function when integrated into designed systems for recombination and reconfiguration. At the risk of overprivileging the metaphors of digital culture, we can say that historiography is an algorithm; as Alex Galloway defines it, "A machine for the motion of parts."[6] This is true both of literally algorithmic systems of history such as Terminal Time or *The Cat and the Coup*, but we may also see the conventions, limitations, and ethics of history proper as metaphorically fulfilling Galloway's model of a machine designed to execute instructions according to predefined rules and parameters. At one level, then, what this book is calling for are some new algorithms, machines, or ways of imagining historical investigation.

"Drunk History"

One such irreverent variation on the concept of visual history is Derek Waters's "Drunk History,"[7] a genuinely bizarre, comedic exercise in which amateur historians get drunk on camera and pontificate about historical events, offering their own interpretations and dialogue pertaining to well-known historical events and people. From obscure beginnings as a video series on YouTube, "Drunk History" was picked up for inclusion in HBO's 2010 *Funny or Die* series. The resulting historical narratives are rambling, digressive, and idiosyncratic, punctuated frequently by the narrators needing to throw up or lament their state of drunkenness. Dialogue scenes are reenacted by well-known actors in poorly costumed period garb, mouthing the words of the narrator, no matter how incoherent.[8] The ventriloquism of "Drunk History" may be understood as a metaphor for the process of more mainstream historical filmmaking as well as a highly accessible model for amateur historians to follow.

Although "Drunk History" episodes are deeply idiosyncratic and played primarily for humor, they are not without substance and genuinely compelling interpretive moments. In the episode devoted to Fredrick Douglass, for example, Jen Kirkman presents a surprisingly nuanced (having completed two bottles of wine) portrayal of Douglass's complex relationship with Abraham Lincoln, as well as Lincoln's often-overlooked support for the containment as opposed to total abolition of slavery. "Drunk History" also brings a refreshing irreverence to its critiques of "great men" of American history, including Benjamin Franklin (played by Jack Black), who is portrayed as a womanizer who recklessly endangers his son's life while experimenting with electricity, and Thomas Edison (Crispin Glover), as a megalomaniac who wantonly executes animals to display the dangers of the alternating current promoted by his rival, Nicola Tesla (John C. Reilly). The real significance of "Drunk History" lies not in these elaborations of relatively minor elements of the historical record but rather in its insouciance. By literally inverting the discourse of sobriety that characterizes much of academic history, "Drunk History" widens the space within which rethinking of and experimentation with the past may take place.

Alternate Realities: *Superstruct*, *World without Oil*, and *The Golden Institute*

In a handful of past- and future-oriented alternate reality games (ARGs), the old binaries of accuracy and inaccuracy give way to forms of historical imagining that are uniquely participatory. Although they share certain characteristics with both "alternate history" and historical reenactments, ARGs are far less beholden to the rational execution of historical chains of cause and effect. Emphasizing social dynamics over historical details and articulation of causal narratives, past and future ARGs encourage players to engage physically in the construction of a jointly authored narrative, making videos, tracking down clues, or sharing information via social networks. In other words, players act as crucial components of a machine with many moving parts, whose goals and outcomes are largely emergent and unpredetermined. As models of historical engagement, the ARGs considered here are particularly promising in their direct endowment of agency in players who are responsible for shaping the game's final outcome.[9] The investment of trust in a participatory mode of narrative construction and the resulting real-world skills that players must develop hold particular promise for the type of empowered historical agency this book seeks to advocate.

I will focus first on two alternate reality games: *Superstruct* and *World without Oil*. Unlike the majority of ARGs produced as part of a transmedial marketing strategy for commercial products of the entertainment industries, *World without Oil* (WWO) was commissioned by ITVS Interactive and designed by Ken Eklund and Jane McGonigal, with funding from the Corporation for Public Broadcasting. The project was billed as

> the world's first serious alternate reality game, a cooperative pre-imagining of a global oil crisis. Over 1900 players collaborated in May 2007 to chronicle the oil crisis with their own personal blog posts, videos, images and voicemails. The game ended after simulating the first 32 weeks of the oil shock, but its effects continue, as game designers analyze its unique gameplay and we all watch the continuing drama with global oil prices and supply.[10]

The basic mode of gameplay in WWO is the creation and sharing of citizen journalism-style video reports, adding richness and specificity to the overall framework of an accelerating energy crisis. Players are urged to report on imaginary solutions and instances of community actions that could actually be mobilized in the event of a real crisis, but perhaps more importantly, they are encouraged to reflect on the interlocking cultural, environmental, and economic systems into which oil is inextricably woven. Players are thus led to think in terms of systemic solutions to contemporary problems and to begin taking actions in an abstract, fictional context that have potential viability in the real world.

Sharing many of the same participatory structures and premises as WWO, the game *Superstruct* launched less than a year later in late 2008. Designer McGonigal, who served as participation architect on WWO, was commissioned to lead the project by the Institute for the Future (IFTF), a nonprofit Silicon Valley–based think tank that describes itself as "committed to building the future by understanding it deeply."[11] A project of the IFTF's Ten-Year Forecast group, *Superstruct* was announced in September 2008 and ran for six weeks beginning in October 2008, drawing over ten thousand participants who contributed their energies to proposing solutions to a series of global catastrophes set ten years in the future. Billed as the first "Massively Multiplayer Forecasting Game," *Superstruct* postulated that

> the existing structures of human civilization—from families and language to corporate society and technological infrastructures—just aren't enough. Superstruct is played on forums, blogs, videos, wikis, and other familiar online spaces. We show you the world as it might look in 2019. You show us what it's like to live there. Bring what you know and who you know, and we'll all figure out how to make 2019 a world we want to live in.[12]

The point of view articulated in *Superstruct* is therefore that of a speculative future anterior, looking backward on actually existing economic and environmental issues to propose solutions for present-day social problems. Challenging players to "Watch the videos. Play the game. Invent the future," *Superstruct* offers a model of collective action and problem solving that encourages players to regard themselves as "Super-Empowered Hopeful Individuals," a way of being in the world that is, presumably, open to a broader range of potential applications. Although neither is framed in terms of historiography, both *Superstruct* and WWO offer compelling models for the kind of collective social action that holds great promise for developing a sense of historical and social agency.

The year after *Superstruct* concluded, German-born artist Sascha Pohlflepp unveiled a project titled *The Golden Institute* that closed the loop between ARG-based participatory gaming and alternate history. *The Golden Institute* is described by Pohlflepp as a fictional "research and development facility for energy technologies in an alternate reality where Jimmy Carter had defeated Ronald Reagan in the US election of 1980." The project postulated a second-term Carter administration that elevated the transformation of American energy dependence to renewable, domestic sources, making it "the most energy-rich nation on the planet."[13] *The Golden Institute* proceeds from a hypothetical past in which a particular problem or set of problems has been solved through a fictional narrative. But in contrast with the fundamental conservatism that plagues much alternate history, *The Golden Institute* does not fetishize the historical causality set in motion by the bifurcation of "real history" and the design fiction it proposes. Pohlflepp's interest is not in the past but rather in the politics of the present. No effort is made to explain Carter's landslide reelection, or to account for the "other" consequences that might have resulted. Conventional alternate histories would surely argue that Carter's focus on domestic energy would have freed the Soviet Union to expand its influence in the Western hemisphere and brought about the downfall of worldwide American military dominance, and so on. The past postulated by *The Golden Institute* is not driven by the logic of digital simulators coded to display and reify the balance of historical forces, plotted along oppositional axes. Indeed, the eccentricity and disengagement from conventions of alternate history in Pohlflepp's work extends to the form of its articulation, including stilted video performances by the institute's purported founder and the creation of model cars and trailers designed for driving into southwestern electrical storms to attract and capture the energy from lightning strikes. *The Golden Institute*, in other words, wants us to think creatively, not literally, about the alternate vision it offers of the present, rather than display the author's virtuosity with historical detail and causal logic.

Despite all efforts to constrain, explain, and domesticate it, the past remains eccentric. These final examples portray different aspects of the kinds of idiosyncratic historiography that this book seeks to valorize. I take it as a given that our ability to think about the past is significantly shaped by the media through which we imagine it, so the forms of media we allow ourselves to consider and what we imagine is possible to do with them are extremely important. The complexity of our awareness about the systems of representation made available to us through media correlates with the sophistication of our thinking about the past. The days of discrete works of history are numbered if not already productively behind us. The future of the past lies in systems of understanding, engagement, and repurposing, informed but not limited to the range of historiographical tendencies sketched here.

The opposite case of neatly packaged histories all too easily reassures us that the injustices of the past are being systematically redressed and overwritten by a more enlightened present. Our own potential complicity in the inequalities of the past need not be interrogated so long as our narratives map the present into a trajectory toward the future that is inevitable, progressive, and self-justifying. We may express momentary outrage at contemporary instances of governmental or corporate corruption, the persistence of racism, gender inequality, or erosion of civil liberties, while experiencing no dissonance over the polite processes by which our own present is textualized and readied for digestion into familiar and reassuring historical narratives. This book presumes that our ability to think critically about the past and to engage the politics of historiography is significantly impacted by our depth of understanding of systems of media representation: film, video, television, games, the internet; and that this understanding will continue to evolve as it collides with future forms, platforms, and technologies of history yet to come. It is in our interest to seize this opportunity to articulate our own values and expectations of what we want our past to look like, the ways we want to understand and judge our actions and the actions of others, and through this insight, more clearly envision the future and our role in it.

Coda

One of cinema's many origin myths goes like this: when D. W. Griffith screened his epic history film *Birth of a Nation* for President Woodrow Wilson at the White House on February 18, 1915, the president was said to have remarked, "It is like writing history with lightning and my only regret is that it is all so terribly true."[14] Derivations of the quote have supplied the title for numerous discussions of the relationship between film and history and are routinely woven into accounts of both Griffith's film and Wilson's presidency. But like all myths, it is also the source of controversy, with a half-dozen different versions of the quote in circulation and active debate over whether the event ever really took place at all. My original plan, in fact, was to title this book *History Written with Lightning*—certainly not in homage to the sentiment of the quote but rather in a gesture of perverse appreciation for its historical uncertainty and ongoing disputation, a case in point for my basic contention that we have much to learn about the past from that which is indigestible to history proper.

Suppose for a moment that finding the truth of what happened on that day in 1915 *were* our goal. We might begin by tracking down footnotes in primary sources, consulting experts whose reputations we respect, or sifting back through the many pages of "history" revisions in Wikipedia articles on Wilson, Griffith, or *Birth of a Nation* to see what the points of popular contestation are. We could search online for commentaries that have already synthesized the controversy or attempt to triangulate conflicting claims from independent sources. We might read books or journal articles or watch movies about Griffith, Wilson, or early film history. We might even rewatch *Birth of a Nation* itself to see if its politics are as appalling as we remember. We could begin to feel that our instincts or increasing knowledge of the historical figures in question can guide us in judging the likelihood that Wilson actually liked the film or that Griffith would or would not have invented the endorsement.

In the course of researching media sources, we might also come across any number of responses to the film, from Oscar Micheaux's *Within Our Gates* (1919) to the digital remixes, DJ Spooky's "Rebirth of a Nation" (2004) and Les LeVeque's "Backwards Birth of a Nation" (2000). These might shift our interest in the controversy over Wilson's utterance to the racial politics of the film and its place in film history, or we might reflect on the reasons that interest in early film history and *Birth of a Nation* in particular seems to resonate more intensely at certain moments than at others. We might also uncover a subset of facts that do not appear to be in dispute—that *Birth of a Nation* was the first film to screen officially at the White House; that it was the longest and most expensive film of its time; that its director is credited with inventing cinematic narrative—and others that occupy positions of greater or lesser relevance and contestation. It might also turn out that secondary texts are as revealing as that which eludes us—digital versions of movie posters for *Birth of a Nation* that allude to the quote in promoting the film; accounts of the controversy stirred up by subsequent screenings; or the widely reported repudiation of the film by members of Wilson's administration. We may conclude that Griffith, the consummate entrepreneur, was perfectly capable of inventing the endorsement in an effort to promote his film and indemnify its sympathetic portrayal of the Ku Klux Klan. Or perhaps the credulousness attributed to Wilson (and by extension the cinematic culture of his time) simply reinforces our innate sense of progress from a naive past to an increasingly sophisticated present.

At this point, we may decide to add our conclusions or speculations to Wikipedia or one of the online forums we have consulted. If we are skilled at Photoshop, we could concoct our own ersatz movie poster and get it in circulation online; a bit of dexterity with video editing, and we could create our own remix for viral distribution. How might this process of fabricating our own evidence or altering historical texts reframe each stage of an historical investigation? Perhaps we have been asking the wrong questions all along. Suppose this simple quote is more useful as a fake—or perhaps its disputed provenance makes little difference to everything we have gained from engaging these questions. We might begin to see our own present in a new light or shift our assumptions about the writing of history. In any case, we will have asked questions and opened doors that might have gone unnoticed or unthought if the lone footnote in this section had simply pointed us to a reputable source and laid our epistephilia calmly to rest. In the end, what actually did or did not come out of the president's mouth on a cold day in 1915—*was it cold in Washington, D.C., that February? Are we sure it was February?*—might be of far less interest and consequence than its subsequent textualization, its role in the discursive rendering of the past, and what we decide to do with and about it as agents in the construction of history.

Notes

Introduction

1 Allan Sekula, "Reading an Archive: Photography between Labour and Capital," in *The Photography Reader*, ed. Liz Wells, 443–52 (London: Routledge, 2003), 447.

2 See, for example, Norman M. Klein, *The History of Forgetting: Los Angeles and the Erasure of Memory* (London: Verso, 1997).

3 This notion of an entangled relationship between memory and historiography comes from Marita Sturken, *Tangled Memories: The Vietnam War, the AIDS Epidemic and the Politics of Remembering* (Berkeley: University of California Press, 1997).

4 Michel de Certeau, *Heterologies: Discourses on the Other* (Minneapolis: University of Minnesota Press, 1986), 215–16.

5 See Roland Barthes, *Camera Lucida: Reflections on Photography* (New York: Noonday Press, 1982).

6 For a discussion of the relationship between time and historiography and the need to historicize time, see Robert Young, *White Mythologies: Writing History and the West* (London: Routledge, 1990), 56–59.

7 The term is used by Georg Lukács in his *Historical Novel* (London: Merlin Press, 1978), 19.

8 See, for example, Leo Braudy, *Narrative Form in History and Fiction: Hume, Fielding and Gibbon* (Princeton, N.J.: Princeton University Press, 1970).

9 Martin Jay marks the beginning of visual culture as a field with the publication in 1988 of Hal Foster's *Vision and Visuality* (Seattle: Bay Press, 1988), a collection of texts based on a conference hosted by the Dia Art Foundation; as well as Foster and Jay, the publication included scholars such as Jacqueline Rose and Jonathan Crary. For a succinct overview of the field, see Martin Jay, "Cultural Relativism and the Visual Turn," *Journal of Visual Culture* 1, no. 3 (2002): 267–78.

10 See, for example, Robert Brent Toplin, *History by Hollywood: The Use and Abuse of the American Past* (Chicago: University of Illinois Press, 1996); Peter C. Rollins, ed., *Hollywood as Historian: American Film in a Cultural Context* (Lexington: University Press of Kentucky, 1983); Robert Rosenstone, *Visions of the Past: The Challenge of Film to Our Idea of History* (Cambridge, Mass.: Harvard University Press, 1995); George MacDonald Fraser, *Hollywood History of the World: From One Million Years B.C. to Apocalypse Now* (Cambridge, Mass.: Harvard University Press, 1988); Vivian Sobchack, ed., *Persistence of History: Cinema, Television and the Modern Event* (New York: Routledge, 1996); Robert Rosenstone, *Revisioning History: Film and the Construction of*

a New Past (Princeton, N.J.: Princeton University Press, 1995); Leger Grindon, *Shadows on the Past: Studies in the Historical Fiction Film* (Philadelphia: Temple University Press, 1994); Mark Carnes, ed., *Past Imperfect: History according to the Movies* (New York: Henry Holt, 1995); Marcia Landy, *Cinematic Uses of the Past* (Minneapolis: University of Minnesota Press, 1996), and *The Historical Film: History and Memory in Media* (New Brunswick, N.J.: Rutgers University Press, 2001); Maria Wyke, *Projecting the Past: Ancient Rome, Cinema and History* (New York: Routledge, 1997); Michael E. Lynch and David Bogen, eds., *The Spectacle of History: Speech, Text, and Memory at the Iran-Contra Hearings* (Durham, N.C.: Duke University Press, 1997); Marnie Hughes-Warrington, *History Goes to the Movies: Studying History on Film* (New York: Routledge, 2006); and Richard Francaviglia and Jerry Rodnitzky, eds., *Lights, Camera, History: Portraying the Past in Film* (College Station: Texas A&M University Press, 2007).

11 Fredric Jameson, *Marxism and Form* (Princeton, N.J.: Princeton University Press, 1971), xviii.

12 This view is echoed in Lutz Niethammer, *Posthistoire: Has History Come to an End?* (London: Verso, 1992).

13 Interestingly, the 1970s also saw a significant increase in historiographical programming on television, culminating with the phenomenal success of the ABC miniseries *Roots* (1978).

14 Of course, the suggestion that history is out of control long predates Vietnam and the Reagan era. In the 1950s, British historian Geoffrey Barraclough argued that, since the world wars, history no longer seemed adequate to explain the present. History, according to these versions of contemporary American culture, is either completely out of control or dominated by evil, unseen, or alien forces. However, even if "the truth is out there," as the *X-Files'* obsessional Fox Mulder maintained, it increasingly seems that a now familiar mélange of carefully constructed narratives, mediated testimonies, and conspiracy theories may be as close to it as we are able to get.

15 Although this is a considerably more cumbersome way of referring to the terror attacks of September 11, 2001, the conventional shorthand terms "9/11" and "September 11" have become too easily and mendaciously associated with the war in Iraq.

16 For human beings in Iraq, of course, the primary manifestation of the war was somewhat more tangible. See Jean Baudrillard, *The Gulf War Did Not Take Place* (Bloomington: Indiana University Press, 1995).

17 It is difficult to resist lapsing into sarcasm in response to the arrogance and cynicism of Francis Fukuyama's *The End of History and the Last Man* (New York: Avon, 1992). The quotes around "free market" are mine, but Fukuyama explains his own strategies of euphemism as follows: "Since the term capitalism has acquired so many pejorative connotations over the years, it has re-

cently become a fashion to speak of 'free-market economics' instead; both are acceptable alternative terms for economic liberalism" (44). As the past two decades of disastrous "free market" economic reforms in the former Soviet Union have demonstrated, the pejorative connotations Fukuyama observes in connection with the term "capitalism" may be more than a matter of fashion.

18 Fukuyama, *The End of History*, xi–xiii.

19 Fukuyama, *The End of History*, 44.

20 See, for example, Klein, *The History of Forgetting*.

21 See, for example, Fredric Jameson, *Postmodernism or the Cultural Logic of Late Capitalism* (Durham, N.C.: Duke University Press, 1988).

22 Walter Benjamin, "Theses on the Philosophy of History," in *Illuminations*, ed. Hannah Arendt, 253–64 (New York: Schocken, 1985).

23 This idea of historical sedimentation is developed in George Lipsitz, *Time Passages: Collective Memory and American Popular Culture* (Minneapolis: University of Minnesota Press, 1990).

24 Hayden White, "The Modernist Event," in *Persistence of History: Cinema, Television and the Modern Event*, ed. Vivian Sobchack, 17–38 (London: Routledge 1996).

25 For more on the question of "unrepresentability" with regard to Disney's America and the controversy over the ability of a theme park to re-create the experience of slavery, see Michel Rolphe Trouillot, *Silencing the Past: Power and the Production of History* (Boston: Beacon, 1997).

26 Christopher Norris, *Uncritical Theory: Postmodernism, Intellectuals and the Gulf War* (Amherst: University of Massachusetts Press, 1992), 90.

27 Young, *White Mythologies*.

28 Tony Bennett, *Outside Literature* (London: Routledge, 1991).

29 Rosenstone, *Revisioning History*, 11.

30 There is nothing specifically cinematic about this mode of observation, however. It is an alternative reading strategy that provides access to information readily available through other sources.

31 See Carlo Ginzberg, *Clues, Myths and the Historical Method* (Baltimore: Johns Hopkins University Press, 1989).

32 A representative example of this debate and the ways in which historians characterize film as a progressive, challenging subject for historians may be found in John E. O'Connor and Martin A. Jackson, eds., *American History/American Film: Interpreting the Hollywood Image* (New York: Frederick Ungar Publishing, 1979).

33 See Rosenstone, *Visions of the Past*.

34 A good example of this is Oliver Stone's *Nixon* (1995), the release of which was preceded by publication of a volume of historical documents, research notes, and generally defensive justifications for the film's many instances of historico-creative license.

35 See, for example, the in-depth analysis of historical signification in realist history films by Landy, *Cinematic Uses of the Past*, and Wyke, *Projecting the Past*.

36 David E. James, *Allegories of Cinema* (Princeton, N.J.: Princeton University Press, 1989), ix.

37 By this I do not mean to discount the possibility of oppositional readings and alternative spectatorial positions, only to deplore the cynicism of an industry that makes them continually necessary.

Chapter 1: Fantastic History

1 Tsvetan Todorov, *The Fantastic: A Structural Approach to a Literary Genre* (Ithaca, N.Y.: Cornell University Press, 1975).

2 Anne Friedberg, *Window Shopping: Cinema and the Postmodern* (Berkeley: University of California Press, 1994), 106.

3 Jameson, *Postmodernism*, 369.

4 This argument is developed and expanded by Foucault throughout his career, but a clear example may be found in *Discipline and Punish: The Birth of the Prison* (New York: Vintage, 1977).

5 See Rosenstone, *Visions of the Past*.

6 See Hayden White, *Tropics of Discourse: Essays in Cultural Criticism* (Baltimore: Johns Hopkins University Press, 1978).

7 White, *Tropics of Discourse*.

8 Dominick LaCapra, *History and Criticism* (Ithaca, N.Y.: Cornell University Press, 1985), 34–35.

9 Rosenstone, *Visions of the Past*, 3.

10 See, for example, Joan Scott, *Gender and the Politics of History* (New York: Columbia University Press, 1999); and Trinh T. Minh-ha, *Women, Native, Other: Writing Postcoloniality and Feminism* (Indianapolis: University of Indiana Press, 1989).

11 This is evidenced in the legacies of "history from below" and oral history movements of the 1960s and '70s.

12 See, for example, Michael Bommes and Patrick Wright, "The Charms of Residence: The Public and the Past," in *Making Histories*, ed. Richard Johnson, Gregor McLennan, Bill Schwarz, and David Sutton, 253–302 (London: Anchor, 1982).

13 See Sturken, *Tangled Memories*.

14 Fukuyama, *The End of History*, 44.

15 See Bill Nichols, *Blurred Boundaries: Questions of Meaning in Contemporary Culture* (Bloomington: Indiana University Press, 1994).

16 Rosenstone, *Revisioning History*, 12.

17 Rosenstone, *Revisioning History*, 3.

18 Rosenstone, *Revisioning History*, 209.

19 Niall Ferguson, ed., *Virtual History: Alternatives and Counterfactuals* (New York: Basic Books, 1999).

20 "Point of divergence" and "divergence point" are terms used in alternative histories to designate the point at which the "true" history and the alternative trajectory split.

21 Point of Divergence: Alternate History, at www.marmotgraphics.com/pod/ pod_what_is.html (accessed May 15, 2008).

22 Though I should note that a number of these works have been adapted to the screen, including Robert Harris's *Fatherland* (1994), an HBO movie set in a Nazi-dominated America of the 1990s.

23 Young, *White Mythologies*, 83.

24 It is interesting to note that "counterfactual thinking" is also a subject of research in the social sciences, where it is studied as a phenomenon linked to decision making and regret—for example, people who are haunted by things that "might have been." Cinematic examples include *It's a Wonderful Life* (1946) and *Back to the Future* (1985).

25 Mary Ann Doane, "Information, Crisis, Catastrophe," in *Logics of Television: Essays in Cultural Criticism*, ed. Patricia Mellencamp, 222–39 (Bloomington: Indiana University Press, 1990), 226–27.

26 Lipsitz, *Time Passages*, 34.

27 Colin McArthur, *Television and History* (London: British Film Institute Press, 1978), 14.

28 McArthur's book is symptomatic of the difficulty of writing about television in terms of content without becoming overwhelmed by issues of institutional practice and economics. Television as an object of study is notoriously intangible. TV criticism must address its status as an amalgam of the physical object in the home, the programming that it makes available, and the commercial infrastructure by which it is subtended. Similarly, the effects of TV watching, diverse circumstances, degrees of attention, and multiple modes of identification that it offers make it very difficult to speak about the cultural role and relevance of TV in general terms.

29 Cited in Jay Leyda, *Films Beget Films: A Study of the Compilation Film* (New York: Hill and Wang, 1964), 16.

30 These include *King* (1978), *Roots: The Next Generations* (1979), *Attica* (1980), and HBO's *I Remember When* (1981).

31 Marginal though Sherman and Mr. Peabody may be, the show was sufficiently inspirational to Internet Archive founder Brewster Kahle that he named his Web preservation engine "The Wayback Machine" in homage to the time travel apparatus named WABAC used by Mr. Peabody to deliver his first-person lessons in history.

32 These include the original *Star Trek* (NBC, 1966–69), *Star Trek: The Next Generation* (UPN, 1987–94), *Star Trek: Deep Space Nine* (UPN, 1994–98), and *Star Trek: Voyager* (UPN, 1994–2001).

33 The show's news format also privileges eyewitness accounts over critical analysis, a tendency that persists in contemporary news, where broadcasting "on location" is unnecessarily fetishized. Another recent manifestation of the fascination with eyewitness accounts is David Colbert's *Eyewitness to America: 500 Years of America in the Words of Those Who Saw It Happen* (New York: Pantheon, 1998).

34 Photographic (or digital) composites offer one form of visual corollary to this type of historical thinking. Bringing together impossible combinations of historical figures allows for representatives of different time periods to speak to each other while partially masking the contemporary sensibilities from which each contrivance originated. In addition to *Meeting of Minds*, this occurs in the collection of historical figures including Abraham Lincoln, Sigmund Freud, and Aristotle that appears in *Bill and Ted's Excellent Adventure* (1989).

35 Steve Allen, *Meeting of Minds: Four Scripts* (New York: Prometheus Books, 1993). In all likelihood, the reason the show was not more widely criticized stems from its structural distance from the sober discourses of history. The obviously fictional contrivance of *Meeting of Minds* situates it safely in the very large cracks between "real" history and Allen's middlebrow, televisual "histo-tainment."

36 In order to find a more sustained and sophisticated critique of racist historiography and its impact on African American images, it is necessary to look outside the sphere of corporate-owned and white-dominated media institutions to independent films such Cheryl Dunye's *Watermelon Woman*, which will be discussed later in this chapter. I would also add here the remarkable distillation of images of racial stereotypes collected in montage form at the end of Spike Lee's digital feature *Bamboozled* (2000).

37 In *Forrest Gump* (1994), the Hanks character helpfully returns a book to one of the students being escorted into the University of Alabama, and on *Quantum Leap*, the Bakula character helps a slave choose a dignified name (King) upon receiving his freedom.

38 According to *Dark Skies*, JFK was killed by a paragovernmental "Black Ops" team when he threatened to expose the alien invasion. Seemingly out of touch with its own irreverence at times, the show goes to absurd extremes to preserve the Camelot mythos, offering repeated assurances that Kennedy was not part of the alien coverup.

39 NBC *Dark Skies* Web site, at www.nbc.com/darkskies (accessed February 3, 1997).

40 Andreas Huyssen, *Twilight Memories: Marking Time in a Culture of Amnesia* (New York: Routledge, 1995), 34.

41 Huyssen, *Twilight Memories*, 94.

42 This conception of historically resistant reading is drawn from Michel de Certeau, "Walking in the City," in *The Practice of Everyday Life* (Berkeley: Uni-

versity of California Press, 1984), a chapter that valorizes the navigation of urban spaces in ways that defy the intentions of urban planners. For de Certeau, this "misappropriation" of public spaces constituted a form of resistance to the prescriptive order of urban planning.

43 David E. James, "The Distinction of Idioms," in *Scratching the Belly of the Beast: Cutting Edge Media in Los Angeles, 1922–94*, ed. Holly Willis, 36–37 (Los Angeles: Filmforum, 1994), 36.

44 Scott MacDonald, *A Critical Cinema: Interviews with Independent Filmmakers* (Berkeley: University of California Press, 1988), 361.

45 Judith Mayne, *Directed by Dorothy Arzner* (Bloomington: Indiana University Press, 1994), 177.

46 Bill Nichols, *Representing Reality: Issues and Concepts in Documentary* (Bloomington: Indiana University Press, 1992), 249.

47 See Marita Sturken, "Reenactment, Fantasy and the Paranoia of History: Oliver Stone's Docudramas," *Spectator* 20, no. 1 (Fall 1999/Winter 2000): 23–37.

48 By this time, the Vietnam film was already practically its own subgenre. Whereas films such as *Apocalypse Now* (1979) and *The Deer Hunter* (1978) had portrayed the experience of combat in Vietnam as "unrepresentable" except by means of elaborately constructed metaphors, in *Platoon* (1986) the war itself remained incomprehensible at some basic level (i.e., "we were fighting ourselves"), but wartime tropes of good and evil, masculinity, and courage were resoundingly recuperated.

49 See also Diane Kunz's "Camelot Continued: What If John F. Kennedy Had Lived?" in *Virtual History: Alternative and Counterfactuals*, ed. Niall Ferguson, 368–91 (New York: Basic Books, 1999).

Chapter 2: Cultural Memory

1 National Geographic, "Pearl Harbor Resources," www.nationalgeographic .com/pearlharbor/images/phlessons.pdf (accessed May 24, 2010).

2 Bommes and Wright, "The Charms of Residence," 256.

3 Friedrich Nietzsche, *Untimely Meditations* (Cambridge: Cambridge University Press, 1997).

4 Huyssen, *Twilight Memories.*

5 Unfortunately, instead of politics, cultural theorists are more apt to deploy the vocabulary of neurology and psychoanalysis in order to talk about popular memory. In *The History of Forgetting*, for example, Norman Klein's use of pseudoscientific terminology such as "distraction," "mytheme," "imago," and "engram" conflates the individual process of remembering and forgetting with that of cultural groups.

6 Marita Sturken writes, "Unlike photographs or film images, memories do not remain static through time—they are reshaped and reconfigured, they fade

and are rescripted. Though an image may fix an event temporally, the meaning of that image is constantly subject to contextual shifts." Marita Sturken, *Tangled Memories*, 21.

7 Michel Foucault, "Film and Popular Memory," *Edinburgh Magazine* 2 (1977): 22.

8 Foucault, "Film and Popular Memory," 22.

9 See, for example, "Intellectuals and Power," a discussion between Foucault and Gilles Deleuze that appears in *Language, Counter-Memory, Practice: Selected Essays and Interviews by Michel Foucault* (Ithaca, N.Y.: Cornell University Press, 1977), 211–17.

10 Jameson contends that, in postmodern culture, TV and other visual media have fostered an increasingly "derealized" sense of presence, identity, and history. And Friedberg writes in her book *Window Shopping*, "In this crucible of philosophic debate, where history and memory are endangered forms, cinematic and televisual apparatuses become readable not just as symptoms of a 'postmodern condition, but as contributing causes. A diminished capacity to retain the past is, as I will argue, a loss that has figured as the price of the cinema's cultural gain" (2).

11 See Jane Feuer, "The Concept of Live Television: Ontology as Ideology," in *Regarding Television*, ed. E. Ann Kaplan, 12–22 (Los Angeles: American Film Institute, 1983).

12 See Doane, "Information, Crisis, Catastrophe," 227.

13 Sturken, *Tangled Memories*, 10.

14 John Caldwell, *Televisuality: Style Crisis and Authority in American Television* (New Brunswick, N.J.: Rutgers University Press, 1995), 166.

15 Mimi White, "Television Liveness: History, Banality, Attractions," *Spectator* 20, no. 1 (Fall 1999/Winter 2000): 37–56.

16 Michael Frisch argues in this regard, "What matters is not so much the history that is placed before us, but rather what we are able to remember and what role that knowledge plays in our lives." Michael Frisch, *A Shared Authority* (Albany: State University of New York Press, 1990), 16.

17 Although *History and Memory* is a short (thirty-minute), experimental video, it has received a remarkable degree of critical attention, for example, with regard to its exemplification of postmodern/ethnic history (Rosenstone) and cultural hybridity (Laura Marks).

18 Homi K. Bhabha, *The Location of Culture* (New York: Routledge, 1994), 310.

19 Bhabha, *Location of Culture*, 310.

20 Foucault, "Film and Popular Memory," 22.

21 Bhabha, *Location of Culture*, 23.

22 This "hybrid form," as Laura Marks notes, "mediates a mixture of documentary, fiction, and experimental genres," which is characteristic of the film work created by "people in transition and cultures in the process of creating identities." Laura U. Marks, "A Deleuzian Politics of Hybrid Cinema," *Screen* 35, no. 3 (Autumn 1994): 245.

23 Janice Tanaka, *Moving the Image*, ed. Russell Leong (Los Angeles: Visual Communications, 1991), 206.

24 David Lowenthal, *The Past Is a Foreign Country* (Cambridge: Cambridge University Press, 1999), xxii.

25 Stan Brakhage, "In Defense of Amateur," in *The Brakhage Scrapbook: Collected Writings 1964–1980*, edited by Robert A. Haller, 162–68 (New York: Documentext, 1982), 167.

26 Nichols, *Representing Reality*, 142.

27 Nichols, *Representing Reality*, 243–55.

28 Nichols, *Representing Reality*, 44.

29 Nichols, *Representing Reality*, 45. Nichols's examples are Ophüls's *Hôtel Terminus* (1988) and Ross McElwee's *Sherman's March* (1986).

30 This image is also known as "Falling Soldier."

31 This is nowhere more apparent than in a contemporary undertaking such as Steven Spielberg's *Survivors of the Shoah* project, discussed in the final chapter. Although Ophüls's work overlaps with this project in many places (the desire to learn something about the past through people's memories; the importance of keeping the past alive; and the significance of the Holocaust as a defining historical moment), the two could not be more different in terms of their historiographical commitments.

Chapter 3: Found Footage

1 James Peterson, *Dreams of Chaos, Visions of Order: Understanding the American Avant-Garde Cinema* (Detroit: Wayne State University Press, 1994).

2 John Tagg, *The Burden of Representation: Essays on Photographies and Histories* (Minneapolis: University of Minnesota Press, 1993); and Brian Winston, *Technologies of Seeing: Photography, Cinematography and Television* (London: British Film Institute, 1997).

3 Michel de Certeau, *The Writing of History* (New York: Columbia University Press, 1988), xxvi.

4 William Wees, *Recycled Images: The Art and Politics of Found Footage Films* (New York: Anthology Film Archives, 1993). Before that, of course, there was Leyda's useful but now dated *Films Beget Films*, published in 1964, a time when it was possible for the author to list every film that incorporated found footage up to that point.

5 One of the primary failings of Wees's work is his adoption of the position that work he labels "postmodern" is ipso facto bad and therefore unworthy of additional critical attention.

6 Bobrow's video may be accessed from his site, at http://negrospaceprogram .com/, or on YouTube, at www.youtube.com/watch?v=lxNAPqGDwCo (accessed July 25, 2010).

7 Paul Arthur touches on this subject in "The Status of Found Footage," *Spectator* 20, no. 1 (Fall 1999/Winter 2000): 57–69.

8 Both of these examples, however, are circumscribed by what Marita Sturken has characterized as the comforting (and therefore conservative) parameters of paranoid culture. See her "Reenactment."

9 The "exhibition" depicted in the animation is loosely based on William Bullock's display of Aztec objects at the Egyptian Hall in London in 1824, a display that included a live Indian, a facsimile of the Codex Boturini, and a possibly fake stone serpent. For more background on this exhibition, see Ian Graham's chapter, "Three Early Collectors in Mesoamerica," in *Collecting the Pre-Columbian Past*, ed. Elizabeth H. Boone, 49–80 (Washington, D.C.: Dumbarton Oaks, 1993).

10 This authorial dispersion stands in contrast with comparable works such as Cheryl Dunye's *Watermelon Woman* (1996) and Marlon Fuentes' *Bontoc Eulogy* (1997), in both of which the filmmaker appears as an on-screen character and provides a focal point of the narrative.

11 This sequence is reminiscent of the rear projection performance sequence in Straub and Huillet's *Chronicle of Anna Magdalena Bach* (1968).

12 This idea of historical sedimentation is developed in Lipsitz, *Time Passages*.

13 Benjamin, "Theses on the Philosophy of History."

14 As Lynne Kirby argues in *Parallel Tracks: The Railroad and Silent Cinema* (Durham, N.C.: Duke University Press, 1997), the advent of widespread train travel marked a key moment in the turn to modernity and proved instrumental in creating the visual sensibility of early cinema.

15 See Tom Gunning, "The Cinema of Attraction: Early Film, Its Spectator and the Avant-Garde," *Wide Angle* 8, nos. 3–4 (1986): 66.

16 This particular performance took place at the University of Colorado, Boulder, in October 1998, and my description of it was first published on the experimental film Web site *Flicker*, at www.hi-beam.net/, in December 1998.

17 This is the term used by Morgan Fisher in an interview with MacDonald in *A Critical Cinema*, 272.

18 Interview with Ken and Flo Jacobs, New York, March 16, 1998.

19 Scott MacDonald, *A Critical Cinema 3* (Berkeley: University of California Press, 1998), 180.

Chapter 4: Home Movies

1 For the purposes of the present discussion, I am not going to attempt a rigorous definition of the term "home movie" or to distinguish it from "home videos," though important differences certainly exist and merit serious consideration. Typically, inadequate definitions of the "home movie" have rested on elusive notions of intentionality or inflexible categories based on film gauge or sophistication of the equipment used. But work by avant-garde filmmakers resists such criteria at every turn. One could easily argue that the intentions behind much of the work of Jonas Mekas or Stan Brakhage are comparable to

that of the "typical" home moviemaker. Likewise, the persistent use of "sub-substandard" gauge and consumer-grade equipment by artists ranging from George Kuchar to Sadie Benning demonstrates the inadequacy of definitions based solely on format or technology.

2 Other examples include R. J. Cutler's *American High* (2000) and Kirby Dick's *Chain Camera* (2001), both of which gave cameras to high school students and then incorporated footage shot by students into a documentary about them. More recently, director Adam Yauch distributed fifty cameras to audience members at a Beastie Boys concert to make the film *Awesome; I Fuckin' Shot That!* (2006). Related efforts have been made using collaborative structures in postproduction, including Bret Gaylor's *Open Source Cinema* (2008), which harvests a range of video footage collected online to create a documentary about the copyright wars.

3 The complete picture is, of course, considerably more complicated. Without entering discussions about the rhetoric of authenticity deployed by reality TV or amateur pornography, I think it is fair to say that home movies derive at least some of their cultural and familial significance from a presumption of spontaneity and authenticity. Obviously, the indeterminacy of the Zapruder footage and the contested meanings of George Holliday's tape of the Rodney King beating show that the inherent power of "authenticity" and "spontaneity" are frequently overshadowed by political or other concerns.

4 Richard Chalfen, "The Home Movie in a World of Reports," *Journal of Film and Video* 38, nos. 3–4 (Summer/Fall 1986): 105–6.

5 Of course, Chalfen's research subjects and the theories he develops from them is anything *but* universal. A troubling theme in much of the published work on home movies is the fatalistic acceptance of and lack of attention to the race and class status of most home movie practitioners.

6 Patricia R. Zimmermann, *Reel Families: A Social History of Amateur Film* (Bloomington: Indiana University Press, 1995). This, of course, is not true in the realm of the self-conscious "personal essay" film, where graphic accounts of personal trauma are the norm rather than the exception.

7 Chalfen, "The Home Movie in a World of Reports," 106.

8 Maureen Turim, "Childhood Memories and Household Events in the Feminist Avant-Garde," *Journal of Film and Video* 38, nos. 3–4 (Summer/Fall 1986): 86.

9 The irony of this assumption, as Fred Camper notes in "Some Notes on the Home Movie," *Journal of Film and Video* 38, nos. 3–4 (Summer/Fall 1986): 9, is that the numerical advantage in terms of hours of footage recorded lies by far in the realm of the amateur film (and certainly, now, video).

10 Christian Metz, *The Imaginary Signifier* (Bloomington: Indiana University Press, 1977), 48.

11 This feeling of nonubiquity is confirmed by the experience of the native subject who feels victimized by the ethnographic gaze. See Trinh T. Minh-ha's

discussion in *Framer Framed* (New York: Routledge, 1992). Also, a parallel argument regarding the relative power invested in on- and off-screen space is developed in Kaja Silverman's *The Acoustic Mirror* (Bloomington: Indiana University Press, 1988). Like the female objects of the male spectatorial gaze, the children subjects of home movies are present only by their appearance in the frame (as opposed to behind the camera, speaking in voice-over, etc.) and are therefore disempowered.

12 Like Benjamin's work of art, the social function of which is transformed through mechanical reproduction, home movies carry with them a diminished but still palpable residue of their ritualistic and familial origins.

13 Slavoj Zizek, *The Sublime Object of Ideology* (New York: Verso, 1989), 105.

14 Zizek, *Sublime Object of Ideology*, 106.

15 I would also make a distinction here between home movies that are truly "refunctioned" through appropriation and the telic shift identified by David James in the work of Jonas Mekas, for whom the lines between home moviemaking and essayistic filmmaking often became indistinguishably blurred: "What before [Mekas] had [been] seen as private, provisional and exergual was now recognized as its own justification and its own telos." David E. James, "Film Diary/Diary Film: Practice and Product in *Walden*," in *To Free the Cinema*, ed. David E. James, 145–79 (Princeton, N.J.: Princeton University Press, 1992), 149. Although Mekas routinely reedited and narrativized footage from his own (sometimes quite distant) past (e.g., *Lost, Lost, Lost* and *Reminiscences of a Journey to Lithuania*), these films do not emphasize his process of reappropriation or the transformation of meaning to which recontextualized images are subjected. Instead, I would argue that Mekas draws on these images as though from a memory pool, using them to weave diaristic details into narratives of personal identity and subjectivity.

16 *Meanwhile Somewhere . . . 1940–1943*, Unknown War series 5/3, www.forgacs peter.hu/prev_version/eng/main/films/meanwhilesomewhere/meanwhile somewhere.htm (accessed May 24, 2010).

17 A brief digression into the multiple layers of authorship in Søren Kierkegaard's *Either/Or* (from which Forgacs drew his title) may serve to illuminate some of these strategies. Danish philosopher Kierkegaard's two-volume study *Either/Or* (Princeton, N.J.: Princeton University Press, 1971) is regarded as one of the author's most autobiographical texts—a philosophical meditation on marriage that coincided with his own broken engagement. Interestingly, however, it is also the work in which Kierkegaard's authorship is most elaborately obfuscated. Published under the pseudonym Victor Eremita, *Either/Or* posits a narrator who is only the "editor" of a group of found texts written by two other individuals to whom the narrator has no connection. The first volume consists of a collection of notes and writings attributed to an anonymous writer known only as "A," which the narrator alleges to have discovered in an old desk. To make things even more confusing, a second layer of anonymous

texts exists among these documents that A claims to have found in *another* desk. The second volume of *Either/Or* consists of a series of letters addressed to A, ascribed to an author known only as "B." The content of the two volumes adds up to a philosophical meditation on the relative merits of leading a life that is guided primarily by aesthetic (romanticist) or ethical (idealist) considerations. Throughout the work, Kierkegaard's surrogate authors resist the possibility that the answer to this conflict may be found in the domestic sphere, through marriage and the life of personal fulfillment that forms the bourgeois family ideal.

18 MacDonald, *A Critical Cinema 3*, 283.

19 MacDonald, *A Critical Cinema 3*, 279.

20 MacDonald, *A Critical Cinema 3*, 281.

21 At this point in the film, the voice-over abruptly switches from the surrogate, child's voice that narrates the rest of the film to Friedrich's own adult voice, further underscoring her personalizing of this final image.

22 The origins of this mode of self-representation may be clearly seen in numerous "classic" texts, from the frank discussion of sexual urges in St. Augustine to Jean-Jacques Rousseau's meditations on masturbation. Equally prevalent in film and video confessions is the practice of transgressing the boundaries of social taboos: William Jones's anonymous sex in *Massillon*; Vanalyn Green's numerous personal traumas, from eating disorders, incestuous impulses, and parental alcoholism to her contraction of herpes; Mindy Faber's mother's mental illness in *Delirium*; Robert Frank's son's mental illness in *Home Improvements*; Lynn Hershman's childhood sexual abuse in *First Person Plural*; Greta Snider's abortion in *Futility*; Marilu Mallet's divorce in *Unfinished Diary*; and innumerable other accounts of formerly off-limits subjects such as parental divorce, coming out as gay or lesbian, or dying of AIDS.

23 Pierre Sorlin noted in *The Film in History: Restaging the Past* that, "if we had to pay to consult Roman inscriptions or medieval documents, and pay again if we quoted them, historical publications would be few in number, and historiography would become the privilege of a few public foundations and wealthy individuals" (Totowa, N.J.: Barnes & Noble Books, 1980), 5.

Chapter 5: Materialist History

1 The conception of "history" as fundamentally textual does not only imply that it may therefore be read, written, and subjected to various forms of erasure and rewriting. In the words of Jacques Derrida, "The age already in the past is in fact constituted in every respect as a text." Jacques Derrida, *Of Grammatology* (Baltimore: Johns Hopkins University Press, 1992), 157. Derrida's rather more extreme assertion that "history is constituted through texts" means we do not arrive at knowledge of "history" *through* texts. When we are dealing with texts—whether filmed, written, recorded, experienced, or re-

membered—we are dealing with "history" itself. While it may be asking a bit much of a word like "history" to include both written documents and lived experiences, there is nothing essential about remembering or living through a moment in time that exempts it from textual or cultural processing (89).

2 Ernesto Laclau and Chantal Mouffe, *Hegemony and Socialist Strategy: Towards a Radical Democratic Politics* (London: Verso, 1985).

3 Young, *White Mythologies.*

4 Dana Polan, *The Political Language of Film and the Avant-Garde* (Ann Arbor: University of Michigan Research Press, 1985), 3.

5 See James, *Allegories of Cinema.*

6 Most notably, Fred Camper in his article "The End of Avant Garde Film," *Millennium Film Journal* 16–18 (Fall/Winter 1986–87): 68–82.

7 If not for the definitive rigor and erudition of Rosenstone's chapter "*Walker*: The Dramatic Film as (Postmodern) History," the indisputable eccentricity of Cox's *Walker* might well have served as a cornerstone case study for this book (in *Revisioning History*, 202–13).

8 I have chosen to follow Barton Byg in adopting "Straub/Huillet" as the conventionalized shorthand for referring to the collective authorship of their film work. As Byg notes in *Landscapes of Resistance* (Berkeley: University of California Press, 1995), 11–16, Danièle Huillet is all too frequently omitted from the collaboration entirely or inexplicably reduced to being one of "the Straubs" despite the consistency with which their creative partnership is characterized as genuinely collaborative (to say nothing of Peter Gidal's cranky intimations in *Materialist Film* [New York: Routledge, 1989] that Danièle is actually the more capable of the two).

9 Even Byg's useful and well-researched book, *Landscapes of Resistance*, privileges formal over political analysis.

10 Martin Walsh, *The Brechtian Aspect of Radical Cinema* (London: British Film Institute, 1981), 37.

11 Maureen Turim, "Textuality and Theatricality in Brecht and Straub/Huillet: *History Lessons* (1972)," in *German Film and Literature: Adaptations and Transformations*, ed. Eric Rentschler, 231–45 (New York: Methuen, 1986).

12 Walsh, *The Brechtian Aspect of Radical Cinema.*

13 Paul Willemen, "An Avant-Garde for the Eighties," *Framework* 24 (Spring 1984): 68.

14 Byg, *Landscapes of Resistance*, 233.

15 Straub/Huillet's use of direct audio suggests an ontological imperative that has been taken up with varying results by film movements as diverse as the cinema vérité or "direct cinema" movements of the 1960s and the group of filmmakers subscribing to Danish filmmakers Lars von Trier and Thomas Vinterberg's Dogme 95 "Vow of Chastity."

16 In certain films (notably *Othon*), Straub and Huillet similarly elect not to do shot-to-shot color corrections in order to draw attention to the constant

but gradual changes in the color temperature and direction of outdoor light. The result is a sometimes very subtle sense of discontinuity and disruption within each scene that works against the illusionist desire for seamlessness and audio/visual continuity. For a bizarre reversal of this argument, see Peter Gidal's mean-spirited and often incoherent attack on Straub/Huillet as being *too* illusionist in his book *Materialist Film*.

17 Rule number 2 of the Vow of Chastity states simply, "The sound must never be produced separately from the images and vice versa (music must not be used unless it is present where the scene is shot)." The complete Vow of Chastity is reproduced in Shari Roman's *Digital Babylon: Hollywood, Indiewood and Dogme 95* (Los Angeles: Lone Eagle Publishing, 2001), 41.

18 Crafton argues that synch sound was present long before 1929 in the form of "part talkies" that emerged during the mid-1920s as well as the precisely synchronized orchestral scores composed for live accompaniment virtually since the beginnings of cinema. See Donald Crafton, *Talkies: American Cinema's Transition to Sound, 1926–31* (Berkeley: University of California Press, 1999).

19 For a meticulously charted, quasimathematical analysis of camera angles and character movement in *History Lessons*, see Walsh, *The Brechtian Aspect of Radical Cinema*.

20 Straub/Huillet invert this shot pattern for the short film *Every Revolution Is a Throw of the Dice* (1977), which is photographed entirely from a single camera position, equidistant from a semicircular arc of performers.

21 Brecht's dictum about characters delivering their lines as if they were reading quotations rather than spontaneously speaking them is quoted at the beginning of Straub/Huillet's *Introduction to Arnold Schoenberg's Accompaniment to a Cinematographic Scene* (1973).

22 In Maureen Turim's otherwise insightful essay on *History Lessons* ("Textuality and Theatricality"), Straub/Huillet's subtitling practices are mischaracterized as "inadequate."

23 For an account of the meticulous attention to historical accuracy and detail in *The Chronicle of Anna Magdalena Bach*, see Walsh, *The Brechtian Aspect of Radical Cinema*.

24 Jacques Derrida, *Positions*, trans. Alan Bass (London: Athlone, 1981), 57–58.

25 Walsh, *The Brechtian Aspect of Radical History*.

26 Turim, "Textuality and Theatricality."

27 Peter Wollen, *Readings and Writings: Semiotic Counter-Strategies* (London: Verso, 1982), 102.

28 Willemen, "An Avant-Garde for the Eighties," 68.

29 Paul Arthur, "The Four Last Things: History, Technology, Hollywood, Apocalypse," in *The End of Cinema as We Know It: American Film in the Nineties*, ed. Jon Lewis, 342–55 (New York: New York University Press, 2001), 343.

30 In the 1990s, some of Godard's work took the construction of history as its

primary theme, including *Germany Year Nine Zero* (1991) and the TV mini-series *Histoire(s) du Cinema* (1998).

31 These include the reenacted witness testimonies in *Used Innocence* and *Landscape Suicide* and occasional intrafilmic tests of short-term memory via displaced sound-image synchronization in *Deseret*, an exercise that reached poetic heights—and may well have served as inspiration for Benning, whose work frequently develops intertextual relations with previous avant-garde films—in Hollis Frampton's *Nostalgia* (1971).

32 Benning's 2000 film *El Valley Centro* performs a similar kind of analysis of the agricultural development in California's Central Valley as that which was applied to the Imperial Valley in *Utopia*.

33 Undoubtedly, Benning's background and abiding interest in mathematics fuels his refusal to abandon structural film entirely. In *Deseret*, for example, each shot is twelve frames shorter than the preceding shot, a variation that creates a perceptible but indeterminate feeling of progressive haste as the film moves forward in time.

34 It is certainly possible to read the discursive practices of these films in Brechtian terms—both Walsh's book *The Brechtian Aspect of Radical Cinema* and Byg's *Landscapes of Resistance* offer useful readings of Straub/Huillet in terms of distanciation and medium reflexivity.

35 It is more important, for example, to the Omaha Beach sequence that opens *Saving Private Ryan* (1998)—a scene much touted for its historical verisimilitude—to make use of a landscape that looks right rather than one that is physically congruent with the site of the actual invasion. This logic was reversed by the makers of *Pearl Harbor* (2001), who received permission to film certain scenes of their re-created attack in the actual waters of Pearl Harbor. This reversal underlines part of the difference between purely fictional and reality-based historiography with regard to cinema's role in national mourning and commemoration.

36 See White, *Tropics of Discourse*.

37 Hayden White, "Historiography and Historiophoty," *American Historical Review* 93, no. 5 (December 1988): 1199.

38 The only example I know of is the Italian television broadcast at the end of *Too Early/Too Late* (*cf.*: Godard's frequent use of preexisting images for purposes of commentary, critique, or historical allusion).

39 The idea that there is an immediate and inevitable connection between the present and the past—that constructions of history speak most clearly about the moment in which they were created—is, of course, nothing new. Pierre Sorlin made this argument explicit with regard to historical filmmaking in the early 1970s, though I would argue that TV's *Star Trek* was articulating much the same argument with sometimes painful clarity nearly a decade earlier.

40 As Benning noted following the Los Angeles premiere of *Deseret*, his images draw equally on the visual aesthetic of the Lumières and Diane Arbus.

41 Benning himself created a shot-for-shot remake of his own film *One-Way Boogie Woogie* (1977) titled *27 Years Later* (2005).

42 Except for a single shot of a graffiti-covered drainage canal that includes the spray-painted slogan "Che Lives!"

Chapter 6: Digital Histories

1 See, for example, Winston, *Technologies of Seeing*, or Jonathan Crary, *Techniques of the Observer* (Cambridge, Mass.: MIT Press, 1992).

2 For a glimpse of the way some historians have viewed computers as tools for communication, archiving, and research, see the American Historical Association's issue "New Technologies and the Practice of History," *Perspectives* 36, no. 2 (February 1998).

3 Hal Foster, "The Archive without Museums," *October* 77 (Summer 1996): 97.

4 Written history's relationship to the novel is perhaps the best documented of these. See, for example, Georg Lukács's 1937 treatise *The Historical Novel*.

5 Rosenstone, *Visions of the Past*, 206.

6 Vivian Sobchack, "Introduction: History Happens," in *Persistence of History: Cinema, Television and the Modern Event*, ed. Vivian Sobchack, 1–14 (New York: Routledge, 1996), 3.

7 Indeed, my earliest inspiration to better understand the entangled relations among cinema, intellectual property, and history may be traced back to my work as a film researcher for Thom Andersen and Noël Burch's revisionist history of the blacklist-era *Red Hollywood* (1996). One lesson, among many others, to be gleaned from this project is that the most honest histories require that control of the material components of visual history should not be left in the hands of media corporations and moving image archives. Andersen's erudite and idiosyncratic essay film *Los Angeles Plays Itself* (2003), which is comprised of clips from more than three hundred (mostly commercial) films, offers the most eloquent case in point.

8 Although it is beyond the scope of the present work to deal in greater depth with these ongoing struggles, their outcomes will doubtless prove crucial to the evolution and preservation of contemporary digital culture.

9 Arthur C. Danto, *Narration and Knowledge* (New York: Columbia University Press, 1985), 155–59.

10 Jorge Luis Borges, "On Exactitude in Science," in *Collected Fictions*, trans. Andrew Hurley, 325 (New York: Viking Penguin, 1998).

11 See White, *Tropics of Discourse*.

12 Jorge Luis Borges, *Ficciones*, ed. John Sturrock (New York: Knopf, 1993), 83–91.

13 In fact, White's point is that even the most disinterested chronicle reveals hints of narrative.

14 The "Eine Kleine Frohike" episode of Fox's short-lived *X-Files* spinoff *The*

Lone Gunmen (2001), which revolves around investigating the identity of a suspected Nazi war criminal, offers a case in point. Additional examples of the close relation between computer geniuses and historical manipulation are evident in the television series *Quantum Leap* (NBC, 1989–93) and *Sliders* (Fox, 1995–2000), among others.

15 Rosenstone, *Visions of the Past*, 24.

16 Dana Polan, "The Professors of History," in *Persistence of History: Cinema, Television and the Modern Event*, ed. Vivian Sobchack, 235–56 (New York: Routledge, 1996), 251.

17 E. D. Hirsch, *Cultural Literacy: What Every American Needs to Know* (New York: Vintage, 1988).

18 Rosenstone, *Visions of the Past*, 199.

19 Another exceptional historian figure may be found in the character played by Nicolas Cage in the *National Treasure* series. In the two films produced by Walt Disney Pictures and directed by Jon Turtletaub, *National Treasure* (2004) and *National Treasure: Book of Secrets* (2007), Cage plays the son of a discredited historian who uses his encyclopedic knowledge of American history, woven into an elaborate conspiracy-oriented counternarrative, to discover hidden treasures.

20 The 1980s trilogy was succeeded by the prequel TV series *The Young Indiana Jones Chronicles* (ABC, 1992–96).

21 *Crystal Skull* is set a decade later than the other films, in 1957, and takes its antagonists as Cold War Soviet agents rather than the erstwhile Nazis of the earlier films.

22 The later film, *Indiana Jones and the Last Crusade* (1989), follows a nearly identical narrative to retrieve the Holy Grail.

23 *Raiders*' final shot is partially comprehensible as homage to the inconclusive investigation into the meaning of "Rosebud" in Orson Welles's *Citizen Kane* (1941), and interestingly this same archive serves as a narrative device opening *Crystal Skull*, when Soviet agents force the professor to retrieve a highly magnetic artifact from the archive.

24 The image of the impossibly comprehensive federal archive also appears with some regularity within the paranoid narratives of *The X-Files*, where smallpox vaccination records secretly double as a genetic map of the world's population in preparation for alien invasion. Originating in the Cold War era, prior to effective computer-based data management, such a total archive was only possible in the form of a massive, top secret government infrastructure, complete with armed guards and impossibly large document warehouses.

25 The videotaping continues at the time of this writing, though at a reduced rate.

26 The final audiovisual display in the U.S. Holocaust Memorial Museum consists of compositionally minimal talking head video projections of survivor testimonies (which may well have provided the stylistic impetus for Spielberg's project). The interviews are entirely unadorned and only minimally

edited, deriving their power not from the use of iconic imagery but rather from the stark simplicity of facial expressions, gesture, and the emotional content of the testimonies.

27 The conventions of documentary editing dictate that an interview subject whose truthfulness is in doubt should be seen on camera, while those who speak in voice-over acquire a degree of authority from their omniscient speaking position.

28 See Michel Foucault, *Archaeology of Knowledge* (New York: Pantheon, 1982), 5.

29 Terminal Time, "Project Information," www.terminaltime.com/project.htm (accessed May 31, 2010).

30 However, Terminal Time's creators note, even if an audience responded with identical responses to each question, the artificial intelligence algorithm would generate slightly varied historical accounts.

31 For a rigorous and insightful reading of a broad range of cultural discourse in art and film surrounding the JFK assassination, see Art Simon's *Dangerous Knowledge* (Philadelphia: Temple University Press, 1996).

32 Of course, digital imaging began long before the nineties. I regard this decade as a key period of transition due to the increasing dissemination of consumer-grade tools for capturing and manipulating digital images along with growing awareness among theorists of visual culture that many long-held assumptions about images and their ontological status would need to be rethought.

33 Large-format internegatives of each frame of the Zapruder film were created in the late 1980s, shortly before digitization came to dominate restoration processes. These frame enlargements were retouched and registered by hand in order to create a reanimated version of the film that was widely distributed.

34 "On February 22, 2005, Stephane Krupa, a user living in France named 'Major Koenig' (named after Erwin König, a famous sniper) won the competition prize of $10,712 with a score of 782 out of 1000. Second and third place went to the users 'Flux' (779) and 'ArrogantB' (777) respectively. After the competition had officially closed, the cost of the simulation was reduced to $4.99, and the 'competition run' option was disabled within the game. Sometime in early August 2005, the official Web site closed but not before offering version 1.1 to the public for free. Version 3.0 was in the making when they closed the Web site. In version 3.0, the player can play the 'controversial side' (that of a shooter on the Grassy Knoll)." Reuter's News wire, November 21, 2004.

35 "Machinima" refers to videos made using game engines or images captured as footage during gameplay. As a form, machinima is extremely varied, and includes documentary-oriented projects, parodies, and narrative works, as well as records of gameplay.

36 Interestingly, Fullerton also claims that her own experience playing the game resulted in insight into the assassination itself, due to the difficulty of making three remotely accurate shots in a matter of only a few seconds. Her comments are refreshing, as the majority of criticism written about *JFK Reloaded*

could easily have been written by people who never played the game. Tracy Fullerton, "Documentary Games: Putting the Player in the Path of History," in *Playing the Past: History and Nostalgia in Video Games*, ed. Zach Whalen and Laurie N. Taylor, 215–38 (Nashville: Vanderbilt University Press, 2008), 228–29.

37 Gareth Schott and Bevin Yeatman, "Subverting Game-Play: *JFK Reloaded* as Performative Space," *Australasian Journal of American Studies* 24, no. 2 (2005): 82–94.

38 Dealey Plaza in Dallas, Texas, http://slurl.com/secondlife/Dealey%20Plaza %20Dallas/120/114/29 (accessed May 24, 2008). Documentation of the Second Life re-creation may be found on Avatar Promotions' Web site at www .avatarpromotions.com/jfk (accessed August 14, 2010).

39 Presumably, this is to prevent accusations of the same kind of tastelessness for which Traffic was excoriated over *JFK Reloaded*. The company's owners were decidedly skittish when asked for additional information about the re-creation scheduled for the forty-fifth anniversary of the assassination on November 22, 2007 (personal correspondence).

40 TimeGlider, "How It Works," http://timeglider.com/how_it_works.php (accessed June 21, 2009).

41 Developer Network, "API Documentation and Tools," *New York Times*, http:// developer.nytimes.com/ (accessed August 14, 2010).

42 Rosemary Comella and Andreas Kratky, with Norman Klein, "Bleeding Through: Layers of Los Angeles, 1920–1986," http://college.usc.edu/labyrinth/ klein/klein.html (accessed August 14, 2010).

43 Museum of London, "Streetmuseum," www.museumoflondon.org.uk/street museum.htm (accessed August 14, 2010).

44 See, for example, Zach Whalen and Laurie N. Taylor, eds., *Playing the Past: History and Nostalgia in Video Games* (Nashville: Vanderbilt University Press, 2008).

45 It is worth noting that a vast majority of these commercial game titles are in fact war themed, with an overwhelming focus on World War II, followed by narratives based on semispecific conflicts related to the Iraq wars, the global "war on terror," and a smaller number related to Vietnam.

46 "Mod" is short for "modification," referring to a version of a PC game that has been modified from its original form. "Modding" may be practiced by individuals, communities, or development companies for commercial or non-commercial purposes.

47 *Rome: Total Realism*, home page, at www.rometotalrealism.org/index-2.html (accessed May 31, 2010).

48 In *Assassin's Creed II*, real historical figures such as Leonardo da Vinci, Niccolo Machiavelli, and Rodrigo Borgia (later Pope Alexander VI) participate in the narrative.

49 In *Turning Point: Fall of Liberty* (2008), for example, victorious Nazi troops

occupy New York in the wake of World War II. Gameplay centers on a character who leads a resistance movement, fighting guerilla style in the streets of New York to liberate icons of the city from Nazi control.

50 Kuma Games, *Kuma\War*, at www.kumawar.com/ (accessed May 24, 2008).

51 The Kuma Web site explains, "Kuma\War is a series of playable re-creations of real events in the War on Terror. Nearly 100 playable missions bring our soldiers' heroic stories to life." Kuma Games, *Kuma\War* home page, at www .kumawar.com/ (accessed May 24, 2008)

52 Fullerton, "Documentary Games," 222.

53 Fullerton, "Documentary Games," 236.

54 Kuma Games, *Kuma\War* downloads page, at www.kumawar.com/downloads .php (accessed May 24, 2008).

55 Kuma Games, *Kuma\War* downloads page, at www.kumawar.com/downloads .php (accessed May 24, 2008).

56 A rare, cognate effort is the U.S. Army's use of the *America's Army* game engine to reenact scenarios in which soldiers were killed in action. This includes a reenactment that was briefly distributed online depicting the heroic actions of the first American soldier to receive the Silver Star during Operation Iraqi Freedom, Sergeant First Class Paul R. Smith. Working from transcripts of military investigations into battlefield deaths, these machinima reenactments use the game engine in conjunction with the voices of soldiers who were in the field under similar circumstances, though they did not necessarily take part in the actual situations depicted.

57 Members of the now defunct C-level collective who were responsible for *Waco Resurrection* are Michael Wilson, Eddo Stern, Jessica Hutchins, Brody Condon, Peter Brinson, and Mark Allen.

58 By using graphic sequences from *Deer Hunter*, Stern humorously invokes Michael Cimino's Vietnam War film of the same title, but the game itself is about deer hunting, not about Vietnam.

59 A similar strategy is in evidence in artist Jon Haddock's *Screenshots* series (2000). Haddock remakes historical photographs using the aesthetics of video games and presents them along with images from Hollywood movies, including such iconic moments as the assassination of Martin Luther King Jr. and Lee Harvey Oswald and film scenes including *The Sound of Music*, *The Godfather*, and *Twelve Angry Men*. Jon Haddock, "The Screenshots," at www .whitelead.com/jrh/screenshots (accessed May 24, 2008). Likewise, artist Kota Ezawa's video *The Unbearable Lightness of Being* (2005) pursues a diminution of historical resolution, using flattened perspective and vectorized images to refute the logic of historical digitization efforts of libraries and archives, for which the goal is to amass searchable data in high-resolution formats. Ezawa's reduction of resolution draws attention to the limitations of the apparatus in its transformation of such iconic imagery as the Zapruder film and *Birth of a Nation*.

60 Peter Brinson, personal communication, May 31, 2010.

61 Likewise, the Green Day song "Wake Me Up When September Ends" offered an equally appropriate soundtrack for multiple memorials of both Katrina and the terror attacks on the World Trade Center and Pentagon buildings in 2001.

62 Marita Sturken, "Memorializing Absence," at www.ssrc.org/sept11/essays/sturken_text_only.htm (accessed May 24, 2008).

63 A parallel example may be seen in the World Trade Center Sonic Memorial, an independently funded and created online collection of sounds, personal recollections, remembrances, and oral histories from and about the World Trade Center. Although the official memorialization of the World Trade Center destruction has been more successful, the Sonic Memorial project continues to allow individuals to participate in the process of public memorialization. Sonic Memorial, "The Sonic Memorial Project," at www.sonicmemorial.org/ (accessed May 24, 2010).

64 Tara McPherson, "I'll Take My Stand in Dixie-Net: White Guys, the South, and Cyberspace," in *Race in Cyberspace*, ed. Beth E. Kolko, Lisa Nakamura, and Gilbert B. Rodman, 117–32 (New York: Routledge, 2000).

65 Michael Warner, "The Mass Public and the Mass Subject," in *The Phantom Public Sphere*, ed. Bruce Robbins, 234–56 (Minneapolis: University of Minnesota Press, 1993), 248.

Conclusion

1 See for example, Carolyn Marvin's *When Old Technologies Were New: Thinking About Electric Communication in the Late Nineteenth Century* (New York: Oxford University Press, 1988); Wolfgang Schivelbusch's *Disenchanted Night: The Industrialization of Light in the Nineteenth Century* (Berkeley: University of California Press, 1988); or Wolfgang Schivelbusch's *The Railway Journey: The Industrialization and Perception of Time and Space in the 19th Century* (Berkeley: University of California Press, 1987).

2 Lisa Gitelman, *Always Already New: Media, History and the Data of Culture* (Cambridge, Mass.: MIT Press, 2006), 147.

3 Center for History and New Media, "H-bot," at http://chnm.gmu.edu/tools/h-bot (accessed May 24, 2010).

4 Gitelman, *Always Already New*, 150.

5 Julian Bleecker, "Design Fiction: A Short Essay on Design, Science, Fact and Fiction," Near Future Laboratory, March 2009, at www.nearfuturelaboratory.com/2009/03/17/design-fiction-a-short-essay-on-design-science-fact-and-fiction (accessed May 24, 2010).

6 Alex Galloway, *Gaming: Essays on Algorithmic Culture* (Minneapolis: University of Minnesota Press, 2006), xi.

7 Derek Waters, "Drunk History," *Funny or Die*, at www.funnyordie.com/drunkhistory (accessed May 24, 2010).

8 The seven episodes released to date have featured actors such as Michael Cera, Jack Black, Will Ferrell, Don Cheadle, Zooey Deschanel, Crispin Glover, and John C. Reilly.

9 As with other forms of media we have considered, not all ARGs are necessarily effective at pursuing these goals; indeed, the category of ARGs is very much open to contestation and likely revision. For now, it is the best placeholder available to denote a kind of gameplay that is insufficiently described by any other term presently available.

10 *World without Oil*, "About *World without Oil*," www.worldwithoutoil.org/metaabout.htm (accessed May 24, 2010).

11 Institute for the Future, "40 Years," at www.iftf.org/about (accessed May 24, 2010).

12 Institute for the Future, "Superstruct: World's First Massively Multiplayer Forecasting Game Announced Today," September 22, 2008, at http://www.iftf.org/node/2318 (accessed July 28, 2010).

13 Sascha Pohflepp, *The Golden Institute*, at www.pohflepp.com/?q=golden institute (accessed May 24, 2010).

14 This would be a good place to insert a reassuring footnote, indicating the source of the quote, the date, and the place of its publication—and an implicit invitation, in case you don't believe me, to look it up for yourself.

Bibliography

Allen, Steve. *Meeting of Minds: Four Scripts.* New York: Prometheus Books, 1993.

American Historical Association. "New Technologies and the Practice of History" issue. *Perspectives* 36, no. 2 (February 1998).

Arthur, Paul. "The Four Last Things: History, Technology, Hollywood, Apocalypse." In *The End of Cinema as We Know It: American Film in the Nineties,* edited by Jon Lewis, 342–55 (New York: New York University Press, 2001).

———. "The Status of Found Footage." *Spectator* 20, no. 1 (Fall 1999/Winter 2000): 57–69.

Barthes, Roland. *Camera Lucida: Reflections on Photography.* New York: Noonday Press, 1982.

Baudrillard, Jean. *The Gulf War Did Not Take Place.* Bloomington: Indiana University Press, 1995.

Benjamin, Walter. "Theses on the Philosophy of History." In *Illuminations,* edited by Hannah Arendt, 253–64. New York: Schocken, 1985.

Bennett, Tony. *Outside Literature.* London: Routledge, 1991.

Bhabha, Homi K. *The Location of Culture.* New York: Routledge, 1994.

Bommes, Michael, and Patrick Wright. "The Charms of Residence: The Public and the Past." In *Making Histories,* edited by Richard Johnson, Gregor McLennan, Bill Schwarz, and David Sutton, 253–302. London: Anchor, 1982.

Borges, Jorge Luis. "On Exactitude in Science." In *Collected Fictions,* 325. Translated by Andrew Hurley. New York: Viking Penguin, 1998.

———. *Ficciones,* edited by John Sturrock. New York: Knopf, 1993.

Brakhage, Stan. "In Defense of Amateur." In *The Brakhage Scrapbook: Collected Writings 1964–1980,* edited by Robert A. Haller, 162–68. New York: Documentext, 1982.

Braudy, Leo. *Narrative Form in History and Fiction: Hume, Fielding and Gibbon.* Princeton, N.J.: Princeton University Press, 1970.

Byg, Barton. *Landscapes of Resistance.* Berkeley: University of California Press, 1995.

Caldwell, John. *Televisuality: Style Crisis and Authority in American Television.* New Brunswick, N.J.: Rutgers University Press, 1995.

Camper, Fred. "Some Notes on the Home Movie." *Journal of Film and Video* 38, nos. 3–4 (Summer/Fall 1986): 9–13.

———. "The End of Avant Garde Film." *Millennium Film Journal* 16–18 (Fall/Winter 1986–87): 68–82.

Carnes, Mark, ed. *Past Imperfect: History according to the Movies.* New York: Henry Holt, 1995.

Chalfen, Richard. "The Home Movie in a World of Reports." *Journal of Film and Video* 38, nos. 3–4 (Summer/Fall 1986): 102–11.

Colbert, David. *Eyewitness to America: 500 Years of America in the Words of Those Who Saw It Happen.* New York: Pantheon, 1998.

Crafton, Donald. *Talkies: American Cinema's Transition to Sound, 1926–31.* Berkeley: University of California Press, 1999.

Crary, Jonathan. *Techniques of the Observer.* Cambridge, Mass.: MIT Press, 1992.

Danto, Arthur C. *Narration and Knowledge.* New York: Columbia University Press, 1985.

de Certeau, Michel. *Heterologies: Discourses on the Other.* Minneapolis: University of Minnesota Press, 1986.

———. *The Practice of Everyday Life.* Berkeley: University of California Press, 1984.

———. *The Writing of History.* New York: Columbia University Press, 1988.

Derrida, Jacques. *Of Grammatology.* Baltimore: Johns Hopkins University Press, 1992.

———. *Positions.* Translated by Alan Bass. London: Athlone, 1981.

Doane, Mary Ann. "Information, Crisis, Catastrophe." In *Logics of Television: Essays in Cultural Criticism*, edited by Patricia Mellencamp, 222–39. Bloomington: Indiana University Press, 1990.

Ferguson, Niall, ed. *Virtual History: Alternatives and Counterfactuals.* New York: Basic Books, 1999.

Ferro, Marc. *Cinema and History.* Translated by Naomi Greene. Detroit: Wayne State University Press, 1988.

Feuer, Jane. "The Concept of Live Television: Ontology as Ideology." In *Regarding Television*, edited by E. Ann Kaplan, 12–22. Los Angeles: American Film Institute, 1983.

Foster, Hal. "The Archive without Museums." *October* 77 (Summer 1996): 97–119.

Foster, Hal, and Dia Art Foundation. *Vision and Visuality.* Seattle: Bay Press, 1988.

Foucault, Michel. *Archaeology of Knowledge.* New York: Pantheon, 1982.

———. *Discipline and Punish: The Birth of the Prison.* New York: Vintage, 1977.

———. "Film and Popular Memory." *Edinburgh Magazine* 2 (1977): 20–25.

———. *Language, Counter-Memory, Practice: Selected Essays and Interviews by Michel Foucault.* Ithaca, N.Y.: Cornell University Press, 1977.

Francaviglia, Richard, and Jerry Rodnitzky, eds. *Lights, Camera, History: Portraying the Past in Film.* College Station: Texas A&M University Press, 2007.

Fraser, George MacDonald. *Hollywood History of the World: From One Million Years B.C. to Apocalypse Now.* Cambridge, Mass.: Harvard University Press, 1988.

Friedberg, Anne. *Window Shopping: Cinema and the Postmodern.* Berkeley: University of California Press, 1994.

Frisch, Michael. *A Shared Authority.* Albany: State University of New York Press, 1990.

Fukuyama, Francis. *The End of History and the Last Man.* New York: Avon, 1992.

Tracy Fullerton, "Documentary Games: Putting the Player in the Path of History," in *Playing the Past: History and Nostalgia in Video Games,* ed. Zach Whalen and Laurie N. Taylor, 215–38 (Nashville: Vanderbilt University Press, 2008.

Galloway, Alex. *Gaming: Essays on Algorithmic Culture.* Minneapolis: University of Minnesota Press, 2006.

Gidal, Peter. *Materialist Film.* New York: Routledge, 1989.

Ginzberg, Carlo. *Clues, Myths and the Historical Method.* Baltimore: Johns Hopkins University Press, 1989.

Gitelman, Lisa. *Always Already New: Media, History and the Data of Culture.* Cambridge, Mass.: MIT Press, 2006.

Graham, Ian. "Three Early Collectors in Mesoamerica." In *Collecting the Pre-Columbian Past,* edited by Elizabeth H. Boone, 49–80. Washington, D.C.: Dumbarton Oaks, 1993.

Grindon, Leger. *Shadows on the Past: Studies in the Historical Fiction Film.* Philadelphia: Temple University Press, 1994.

Gunning, Tom. "The Cinema of Attraction: Early Film, Its Spectator and the Avant-Garde." *Wide Angle* 8, nos. 3–4 (1986): 63–70.

Hirsch, E. D. *Cultural Literacy: What Every American Needs to Know.* New York: Vintage, 1988.

Hughes-Warrington, Marnie. *History Goes to the Movies: Studying History on Film.* New York: Routledge, 2006.

Huyssen, Andreas. *Twilight Memories: Marking Time in a Culture of Amnesia.* New York: Routledge, 1995.

James, David E. *Allegories of Cinema.* Princeton, N.J.: Princeton University Press, 1989.

———. "The Distinction of Idioms." In *Scratching the Belly of the Beast: Cutting Edge Media in Los Angeles, 1922–94,* edited by Holly Willis, 36–37. Los Angeles: Filmforum, 1994.

———. "Film Diary/Diary Film: Practice and Product in *Walden.*" In *To Free the Cinema,* edited by David E. James, 145–79. Princeton, N.J.: Princeton University Press, 1992.

———. *To Free the Cinema,* edited by David E. James. Princeton, N.J.: Princeton University Press, 1992.

Jameson, Fredric. *Marxism and Form*. Princeton, N.J.: Princeton University Press, 1971.

———. *Postmodernism or the Cultural Logic of Late Capitalism*. Durham, N.C.: Duke University Press, 1988.

Jay, Martin. "Cultural Relativism and the Visual Turn." *Journal of Visual Culture* 1, no. 3 (2002): 267–78.

Kierkegaard, Søren. *Either/Or*. Princeton, N.J.: Princeton University Press, 1971.

Kirby, Lynne. *Parallel Tracks: The Railroad and Silent Cinema*. Durham, N.C.: Duke University Press, 1997.

Klein, Norman M. *The History of Forgetting: Los Angeles and the Erasure of Memory*. London: Verso, 1997.

Kunz, Diane. "Camelot Continued: What If John F. Kennedy Had Lived?" In *Virtual History: Alternatives and Counterfactuals*, edited by Niall Ferguson, 368–91. New York: Basic Books, 1999.

LaCapra, Dominick. *History and Criticism*. Ithaca, N.Y.: Cornell University Press, 1985.

Laclau, Ernesto, and Chantal Mouffe. *Hegemony and Socialist Strategy: Towards a Radical Democratic Politics*. London: Verso, 1985.

Landy, Marcia. *Cinematic Uses of the Past*. Minneapolis: University of Minnesota Press, 1996.

———. *The Historical Film: History and Memory in Media*. New Brunswick, N.J.: Rutgers University Press, 2001.

Leyda, Jay. *Films Beget Films: A Study of the Compilation Film*. New York: Hill and Wang, 1964.

Lipsitz, George. *Time Passages: Collective Memory and American Popular Culture*. Minneapolis: University of Minnesota Press, 1990.

Lowenthal, David. *The Past Is a Foreign Country*. Cambridge: Cambridge University Press, 1999.

Lukács, Georg. *The Historical Novel*. London: Merlin Press, 1978.

Lynch, Michael E., and David Bogen, eds. *The Spectacle of History: Speech, Text, and Memory at the Iran-Contra Hearings*. Durham, N.C.: Duke University Press, 1997.

MacDonald, Scott. *A Critical Cinema: Interviews with Independent Filmmakers*. Berkeley: University of California Press, 1988.

———. *A Critical Cinema 3*. Berkeley: University of California Press, 1998.

Marks, Laura U. "A Deleuzian Politics of Hybrid Cinema." *Screen* 35, no. 3 (Autumn 1994): 244–64.

Marvin, Carolyn. *When Old Technologies Were New: Thinking About Electric Communication in the Late Nineteenth Century*. New York: Oxford University Press, 1988.

Mayne, Judith. *Directed by Dorothy Arzner*. Bloomington: Indiana University Press, 1994.

McArthur, Colin. *Television and History*. London: British Film Institute Press, 1978.

McPherson, Tara. "I'll Take My Stand in Dixie-Net: White Guys, the South, and Cyberspace." In *Race in Cyberspace*, edited by Beth E. Kolko, Lisa Nakamura, and Gilbert B. Rodman, 117–32. New York: Routledge, 2000.

Metz, Christian. *The Imaginary Signifier*. Bloomington: Indiana University Press, 1977.

Minh-ha, Trinh T. *Framer Framed*. New York: Routledge, 1992.

———. *Women, Native, Other: Writing Postcoloniality and Feminism*. Indianapolis: University of Indiana Press, 1989.

Nichols, Bill. *Blurred Boundaries: Questions of Meaning in Contemporary Culture*. Bloomington: Indiana University Press, 1994.

———. *Representing Reality: Issues and Concepts in Documentary*. Bloomington: Indiana University Press, 1992.

Niethammer, Lutz. *Posthistoire: Has History Come to an End?* London: Verso, 1992.

Nietzsche, Friedrich. *Untimely Meditations*. Cambridge: Cambridge University Press, 1997.

Norris, Christopher. *Uncritical Theory: Postmodernism, Intellectuals and the Gulf War*. Amherst: University of Massachusetts Press, 1992.

O'Connor, John E., and Martin A. Jackson, eds. *American History/American Film: Interpreting the Hollywood Image*. New York: Frederick Ungar Publishing, 1979.

Peterson, James. *Dreams of Chaos, Visions of Order: Understanding the American Avant-Garde Cinema*. Detroit: Wayne State University Press, 1994.

Polan, Dana. *The Political Language of Film and the Avant-Garde*. Ann Arbor: University of Michigan Research Press, 1985.

———. "The Professors of History." In *Persistence of History: Cinema, Television and the Modern Event*, edited by Vivian Sobchack, 235–56. New York: Routledge, 1996.

Rollins, Peter C., ed. *Hollywood as Historian: American Film in a Cultural Context*. Lexington: University Press of Kentucky, 1983.

Roman, Shari. *Digital Babylon: Hollywood, Indiewood and Dogme 95*. Los Angeles: Lone Eagle Publishing, 2001.

Rosenstone, Robert. *Revisioning History: Film and the Construction of a New Past*. Princeton, N.J.: Princeton University Press, 1995.

———. *Visions of the Past: The Challenge of Film to Our Idea of History*. Cambridge, Mass.: Harvard University Press, 1995.

Schivelbusch, Wolfgang. *Disenchanted Night: The Industrialization of Light in the Nineteenth Century*. Berkeley: University of California Press, 1988.

———. *Railway Journey: The Industrialization and Perception of Time and Space in the 19th Century*. Berkeley: University of California Press, 1987.

Schott, Gareth, and Bevin Yeatman. "Subverting Game-Play: *JFK Reloaded* as Performative Space." *Australasian Journal of American Studies* 24, no. 2 (2005): 82–94.

Scott, Joan. *Gender and the Politics of History.* New York: Columbia University Press, 1999.

Sekula, Allan. "Reading an Archive: Photography between Labour and Capital." In *The Photography Reader*, edited by Liz Wells, 443–52. London: Routledge, 2003.

Silverman, Kaja. *The Acoustic Mirror.* Bloomington: Indiana University Press, 1988.

Simon, Art. *Dangerous Knowledge.* Philadelphia: Temple University Press, 1996.

Sobchack, Vivian. "Introduction: History Happens." In *Persistence of History: Cinema, Television and the Modern Event*, edited by Vivian Sobchack, 1–14. New York: Routledge, 1996.

———, ed. *Persistence of History: Cinema, Television and the Modern Event.* New York: Routledge, 1996.

Sorlin, Pierre. *The Film in History: Restaging the Past.* Totowa, N.J.: Barnes & Noble Books, 1980.

Sturken, Marita. "Reenactment, Fantasy and the Paranoia of History: Oliver Stone's Docudramas." *Spectator* 20, no. 1 (Fall 1999/Winter 2000): 23–37.

———. *Tangled Memories: The Vietnam War, the AIDS Epidemic and the Politics of Remembering.* Berkeley: University of California Press, 1997.

Tagg, John. *The Burden of Representation: Essays on Photographies and Histories.* Minneapolis: University of Minnesota Press, 1993.

Tanaka, Janice. *Moving the Image*, edited by Russell Leong. Los Angeles: Visual Communications, 1991.

Todorov, Tsvetan. *The Fantastic: A Structural Approach to a Literary Genre.* Ithaca, N.Y.: Cornell University Press, 1975.

Toplin, Robert Brent. *History by Hollywood: The Use and Abuse of the American Past.* Chicago: University of Illinois Press, 1996.

Trouillot, Michel Rolphe. *Silencing the Past: Power and the Production of History.* Boston: Beacon, 1997.

Turim, Maureen. "Childhood Memories and Household Events in the Feminist Avant-Garde." *Journal of Film and Video* 38, nos. 3–4 (Summer/Fall 1986): 86–92.

———. "Textuality and Theatricality in Brecht and Straub/Huillet: *History Lessons* (1972)." In *German Film and Literature: Adaptations and Transformations*, edited by Eric Rentschler, 231–45. New York: Methuen, 1986.

Walsh, Martin. *The Brechtian Aspect of Radical Cinema.* London: British Film Institute, 1981.

Warner, Michael. "The Mass Public and the Mass Subject." In *The Phantom Public Sphere*, edited by Bruce Robbins, 234–56. Minneapolis: University of Minnesota Press, 1993.

Wees, William. *Recycled Images: The Art and Politics of Found Footage Films*. New York: Anthology Film Archives, 1993.

Whalen, Zach, and Laurie N. Taylor, eds. *Playing the Past: History and Nostalgia in Video Games*. Nashville: Vanderbilt University Press, 2008.

White, Hayden. *Content of the Form: Narrative Discourse and Historical Representation*. Baltimore: Johns Hopkins University Press, 1990.

———. "Historiography and Historiophoty." *American Historical Review* 93, no. 5 (December 1988): 1193–99.

———. "The Modernist Event." In *Persistence of History: Cinema, Television and the Modern Event*, edited by Vivian Sobchack, 17–38. London: Routledge 1996.

———. *Tropics of Discourse: Essays in Cultural Criticism*. Baltimore: Johns Hopkins University Press, 1978.

White, Mimi. "Television Liveness: History, Banality, Attractions." *Spectator* 20, no. 1 (Fall 1999/Winter 2000): 37–56.

Willemen, Paul. "An Avant-Garde for the Eighties." *Framework* 24 (Spring 1984): 53–73.

Winston, Brian. *Technologies of Seeing: Photography, Cinematography and Television*. London: British Film Institute, 1997.

Wollen, Peter. *Readings and Writings: Semiotic Counter-Strategies*. London: Verso, 1982.

Wyke, Maria. *Projecting the Past: Ancient Rome, Cinema and History*. New York: Routledge, 1997.

Young, Robert. *White Mythologies: Writing History and the West*. London: Routledge, 1990.

Zimmermann, Patricia R. *Reel Families: A Social History of Amateur Film*. Bloomington: Indiana University Press, 1995.

Zizek, Slavoj. *The Sublime Object of Ideology*. New York: Verso, 1989.

Index

Italicized page numbers indicate illustrations.

Library of Congress Cataloging-in-Publication Data

Anderson, Steve F.

Technologies of history: visual media and the eccentricity
of the past / Steve F. Anderson.

   p. cm.—(Interfaces: studies in visual culture)

Includes bibliographical references and index.

ISBN 978-1-58465-901-3 (cloth: alk. paper)—

ISBN 978-1-61168-003-4 (pbk.: alk. paper)—

ISBN 978-1-61168-008-9 (e-book)

1. Mass media and history. 2. Memory—Social aspects.

3. Visual communication. I. Title. II. Series.

P96.H55A53   2011

900—dc22   2010044871